First-Time Parenting Journeys

All too often heterosexual first-time parents are treated as the unmarked norm within research on reproduction. *First-Time Parenting Journeys* maps out what it means to be situated within the norm, while providing a critical account of how social norms about parenthood shape, regulate, and potentially delimit experiences of new parenthood for heterosexual couples. Based on qualitative longitudinal research, this book tells the story of journeys to parenthood, highlighting the impact of gender norms, moral claims, emotion work, and generativity. While drawing on Australian data, the critical conceptual framework has broader applicability across Western contexts in terms of understanding normative family structures and parenting practices. By focusing on expectations about, and the reality of, new parenthood, it explicates the ways in which institutionalised norms about parenthood are internalised and explores what this can tell us about the broader contours of parenthood discourses.

DAMIEN W. RIGGS is Professor of Psychology at Flinders University, Australia. He is also a Fellow of the Australian Psychological Society and a psychotherapist who specialises in work with trans children. He has authored more than twenty books, including *Diverse Pathways to Parenthood: From Narratives to Practice* (2020).

CLARE BARTHOLOMAEUS is an Adjunct Research Fellow at Flinders University, Australia. Her previous books include *Home and Away: Mothers and Babies in Institutional Spaces* (with Kathleen Connellan, Clemence Due, and Damien Riggs, 2021) and *Transgender People and Education* (with Damien Riggs, 2017).

First-Time Parenting Journeys

Expectations and Realities

DAMIEN W. RIGGS
Flinders University of South Australia

CLARE BARTHOLOMAEUS
Flinders University of South Australia

Shaftesbury Road, Cambridge CB2 8EA, United Kingdom

One Liberty Plaza, 20th Floor, New York, NY 10006, USA

477 Williamstown Road, Port Melbourne, VIC 3207, Australia

314–321, 3rd Floor, Plot 3, Splendor Forum, Jasola District Centre,
New Delhi – 110025, India

103 Penang Road, #05–06/07, Visioncrest Commercial, Singapore 238467

Cambridge University Press is part of Cambridge University Press & Assessment,
a department of the University of Cambridge.

We share the University's mission to contribute to society through the pursuit of
education, learning and research at the highest international levels of excellence.

www.cambridge.org
Information on this title: www.cambridge.org/9781316513989

DOI: 10.1017/9781009076449

First published 2023

A catalogue record for this publication is available from the British Library

Library of Congress Cataloging-in-Publication Data
Names: Riggs, Damien W., author. | Bartholomaeus, Clare, author.
Title: First-time parenting journeys : expectations and realities /
Damien W. Riggs, Clare Bartholomaeus.
Description: New York, NY : Cambridge University Press, [2023] |
Includes bibliographical references and index.
Identifiers: LCCN 2022043426 | ISBN 9781316513989 (hardback) |
ISBN 9781009076449 (ebook)
Subjects: LCSH: Parenthood. | Parenting. | Parent and child.
Classification: LCC HQ755.8 .R53135 2023 |
DDC 306.874–dc23/eng/20221021
LC record available at https://lccn.loc.gov/2022043426

ISBN 978-1-316-51398-9 Hardback

Damien would like to dedicate this book to Leo and Geremyah.

Contents

Acknowledgements

We begin by acknowledging that we live and work on the lands of the Kaurna people, and we acknowledge their sovereignty as First Nations people.

We offer our sincere thanks to the couples and parents we interviewed and to their babies and animals for often having to be very patient while they spoke to us. This project could not have happened without their commitment to speaking to us over multiple years, and it was a great privilege for us to be entrusted with their stories during an important time in their lives.

We are very thankful to Janka Romero from Cambridge University Press for providing such strong support for this book from the very first email and to Emily Watton and Rowan Groat from Cambridge for their editorial support.

Funding for the project was received from the Australian Research Council in the form of a future fellowship awarded to Damien, FT130100087.

Damien would like to thank Helen Lux-Bridges, Shoshana Rosenberg, Sophie de Rohan, Clemmi Due, Kate Travers, Sharon Riggs, and Mia Mandara for conversations that influenced this book. We would also like to thank Anna Worth for working with us on an earlier paper exploring partner relationships. Thanks to Danielle Navarro for allowing us to use the image that appears on the cover.

1   Introduction

1.1   JOURNEYS TO THE PROJECT

As is fitting for a book on parenthood, this book has undergone a
long gestation period. In order to understand the genesis of our project focusing on heterosexual couples' pathways to parenthood, it is
important to map the work that Damien, in particular, has conducted
on parenting and kinship in many forms. Over fifteen years ago,
Damien started a programme of research involving two interrelated
studies. The first focused on foster parenting, and the second focused
on lesbian and gay parents. The study on foster parenting sought to
examine how people create kinship with people to whom they are
not genetically related (e.g., Riggs, Augoustinos & Delfabbro, 2007). It
examined kinship through the lens of chosen families, explicitly challenging what Finkler (2000) refers to as the 'hegemony of the gene'.
Yet this study was not without its challenges. A key challenge was
the imperative to balance out chosen families in the context of foster care with the relationships that children in foster care continue
to have with their birth families (Riggs, Delfabbro, & Augoustinos,
2009). In other words, the challenge was to be mindful and respectful of genetic relationships without discounting the forms of kinship
engaged in by foster families. Doing this required a close examination
of how genetic relationships are treated as sacrosanct within child
protection laws, and, at the same time, why birth families are treated
as inadequate in the context of child protection. Similarly, it required
close attention to the exaltation of foster parents as 'saints' and, at
the same time, why such parents are often viewed as second best.

The second study focused on lesbian and gay parents and
occurred at a time in both the Australian and global contexts where
significant change was taking place in terms of the rights of this

group of parents. As part of that shift, there was a move within academic research to challenge the idea that the only way to support the rights of lesbian and gay parents was to claim that such parents were 'just like' heterosexual parents (e.g., Clarke, 2002). The research that Damien undertook was part of this critical movement to emphasise the unique experiences of lesbian and gay parents and to refuse forms of homonormativity (defined as the insistence that lesbian and gay lives mirror those of heterosexual lives, especially with regard to marriage and parenting; Duggan, 2012). Similar to the study on foster parenting, this study was certainly not without tensions. As much as lesbian and gay parents themselves have often recognised and celebrated their unique experiences, the push for equal rights very much rested on assumptions of equality, often requiring the reinstatement of normative comparisons (Riggs, 2010). This can be seen in an oft-repeated phrase of the time, namely that children of lesbian and gay parents do *at least as good as* children of heterosexual parents (e.g., Gartrell & Bos, 2010).

These two projects led Damien to additional research areas. In a series of studies undertaken with Clemence Due, Damien explored families formed through commercial surrogacy (i.e., surrogacy where the woman who carries the child is paid), families formed through adoption, and the experiences of refugee families in Australia. The research that Damien and Clemence undertook on commercial surrogacy was just as fraught as were the two earlier studies by Damien. At the time of this study, significant debates were occurring both within Australia and internationally about the ethics of commercial surrogacy, with a number of countries that had previously allowed citizens of other countries to commission surrogacy arrangements (e.g., India and Thailand), closing their borders to foreign nationals. Media stories about commercial surrogacy emphasised the ethical precarity of women who act as surrogates, focusing on the commercial aspects of such surrogacy arrangements (Riggs & Due, 2013). In the face of this, Clemence and Damien sought to balance out a feminist critique of the commodification of women's bodies, with the precarity experienced by people who felt the injunction to have children but who perceived no other way to have children to whom they were genetically related (primarily cisgender gay men and heterosexual couples experiencing infertility) than to enter into a commercial surrogacy arrangement.

Clemence and Damien's research on adoption took up the topic of genetics and birth families raised in Damien's previous research on foster parents, and it added an additional layer to this by looking at transnational adoptions. In this context, the topic of cultural differences was especially salient, and this study examined how white adoptive parents speak about and navigate cultural differences, whilst at the same time trying to lay claim to legitimacy for their adoptive families (Riggs & Due, 2015). Clemence and Damien's research on adoption sat within a broader tradition of research on transnational adoption, starting with adoptions that occurred within the context of the Vietnam War (e.g., Willing, 2004), spanning to events happening at the time Clemence and Damien undertook their research, including those involving celebrities such as Madonna and Angelina Jolie adopting children from the African continent. Woven across these diverse topic areas is a consistent thread of the relative privilege of adoptive parents, and the relative disadvantage experienced by both birth parents (for whom war or famine often means that their capacity to care for their children is diminished) and adopted children (who often report experiencing racism in their adoptive countries). In a similar vein, the research that Clemence and Damien undertook on refugee families in Australia explored how transnational movement draws attention to binaries of privilege and disadvantage, and how both are shaped by cultural norms within host countries that serve to emphasise narratives of benevolence (on the part of host countries) at the expense of critical attention to the social and political factors that lead to (in this case forced) migration (Due & Riggs, 2009).

Across these research projects, we drew on previous research on predominately white, middle-class heterosexual couples who had children via heterosex to explore how families whose form or reproductive journeys differ from the norm are shaped by the norm itself. Using Turner's (2001) work on reproductive citizenship, we examined how the injunction to reproduce is widely felt, even if its effects are differentially distributed. Yet, time and time again, reviewers of this work asked how we can truly 'know' if heterosexual couples really are part of a norm. Reviewers pointed out that there are clear inequalities among heterosexual couples, specifically when it comes to socio-economic status and cultural background. To suggest that heterosexual couples constitute a norm against which all others are compared, it was suggested, was thus problematic, especially as our own research was not comparative. In other words, some of our reviewers suggested that it did not suffice to make recourse to other research about heterosexual couples to make a case for a norm against which our own research samples could be compared.

Of course, Damien's concerns about the injunction placed on lesbian and gay parents to be 'just like' heterosexual parents were amplified when it came to the expectation that only comparative research could adequately examine a norm. Clemence and Damien typically made the argument that examining a norm is about examining how a norm functions: as much as to whose disbenefit and as much as to whose benefit. Having a heterosexual 'control group' is not necessary in order to examine the norms experienced by, for example, lesbian and gay parents or parents who have their children via commercial surrogacy. Norms are evident in media stories about families, in public debates, in legislation, and of course in the stories of those families positioned as outside of the norm. An opportunity arose, however, for Clemence and Damien, in collaboration with Clare, to make a direct comparison between families formed through fostering, intercountry adoption, surrogacy, and reproductive heterosex. We took up this opportunity by drawing on some interviews we had done with the latter group and comparing them with our other samples.

What we found in this comparative research was a continuum on which families were located, depending on the degree to which their lives were treated as either a public or private matter (Riggs, Bartholomaeus, & Due, 2016). Drawing on our interviews, we found that families formed through reproductive heterosex were those who were most likely to perceive little scrutiny from their community and little negative impact of government policy on their lives (though for some, there was a benefit, such as government subsidies for new parents). Families formed through commercial surrogacy reported a mix of feelings both private and public. They were very much aware that their families were a topic of public debate, but they largely found that – because at least one of the parents had a genetic relationship to their children – government bodies largely left them alone, and sometimes were instrumental in providing support (such as issuing passports for children born overseas). Foster families reported a perception of being 'public families', subject to scrutiny by the media, by government agencies, and without the legal protection afforded by genetic relations. In utilising a comparative approach, we were able to speak to the effects of a number of norms, specifically genetic relatedness, government intervention, and public scrutiny of families. We also explored the meaning of family to participants, finding similarities and differences within and between the samples, with an overall privileging of genetic relatedness and cohabitation (Bartholomaeus & Riggs, 2017b). Again, this analysis highlighted the relative privileging of some samples (families formed through reproductive heterosex) over others (e.g., families formed through fostering).

Yet as much as these earlier studies allowed us to explore the differential effects of social norms about kinship, we were left with a keen interest in what it means for families formed via reproductive heterosex to live in relation to a norm of which they are a part. How, in other words, do such families understand the norm of which they are notionally a part? How does it shape their lives, and indeed do they have an awareness of their normative (and privileged) status? In particular, we were interested in how people imagine for themselves a place within a norm that may largely be invisible to them and the affective dimensions of being part of this norm. Damien and Clare thus devised a study that sought to focus concertedly on heterosexual couples planning for a first child. The *Feeling, Wanting, Having: The Meaning of Children to Heterosexual Couples* study, which is the focus of this book, involved interviews – conducted from 2015 to 2020 – with nine heterosexual couples living in the state of South Australia. In addition, we interviewed 10 parents of these participants to explore their experiences of becoming parents and grandparents. In Chapter 2, we provide a more detailed overview of the study, our approach, and the participants, but here we note that our focus was on the relationship between the expectations and reality of first-time parents, a focus that shapes the later chapters in this book. In order to provide some contexts for our study, we now provide a brief overview of Australian families, drawing on available government data.

1.2 AUSTRALIAN FAMILIES IN CONTEXT

Australian families over the past half century have been marked by change as much as they have been marked by significant continuity. In terms of change, there has been a diversification of family forms, as indicated by some of the research studies that we have undertaken, including the one with Clemence Due, outlined earlier. However, there are also significant elements of continuity in the shape of Australian families. This is perhaps not surprising, given that while there are generational changes across the globe, including in regard to attitudes towards differing family forms, in the Australian context specifically, a number of factors have remained relatively constant. These include the availability of social healthcare, including both coverage for fertility-related medical treatment and the availability of welfare payments. Furthermore, although the introduction of no-fault divorce opened up possibilities in regard to the constitution and reconstitution of families, this does not automatically mean that all people will have shifted their views about marriage and families. While Australia is a secular nation, it is certainly comprised of a significant Christian majority (comprising just over half of the population who responded to an optional Census question about religious beliefs) (Australian Bureau of Statistics, 2017). While Christianity encompasses a diversity of views, heterosexual marriage and reproduction remain central to the values of many people who adhere to a Christian faith. Such religious views in the context of a secular nation are reflected in the views of several Australian politicians, including prime ministers, whose views have directly impacted support availability to families, along with support that could arguably be framed as pronatalist (Kevin, 2005).

Pronatalism refers to the injunction placed on people to reproduce. This injunction appears in political messaging, public policy, education and healthcare, through public discourse, and in the values held by individual people. Pronatalism is arguably evident in the Australian context in the form of payments made to people who reproduce. Specifically, a government 'baby bonus' was introduced in 2004, offering a one-off payment of $5,000 (Australian dollars) for each child born to, or adopted by, parents who were not otherwise eligible for paid parental leave and who had an annual income of under $75,000 (Klapdor, 2013). A decade later, this payment was reviewed and paid as an initial lump sum of $560 and then fortnightly payments totalling to $1,679 (Centrelink, 2019a). The payment is means tested and again is not available for those in receipt of paid parental leave. Government-paid parental leave is available to families with an annual income of under $150,000, though only where parents were working prior to the birth or adoption of a child (Centrelink, 2019b). This leave is available for up to eighteen weeks for the primary caregiver, and an additional two weeks to the second parent (typically referred to as 'dad and partner pay') is also available (Centrelink, 2019b).

Around the time we started the *Feeling, Wanting, Having* study, we produced a summary of available Australian data on families (Riggs & Bartholomaeus, 2016a). Our summary documented both changes and continuities in the Australian context between 1960 and

2015. We noted that the number of single-parent families had consistently risen over the time period; however, the number of couples with or without children remained relatively stable. Specifically, the overwhelming majority of families (almost two-thirds) reported in the Australian Census continue to be comprised of heterosexual couples (who have not separated) and their children. In terms of birth rates, we noted that the total number of births continues to grow each year; however, the fertility rate has decreased, indicating that fewer women are having fewer children each year (as the fertility rate is measured in relation to women). In other words, historically there were fewer women, but each had a relatively high number of children. The population of people who can give birth is now higher, but fewer are having as many children.

Further in terms of change, and specifically focusing on first-time mothers, over a 21-year period of the broader 50-year period we examined, the mean age of such mothers rose sharply. This is related to the drop in women under 20 giving birth to their first child and, simultaneously, the rise in women over 40 giving birth to their first child. Further, we also noted that the number of children born to parents who are not married has increased within a 50-year period, and the number born to parents who are married has decreased. Nonetheless, more children are stillborn in the context of heterosexual marriage than not. This is interesting, given that whilst the number of marriages increased across the same time period, the actual marriage rate decreased. With regard to divorce, whilst there was an initial spike in divorces following the introduction of no-fault divorces in 1976, the number of divorces has fallen in line with the number of marriages. The full impact of COVID-19 has yet to be seen, but early figures suggest that the number of births has remained relatively stable (Australian Bureau of Statistics, 2020). Qualitative research, however, indicates that the pandemic may impact on the timing of when people have children, with some people delaying parenthood (Qu, 2021).

As this brief summary would suggest, there have most certainly been changes in the Australian context with regard to families, specifically in terms of divorce and single-parent families, and the age at which women have a first child. Yet at the same time, the predominance of the heterosexual nuclear family has remained relatively stable. This is perhaps not surprising given that heterosexual people of reproductive age constitute a large proportion of the adult population. Yet as we explore in Section 1.3, where we outline the theoretical frameworks that we use in the analytic chapters of this book, the mere existence of heterosexual people of reproductive age does not explain why it is that this group of people have children.

1.3 CONCEPTUAL FRAMEWORKS

Given the study reported in this book focuses on a sample of parents notionally located within the norm, it is not surprising that a long tradition of research informs this book, some of which we briefly overview in the following text, noting though that in each of the subsequent chapters, we summarise the relevant literature in more detail. At its broadest, it is fair to say that a great majority of literature in the field of parenting studies focuses on heterosexual parents. Even with the diversification of parenting studies over the past two decades, it remains the case that many studies of 'parents' are actually studies of cisgender heterosexual parents, who are often unmarked as such. At the same time, however, many of the studies that we summarise briefly in the following text, and which have focused specifically on first-time parents, have explicitly oriented to the norms that such parents face. With specific reference to normative assumptions about women and motherhood, and gender imbalances in the division of household labour, the literature on first-time parents has been far from silent on the topic of social norms. Yet as we argue later in this section, often missing from the literature is a focus on how heterosexual first-time parents understand their location within a norm, the potential discrepancies between their positionality within a norm and their actual experiences of first-time parenthood, and the affective dimensions of being situated within the norm.

Earlier work on the transition to parenthood for heterosexual couples in the 1980s was centrally focused on the normalisation of parenthood for such couples in the context of the United States (e.g., Daniels & Weingarten, 1982). Couples interviewed struggled to account for their desire to have children, resorting to the idea that it is 'natural' or indeed 'normal' to want children. A central focus in these earlier studies was on normative expectations placed on women, the assumption being that all women should want to become mothers, and moreover that mothering comes 'naturally' to women. This early research also introduced a focus on shifts in fatherhood – what in this case Daniels and Weingarten referred to as the 'fatherhood click' (i.e., when some men become 'involved' fathers) – where they identified a move from men solely being breadwinners, to some men at the time being more actively engaged with their children. As they note, the 'fatherhood click' is shaped by 'what the culture asks of its fathers – whether they are expected to be participants or observers at home' (Daniels & Weingarten, 1982, p. 150).

Moving ahead more than two decades, the work of Miller has focused closely on similar themes, whilst also adding new dimensions to how social norms are understood to impact on heterosexual first-time parents. First, in her study of mothers in the United Kingdom, Miller (2005) drew a distinction between mothering as personal experience and motherhood as a product of institutionalised discourses that provide moral dictates about what mothering should look like in practice. As Miller highlighted, for many women, the assumption that mothering is 'natural' for women stands in stark contrast to the experiences of many women who struggle to identify as mothers or to know what is expected of them beyond normative assumptions. Indeed, in her interviews with mothers, Miller found that many of the women in the context of the United Kingdom reported shifting and indeed at times contradictory narratives about what it means to be a mother. As Miller argued, such shifts and contradictions are not a matter for concern. Rather, they demonstrate the disjuncture between motherhood narratives and the actual practices of mothering, with the latter being in many ways impeded by the normative impact of the former.

Miller (2011) then shifted her focus to fathers in the United Kingdom, producing an account of fatherhood that is still salient, namely that 'fatherhood and its associated responsibilities and practices are not so clearly defined or morally "policed" as motherhood' (p. 2). Our own work, as reported in this book and elsewhere (e.g., Bartholomaeus & Riggs, 2020), supports this claim, in the finding that men commonly experience greater latitude in how they engage with discourses of fatherhood as compared to women and discourses of motherhood. At the same time, however, the findings we share in this book differ in one key respect from the work of Miller, particularly with regard to the following claim: 'While "myths of motherhood" denote the ways in which individual mothering experiences so often do not resonate with the category "motherhood", an equivalent gulf has not (so far) been articulated in relation to the misfit between individual fathering experiences and the category "fatherhood"' (p. 6). Certainly, while for some of the men we interviewed there was not a gap between fathering experiences and norms of fatherhood, this gap did appear for some of the participants in our study.

In a similar time period as Miller (2011), though in the context of the United States, Goldberg (2014) argued that while men may not be subjected to the exact same social pressures as women – because of the 'naturalisation' of motherhood for women via an emphasis on gestation – men are nonetheless subjected to social forces that determine whether or not they will become parents. Building on the common cultural narrative of the 'biological clock' shaping the parenthood decisions of women, Goldberg argues that men are subject to both a social clock and a psychological clock. The social clock refers to men having an awareness that other people expect them to become fathers, and that there are normative assumptions about the age at which this should occur. The psychological clock refers to how men internalise societal expectations and the pressures they place on themselves to become parents. Similar to Miller, Goldberg argues that while men are subjected to social and psychological clocks, the moral imperative is different than it is for women. Mothering is expected to be all encompassing for women, while for men, fathering *can* be all encompassing, but the moral imperative for it to be so for men is much less evident. Even with the shift to discourses of 'involved fathering' since the 1970s, there is still very much a sense in which the role that men play as fathers is up for negotiation (Finn & Henwood, 2009; Hunter, Riggs, & Augoustinos, 2017).

Yet while it is very much the case that in all of the studies summarised earlier, and many others like them, the normative expectation of parenthood is the focus, it is less often the case that such research has focused on theorising why it is that heterosexual couples become parents. As we noted earlier, it does not suffice to say that heterosexual people constitute a majority, that reproduction for many heterosexual couples is possible without medical intervention, and hence that they will do so. A focus on accounts provided by heterosexual couples in which they attempt to naturalise their reproductive desires does not go beyond such individual accounts to situate them within a broader social context. A notable exception to this is the work of Morison (Morison, 2013; Morison & Macleod, 2015), who has examined how white heterosexual men in the South African context account for their location within what she terms the 'invisible norm'. Importantly, Morison moves beyond focusing on the norm itself, to unpacking the ways in which the norm works. Certainly, as we noted above, many other studies have focused on social norms about motherhood and fatherhood, but this is different to focusing on the norm of heterosexual parenthood. As Morison argues, it is at the intersections of heteronormativity, pronatalism, and moralism that heterosexual couples make decisions about having children. Heteronormativity includes the assumption of reproduction, such that having children is seen as axiomatic for many heterosexual couples, even if in practice it is not easy for all. Pronatalism emphasises reproduction as a moral duty placed primarily on the shoulders of heterosexual people. Heteronormativity and pronatalism combine to produce normative moral discourse about reproduction in which such a significant act (i.e., having a child) can be passed off as axiomatic, rather than a major life decision.

Building on the work of Morison, then, our work in this book seeks to focus both on the individual decisions that heterosexual couples make about having a first child, and how such decisions sit in the context of broader social norms. In this book, we are guided by the work of Ahmed (2010), who in her work on happiness suggests that 'feelings might be how structures get under our skin' (p. 216). This brief statement carries with it considerable import for our work in this book. Given our emphasis above on motherhood and fatherhood as reflecting institutional and gendered discourses about what is expected of mothers and fathers, part of our interest in this book is how the feelings associated with becoming a mother or father constitute a mechanism through which social norms are taken up as one's own. This, we believe, will help to more explicitly explore the difference between participants in previous research being mindful of social norms, and how they come to take up such norms as their own. A focus on feelings associated with first-time parenthood, then, allows for the necessary analytic leverage to examine how feelings are reflective of social norms (i.e., certain feelings are culturally endorsed, in potentially differing ways for women and men). It also allows us to examine how the lived experience of feelings associated with first-time parenthood – both feelings that reflect or resist normative expectations – bring social structures under the skin. This includes where there is a notional alignment between individual experiences and social expectations, and when there is a mismatch between the feelings that an individual experiences and the feelings they are expected to have about first-time parenting.

This focus on feelings being the mechanism through which structures get under the skin provides us with a way to situate the norm of parenthood for heterosexual couples within a specific context in which it is made possible, a context that we may frame as the social flesh. Beasley and Bacchi (2007) introduce the concept of 'social flesh' to evoke a political metaphor that emphasises new ways of thinking about the intersections of human bodies and the body politic. It resists a simplistic focus on the individual citizen enacting (or not) rights determined by the state, and instead emphasises the idea that both interpersonal relationships and relationships between the individuals and the state are fleshy experiences. Here the term flesh does not refer simply to the human body, but rather to how relationships between humans and between humans and the state are given 'thickness' or 'flesh' by a plethora of social norms, legislative practices, embodied experiences, and individual interactions. Beasley and Bacchi's work does not focus on parenting, but we believe it has direct application to our work in this book and take it up to use in this context. Specifically, it allows us to think about how the relationship between individual mothers and fathers and the social norms and legislative practices that relate to motherhood and fatherhood constitutes a specific form of social flesh, one through which individual people come to experience their journey into parenthood. In other words, part of our argument in this book is that specific individual experiences of first-time parenthood are always formed through the social flesh of parenthood, motherhood and fatherhood.

In order to draw attention to the role of feelings in bringing structures under our skin, and how that skin forms part of a social flesh that fundamentally shapes people's experiences of parenting, in the analytic chapters of this book, we use a comparative approach as utilised previously in Damien's work on critical kinship studies (Riggs & Peel, 2016). Specifically of relevance to this book is the practice of juxtaposition (see also Laurent et al., 2021; Vogel, 2021). Being critical of normative accounts of kinship requires placing diverse accounts of reproduction and parenthood in conversation with one another in ways that do not often occur. In a book that Damien wrote with Elizabeth Peel (Riggs & Peel, 2016), for example, they juxtaposed caring for parents living with dementia with mothers and their babies staying in psychiatric units. They juxtaposed the experiences of transgender mothers with those of cisgender mothers living with dementia. And they juxtaposed donor conception with organ donation. These juxtapositions allowed Damien and Elizabeth to explore the often kin-like discursive relations between seemingly disparate experiences of kinship, including how they intersect with one another despite their seeming differences, and how they draw upon similar discursive framings. In this book, we use juxtaposition as a way to compare and contrast experiences of first-time parent-hood, reflecting on both similarities and differences between women and men, within couples and between couples, and amongst the grandparents we interviewed. In juxtaposing these differing pairs, we examine how the social flesh is differentially experienced, and how feelings may fail to bring structures under our skin, either because we resist the restructures or are unable to comply with their demands. We also consider what it means to feel like one has 'failed' when one's experiences or feelings do not align with what social structures tell us they should be.

Finally, in terms of our conceptual frameworks, our interest in this book is to explore shifts in the social flesh of parenthood across time. As we noted earlier, and as we explore in more detail in Chapter 2, we also interviewed the parents of some of the participants. In many respects, we saw considerable continuity between generations. Yet at the same time, we also saw a process of intensification of pronatalism occurring. It is certainly the case that pronatalism has long framed parenthood as a must for heterosexual couples. What we argue has changed, is that along with this injunction to parenthood, there is also a moral requirement. For previous generations, the injunction to parenthood was accompanied by normative gendered prescriptions about what parents should morally do. Now, additionally, we argue that parents, particularly mothers, are expected to make additional moral 'choices'. This constitutes another normative moral prescription, albeit one wrapped up in the guise of neoliberal 'choice'. Different in many ways to previous generations, there is increasing significance placed on 'choice' in relation to parents deciding about the kind of birth they want, whether or not they want to know the sex of their child, what they will feed their child, what roles they will adopt, how they will engage with digital technologies such as mobile apps to track the pregnancy, what their paid work will look like after becoming a parent, and so forth (e.g., Lowe, 2016; Lupton, 2020; Miller, 2012a). This is not to say that previous generations did not have to make choices. Rather, it is to suggest a proliferation of choices, accompanied by a moral imperative to make a 'choice'. Intensification of 'choice', then, constitutes a point of difference across generations.

1.4   CHAPTER OVERVIEWS

In Chapter 2, we outline in detail our research methods, our analytic approach, and the participants. We provide commentary on our assumptions as researchers, gaining and maintaining consent, the challenges in interviewing, our decision to interview women and men separately, the challenges we faced in finding people to participate in the study, the burden we feel women were faced with in terms of ensuring their partners' participation, and the emotion work for Clare in being in close contact with the participants across a five and a half-year time frame. Given the size of our sample, we provide a very broad-brush picture of the participants, due to concerns around confidentiality (as much as we realise they will be able to identify themselves in the stories that we share). We also briefly outline our approach to analysing and reporting participant narratives in the subsequent analytic chapters.

In Chapters 3 and 5, we focus solely on the first-time mothers we interviewed. We do this for a number of reasons. First, while in the book more broadly we are interested in how gender differentiates experiences, in these two chapters, we specifically focus on women due to the ways in which gendered norms about parenthood impact most clearly on women. Second, and on a related note, our approach to understanding first-time parents adopts a feminist focus, highlighting how gendered norms directed towards women as mothers serve to prop up existing social structures. Finally, when it came to talking about intending parenthood and the work associated with new parenthood, it was women who had the most to say about both topics. The two chapters thus focus on these areas. Chapter 3 considers some of the normative moral assumptions that women are often directed to invest in when it comes to thinking about (intending) motherhood. And Chapter 5 contrasts these assumptions with the reality of what it means to become a mother. This focus on reality versus expectations is a thread that we follow throughout the book.

Sitting in between Chapters 3 and 5 is a chapter that focuses on birthing experiences. In Chapter 4, we explore how the people we spoke with narrated the experience of birth. Specifically, we explore how some women spoke about the idea of 'natural birth', the less than positive experiences that some people had, and particularly traumatic experiences of birthing. We also focus on how men spoke about their experiences of birthing, including in terms of their emotional responses and their thoughts about cutting the umbilical cord. In Chapter 6, we continue with our focus on both women and men by exploring how the people we spoke to account for the development of a parental identity. Specifically, we compare and contrast accounts of parenthood during pregnancy, and accounts shared with us after the birth. During pregnancy, unborn children were either seen as part of the family or as an abstract concept. After the birth, some of the people we interviewed struggled to see themselves as parents, while others had a very clear sense of themselves as parents.

In Chapter 7, we turn to consider what the people we spoke to thought about having more children at the time of their final interview, reflecting on this in relation to their earlier responses. We map out a number of different accounts of the idea of having more children. Some couples had only ever wanted one child, and were steadfast in that position. Some had planned to have more than one child, and had since decided that one child would be enough. Conversely, some couples had planned for only one child, but had since decided they might have more than one. Some couples were as yet undecided about whether or not to have more children, and one couple had already had a second child, and another couple were pregnant with their second child. For some of the couples we interviewed, decisions about having more children were impacted by changes to the couple relationship through the transition to parenthood. As such, in Chapter 8, we consider such changes. While the couples we interviewed all stayed in their relationships after the birth of their first child, some certainly struggled with the transition to parenthood, while other couples felt that the arrival of a child had strengthened the relationship. For some couples, it was a mix of both, with both benefits and challenges for the couple relationship as a result of the birth of their first child.

Chapter 9 changes focus to explore the interviews we undertook with the parents of the first-time parents. Some of these parents were already grandparents several times over, but many were looking forward to becoming grandparents for the first time. In Chapter 9, we consider how the parents we interviewed thought the arrival of a grandchild might change their relationship with their adult child, the role they thought they would play (or were already playing) in the lives of their adult children and grandchildren, and whether or not becoming a grandparent was likely to change how they saw themselves. In the final chapter of the book, we provide a synthesis of the key insights from the book, before exploring what the first-time parents we interviewed had to say about what it meant to them to be involved in this study, looking at both how the couple reflected on their involvement, and what benefits they felt they had gained from being involved in the study.

I.5 CONCLUDING THOUGHTS

We started this chapter by providing a brief overview of the research journey that brought us to the project reported in this book. Much like the gestational journey towards this project, our writing of this book has itself been its own gestational journey. With such a large number of interviews, we have had many conversations about how to analyse and work with our data in a way that would make a useful contribution to the literature, and might be of interest to the people we spoke to. When the project began and we had completed the first round of interviews (i.e., before the conception of a child), and then the second round, we began publishing on topics that we found both important and interesting. But as the years went by, more and more possible topics of interest became evident to us. Writing a book, then, seemed like a useful way to bring together the stories we were told across the entire project, and to be able to say something about the larger picture that is not as easy to capture in a single journal article focused on a single area of interest.

Having been offered a book contract, we then were faced with the task of reading over hundreds of hours of interview transcripts, and finding a way to do justice to them. We acknowledge that all of the stories we share in this book are partial, but we hope that they give readers an insight into the journey to, and beginning of, first-time parenthood, and how that sits in a relationship to social norms about reproduction, parenthood, motherhood, and fatherhood. Given the long history of research on parenting – including first-time parenting – our focus on a group of Australian first-time parents can only tell part of the story. But as we outlined earlier in this chapter, we believe that a focus on affect, the taking up of social norms and the intersections of feelings and social flesh make an important contribution to understanding the ways in which heterosexual couples navigate first-time parenthood.

2 Undertaking a Qualitative Longitudinal Research Study with Intending Parents

2.1 INTRODUCTION

Qualitative longitudinal research has been extensively used to examine individual people's experiences across time, including in relation to key life transitions (Henwood et al., 2012; Holland, Thomson, & Henderson, 2006; Saldaña, 2003; Thomson & McLeod, 2015). Situating individuals within a relational context through qualitative longitudinal research offers the opportunity to consider how relationships change and are changed by the individuals within them (e.g., Thomson et al., 2011). In this chapter, we introduce our qualitative longitudinal research project with heterosexual first-time parents. As we noted in Chapter 1, and as we explore further in the following text, while much has been written about heterosexual couples having a first child (given they constitute a norm with regard to reproduction), there is little research on how heterosexual couples planning for a first child negotiate their place within the norm of which they are notionally a part, and even less research on how such negotiations change over time. Our study *Feeling, Wanting, Having: The Meaning of Children to Heterosexual Couples* has afforded us the opportunity to consider some of the relational contexts in which people in heterosexual couples negotiate the injunction to reproduce, and how this injunction shifts over time.

Importantly, the insights that we have gained from this study have implications for qualitative longitudinal research that focuses on relationships rather than solely individuals. Our aim in this chapter is thus to explore some of the general principles that might be of interest to other researchers, particularly in the social sciences, undertaking or planning to undertake a qualitative longitudinal research project that focuses on relationships, or the relational contexts in which individuals exist. Specifically, we canvas issues related to establishing a qualitative longitudinal research project focused on relationships, the challenges that may arise and potential strategies for managing these, and the emotion work associated with undertaking a qualitative longitudinal research project focused on relationships. We then provide a broad overview of the study participants and conclude the chapter with an overview of how we analysed our interview data for the current book. Before focusing on each of these areas, we first provide a brief background to the study itself.

2.2 BACKGROUND TO THE STUDY

The key aims of the *Feeling, Wanting, Having* study were to examine the decision-making, expectations, and desires related to planning for (and then having) a first child amongst a normative sample of middle-class heterosexual Australian couples. While such couples are typically treated as the norm in terms of becoming parents, their experiences are less often examined explicitly (Morison & Macleod, 2015). Specifically, the naturalisation of reproductive heterosex often means that the reasons for why heterosexual couples desire to have children are left unexamined. We argue that the value of such research lies in its usefulness to examine how people are enmeshed in dominant discourses relating to having children, particularly in the context of heterosexual relationships.

The study involved interviews with members of nine couples at four stages:

1) when the couples were planning a pregnancy via reproductive heterosex (i.e., without the assistance of reproductive technologies),
2) at the six-month mark of pregnancy,
3) six months after the birth of the child, and
4) eighteen months after the birth of the child.

Semi-structured interviews were undertaken individually with each member of the couple by Clare. The early interviews tended to take place in person, whereas the later interviews (particularly the third interview) were more often via telephone or video call (e.g., Skype), to suit the participants. Each member of the couple was interviewed at each stage of the research (four times each, for a total of seventy-two interviews), as we explore further in the following text. All of the participants in the nine couples completed the interviews at each stage of the study, including one couple who re-joined the study after they were able to conceive. We chose these time points in order to provide us with a broad view of heterosexual couples' journeys to parenthood, being mindful of not requiring time too late in the pregnancy or too soon after the birth of their child.

The study additionally involved interviews with ten of the parents of the couples, at one time point. Couple participants were provided with information for their parents to participate, and it was up to them if they were willing to invite their parents to be part of the study. This additional cross-sectional focus adds breadth to the study by considering how parents account for their own experiences of becoming parents, as well as their views about their child becoming a parent. As such, these interviews add a further focus on the relational aspects of individual experiences of reproduction, and help to situate the experiences of the couple within some of their broader relational contexts. Institutional ethics approval for the research was granted by our university.

2.3 ESTABLISHING A QUALITATIVE LONGITUDINAL STUDY FOCUSED ON RELATIONSHIPS

In this section, we focus on some of the considerations that we see as important when planning for and establishing a qualitative longitudinal research project that focuses on relationships. Specifically, we address (1) the need to reflect on the assumptions and perspectives of the research team, (2) how consent is gained and maintained in a longitudinal project, and (3) decisions about the interviewing approach.

2.3.1 Researcher Assumptions and Perspectives

Research projects typically arise from topics or experiences that researchers are invested in, whether that investment be personal or political or both, and is particularly the case with feminist research (e.g., Haggis, 1990/2013; Letherby, 2002). From the onset of this project as researchers, we were mindful of our own relationships to pronatalism, and how our personal critiques of the injunction to reproduce were likely to shape the project. Yet, despite our awareness of the potential impact of our personal positions, we felt it important to undertake a project that, for both of us, was outside of our usual focus on 'family diversity', as we outlined in Chapter 1. Indeed, adding a focus on heterosexual couples to our previous research areas seemed an important way to bring such couples into a 'diversity' framework, rather than leaving their motivations and decision-making as the (unexplored) norm.

As a strategy to maintain a balance between our critique of pronatalism with respect for the participants, we have sought in our analyses of the data to focus on investments in reproduction in two key ways. The first of these involves a focus on investments in a norm, and occupying a place within it. The second explores the affective dimensions of this investment. This latter dimension is, in many ways, much harder to articulate and explain, as we found in our interviews. Having interview questions that were, from the onset, designed to elicit affect has been an important part of our research design, so as to avoid producing data that simplistically repeat normative assumptions about reproduction. By gently encouraging the participants to explore more deeply the accounts that they provided, we now have access to a rich set of data that allow us to consider what it means to be affected by the injunction to reproduce, and how this is shaped by the relational contexts in which the participants existed.

2.3.2 Consent to Participate in a Longitudinal Study

In all research projects, researchers must find ways to ensure that participants can meaningfully give informed consent, which goes beyond signing a consent form. The idea of informed consent, however, is vexed in the context of longitudinal research, as participants are being asked well in advance to agree to give up their time over a number of years and to talk about experiences they cannot anticipate at the start of the study (Miller & Bell, 2012). We would suggest that this issue of time demand and the extent to which any individual can foresee their ability to make a time and emotional commitment into the future is exacerbated in the context of research with a relational focus, given the very premise of such research is that relationships change with time. That any individual might feel comfortable sharing the details of their relationship in the present is not necessarily a guarantee that they will be willing to do so in the future.

In the context of our research, it was important to be aware from the onset that we might need to say goodbye to some participants if they faced unexpected events. One couple decided to leave the study more than six months after the first interview because of the fertility issues they were experiencing. It is interesting to note that when communicating this to us, the woman in the couple expressed her 'embarrassment' at 'wasting' our time and their time by participating in the study, clearly speaking to the impact of pronatalism and the pressures of conceiving in a straightforward way. Our ethically informed response to this was not to try to convince them to stay, but rather to leave it open to them to re-join the study at a later stage if they desired (and, of course, to reassure them that they had made a valuable contribution to the project and had certainly not wasted our time). It was also important that the participants knew we would not contact them again, but that they were welcome to contact us. In this instance, the couple later re-joined the study after conceiving and proceeded with the subsequent interviews.

2.3.3 Benefits and Challenges of Having the Same Interviewer

It was important in the context of a longitudinal project focused on relationships for us to consider how the interviews would be conducted. While we could have taken turns at interviewing different couples, or each interviewing either women or men, we agreed with Forbat and Henderson's suggestion that having the same interviewer allows for 'making connections in the analysis of both stories that might otherwise remain implicit or underexplored' (2003, p. 1458). We also felt it was particularly important to have the same interviewer conduct all of the interviews to build connections with both members of each couple.

If the decision is made that one researcher will conduct all of the interviews, a number of potential issues need to be thought through, particularly with regard to maintaining confidentiality. Forbat and Henderson (2003) raise a number of questions about the ethics of introducing topics or issues mentioned by one member of an intimate relationship with the other. In our study, we were fortunate in that participants rarely asked what their partners had told Clare, although they sometimes asked if their partner had mentioned a certain topic, usually with the sense that they did not need to go into detail about it if she was already aware of the 'facts'. As we were focused on hearing about experiences from both partners, Clare emphasised that she was interested in each participant's perspectives and experiences, even if their partner had already discussed the topic in their interview.

Another challenge associated with the same person interviewing both members of a couple is that a greater rapport may be built with one member of the couple than the other. Forbat and Henderson (2003) suggest that interviewers may often be 'stuck in the middle' of two participants, meaning that they may develop a closer relationship with one participant more than the other. While this may occur in any project, we would suggest that it is especially important in qualitative longitudinal research focused on relationships, where the work of both building rapport and coming to understand the relationship (and the individuals within it) may at times be at odds with one another. In the context of feminist research on heterosexual relationships, rapport may also be impacted on when researchers are confronted with examples of gender inequality within the relationship (see also Hubbard, Backett-Milburn, & Kemmer, 2001). This certainly occurred within our study, but the general pattern of the interviews where Clare asked questions (and further prompts) and participants responded in ways they felt comfortable meant that rapport was maintained in a non-judgemental environment.

2.3.4 Interviewing Women and Men Separately

Another decision that must be made when conducting qualitative longitudinal research that focuses on relationships is whether the individuals in the relationship will be interviewed together or separately. Existing research suggests that individuals within couples are likely to have different investments in, and desires to have, children (Miller, Severy, & Pasta, 2004). Thus, for the present study, members of each couple were interviewed separately to explore their views and feelings in depth so they could talk more freely without the presence of their partner. This also allowed us to analyse how sense was made of the relationship absent of it being physically present in the interview space.

As we found, interviewing couples separately has a number of other benefits including (1) being able to ask about topics that participants might not have discussed with each other, (2) enabling participants to be more open to discussing topics separately, particularly if they are sensitive, relate to different opinions than their partner, or involve things that would be uncomfortable to talk about in the presence of their partner, (3) preventing one member of the couple dominating the interview, (4) avoiding couples giving a sanctioned 'couple narrative' and/or reaching consensus on topics in the interview, and (5) going beyond the idea of couples as unified units of analysis (Eisikovits & Koren, 2010; Heaphy & Einarsdottir, 2012; Hertz, 1995; Mellor et al., 2013; Miller et al., 2004). In addition, in our study, we found that interviewing members of each couple separately turned out to be an important decision, given that, for the most part, men spent more time thinking about their responses before speaking, and benefited from more follow-up questions than did women. The power dynamics within couples would also likely have impacted on the responses we received to our questions.

A potentially significant ethical challenge with interviewing both members of the same couple separately is that, if reading any resulting publications or outputs from the study, participants may be able to identify their partner. This is particularly the case if quotes from both members of a couple are placed side by side in a publication where participants may recognise what they said and thus can easily identify their partner (Forbat & Henderson, 2003), but may also be an issue if a couple has experienced events that are specific to them and thus more identifiable (e.g., less common experiences relating to conception, birth, and so on). Thus, it is important that participants are informed about the possibilities that their partner may identify them (Peters et al., 2008). On the information letter given to all participants in our study, we highlighted that while participants' confidentiality was guaranteed in the context of the general public, it was possible that particular aspects of the experiences they shared (if reported in subsequent publications) may be identifiable to their partners, but potentially also to any family members or close friends who read them. This was a point which we also reiterated in the interviews. As we discuss in Chapter 10, participants were generally open with their partners about what they had shared in the interviews, so this was less of an issue for our project. There was also the issue of the first-time parents and their parents potentially identifying each other in publications, which we also raised with participants. However, as we asked the first-time parents to invite their parents only if they were comfortable with including them in the study, and participation of the parents was predicated on their children participating, they were able to reflect on any potential confidentiality issues prior to consenting to being interviewed.

2.4   CHALLENGES IN ESTABLISHING AND MANAGING A QUALITATIVE LONGITUDINAL STUDY FOCUSED ON RELATIONSHIPS

As we noted in Section 2.3, there are many factors requiring consideration when establishing a qualitative longitudinal research project that focuses on relationships. Yet, even having considered these factors in the planning stages, this does not necessarily mitigate against challenges arising once the project begins. Specifically, we now focus on challenges in (1) identifying outlets through which to find potential participants, (2) the burden often assumed by women in relationship-focused research, and (3) researching topics that by their very nature are 'aspirational'.

2.4.1 Identifying Outlets for Finding Potential Participants

Having considered the factors outlined earlier with regard to establishing a qualitative longitudinal project focused on relationships, and having been granted institutional ethics approval, the next challenge is then to explore ways to find potential participants and invite them to participate. This requires targeted strategies that place information about the study in front of people fitting the target demographics. As we came to advertise the study, we realised that many parenting-related outlets focus on people who already have children or at least have already conceived. Our challenge, then, was to try to reach people who were planning to have children, but who had not yet conceived. We advertised in local media and community newspapers and on Facebook and Twitter, organised for a news story to be run in the main newspaper in our state, and posted details about the study on a range of forums that focus on parents and pregnancy planning. While over 2,000 people visited the study website in the space of a month, only sixteen made contact asking for more information. People who contacted us but did not take part in the study told us that they had decided not to participate without giving a reason or because they did not have time, did not reply to our follow-up emails, or, in the case of one couple, a recent miscarriage meant they were not yet ready to participate in such a study.

We have spent a lot of time talking and reflecting about the possible barriers to finding participants. One issue may have been that we focused only on one state in Australia (largely in order to be able to conduct face-to-face interviews), although considering the normative sample this still left us with a large potential participant pool. We suggest there were likely two key reasons behind our difficulties: that both members of couples were required to participate (which often meant that women acted as 'managers' of the couple) and that we sought the participation of couples prior to pregnancy. We consider the implications of these two reasons now.

2.4.2 Burden Placed upon Women in Relationship-Focused Research

While we were not gender specific in our targeting (unlike other research such as Mellor et al.'s (2013) study, which recruited heterosexual couples from contraceptive clinics that primarily provide services for women), it was clear that women acted as 'managers' of the couple, a phenomenon that is useful to explore further. Mellor et al. (2013) suggest that men may be involved in heterosexual couple research to please their partners who are keen to participate, and may become involved because they have no objections to participating, rather than explicitly desiring to participate. In the context of our study, this may have meant that women often strongly encouraged or influenced their partners to participate, potentially meaning that partners were less purposively involved when they were recruited in this way (Mellor et al., 2013).

In our study, it was usually the woman in the couple who first learnt about the study. For example, this occurred by seeing a story about the study in the state-wide newspaper, a woman's mother seeing a paid advertisement for the study in the local newspaper, and via online promotion by our university. However, three couples were found via snowballing where both members of the couple said they had heard about the study from a friend or family member, and wanted to participate.

After finding participants, in some couples, women continued to act as 'managers', with some organising interviews for their partners or making sure their partners replied to Clare's emails to arrange interview times. This was also the case with regard to the interviews with the parents of the participants, which were typically facilitated by women and were primarily the parent(s) of women. For this part of the project, we interviewed six mothers and four fathers of participants. Notably, fathers were only involved if their wives were also being interviewed. This again showed the work that women did in organising participation in the research. Only one father was directly in touch with us to organise the interviews with himself and his wife, whereas all other interviews were arranged by women (mothers in all but one case where the daughter arranged the interviews).

Of course, it is important to note that while the role of 'manager' may at first glance appear to suggest that women were controlling of their partners, we would suggest that in fact the work of relationship 'management' is often a highly gendered activity in heterosexual relationships, with women often expected to take up the work of managing the day-to-day running of the relationship, especially with regard to emotion work (e.g., DeVault, 1999). That the women in our sample were those most likely to be actively involved in organising participation is thus likely a result of this normative gendered expectation. This has implications for qualitative longitudinal research focused on heterosexual relationships, particularly where such research seeks to trouble gender inequalities within a feminist framework. In the context of our study that the very dynamics we sought to investigate with regard to gender and pronatalism were repeated when communicating with participants highlights the endemic nature of the phenomena we are trying to investigate.

2.4.3 Seeking Participants prior to an Event

There are particular challenges in finding participants for a qualitative longitudinal study that involves participant aspirations or anticipation of an 'event'. For both potential researchers and participants, there will likely be concerns about the possibility that the 'event' may not happen at all, or at least may not happen in an expected time frame. While in our case the 'event' was pregnancy, followed by childbirth, this issue is useful to reflect on more broadly for other qualitative longitudinal studies such as those related to health issues and other transitions.

In the context of our research focusing on heterosexual couples intending to conceive in the near future, rather than couples who are already pregnant, we encountered issues that other studies focusing on the journey to parenthood avoid. Longitudinal studies of first-time parenthood beginning during (usually late) pregnancy have more obvious sites from which to seek participants, such as antenatal classes (Lupton & Barclay, 1997) and childbirth courses (Fox, 2009), although some researchers have still reported difficulties in finding participants during pregnancy (Miller, 2012b). In the context of our study, we would suggest that many people in the planning stages might be concerned about what lies ahead, and might not want to jinx things by talking to us before they conceive, hence limiting our sample. We could also only interview couples who were planning to conceive, rather than those who were open to having a child but not specifically intending to have a child. Finally, we were looking specifically for first-time parents, where both members of the couple did not have children.

Despite our awareness of these potential concerns, we nonetheless made the assumption that couples would conceive during the first year of the study, highlighting how we as the researchers were caught up in dominant discourses that silence infertility. Our study advertisements explicitly sought participants with 'no significant history of fertility concerns', which reduced the possibility of including couples with *known* fertility issues, but, as it turned out, several of the couples had fertility issues that were not yet known to them. While we had an optional 'exit interview' planned for participants who left the study if they had not conceived a year from the initial interview, we had really expected this to come into effect more in terms of couples deciding not to have children or postponing this until later. As we discussed in the section on emotion work with participants, these assumptions had the potential to cause issues when we contacted participants after the first interview to check when they would be ready for the second interview.

2.5 EMOTION WORK IN A QUALITATIVE LONGITUDINAL STUDY FOCUSED ON RELATIONSHIPS

Much of this book is about affect and emotion in relation to wanting and having a child. In this section, we focus on the emotion work involved in conducting qualitative longitudinal research, particularly in terms of the topic of our research and relationships built with participants.

Hochschild (1979, 1983/2003) defines emotion work as the practice of managing feeling (evoking or suppressing emotions) for a particular use, which can be for payment or in private contexts. In the context of qualitative longitudinal research that focuses on relationships, emotion work is undertaken by both researchers and participants. It was always likely to be the case that our study would involve a significant degree of emotion work, given we first met participants when they were planning to have a child (rather than when they were already pregnant) and hence their aspirations and anxieties would be very much at the forefront from the beginning. Given we know from previous research that significant life events can at times bring with them relationship dissolution, including in relation to pregnancy loss (Gold, Sen, & Hayward, 2010) and the birth of a first child (Gamgam Leanderz et al., 2021), we were also likely to be privy to emotion work arising from the relational nature of the research. In Sections 2.5.1 and 2.5.2, we reflect on the emotion work associated with (1) ongoing contact with participants in the face of (in)fertility and pregnancy loss, and (2) relationships of trust with participants.

2.5.1 Ongoing Contact with Participants in the Face of (In)fertility and Pregnancy Loss

Unlike other qualitative longitudinal studies, starting a study prior to pregnancy meant we had to take particular care when contacting participants to check when they would be ready for their second interview (at the six-month pregnancy mark). While we had originally asked participants to tell us when they were three months pregnant, an increasing amount of time often passed after the first interview without hearing back from them. Thus, participants seemed to be experiencing what Sweeny et al. call 'a series of uncertain waiting periods' during the process of trying to conceive (2015, p. 131). As the study progressed, and we realised the difficulty some participants were having conceiving, we sent infrequent emails (approximately every six months) to say we were just 'checking in' to see how they were going, without asking the question of whether they had conceived. The use of email rather than telephone meant participants could respond in their own time, which we argue is particularly important when studying potentially sensitive topics.

Again, it was notable that while both members of the couple were emailed (aside from two men who did not provide their email addresses until later in the study), in all cases it was women who first responded to these emails and maintained ongoing contact with Clare, thus undertaking the bulk of the emotion work for the couple in this context. The emails we sent were generally well received, with participants commenting that they appreciated us keeping in touch and, in some cases, had been thinking about the study, and either telling us that they had nothing to report yet, or detailing some of the fertility issues (and sometimes treatments) they were having. We were particularly concerned to respond in a caring manner, so we discussed between us the issues raised in the emails (particularly when fertility problems or pregnancy loss was mentioned) before Clare then replied to participants. The cumulative effect of these emails certainly had an impact on us, as we became less concerned about the progress of the study and more concerned about the couples and the challenges they were facing. To our surprise, sometimes participants expressed to us that they were sorry their fertility issues were delaying our research. While we had provided participants with a comprehensive support services and information sheet prior to the first interview (with supports for infertility, pregnancy loss, and child loss), we were also available as ongoing support for the participants, and reassured them that their main focus should be themselves and their family, rather than our study.

Our focus here on our communication with participants outside of the interviews raises a broader issue about what participants consent to. Miller (2012b) argues that it is unclear what constitutes 'the data' in studies which produce additional communication such as emails, mobile phone text messages, and voicemail messages. For our study, participants consented specifically to participation in interviews, which would be audio-recorded and this is what we gained institutional ethics approval to use. We, therefore, have not included excerpts of email text in our analytic chapters (unlike e.g., Miller, 2015), but instead have spoken broadly about the email communication between us and the participants here in order to highlight the need for sensitive responses. However, as Miller (2012b) also argues, even if this additional communication is not used as data, it influences the ways in which researchers engage with the data collected formally.

2.5.2   *Relationships of Trust with Participants*

For qualitative longitudinal research that focuses on relationships, researchers are privy to a certain period of time in a relationship. As a significant life event, the birth (or desired birth) of a child provides us entry into an important part of the relationship narrative, thus positioning us in a significant relationship of trust with the participants. Specifically in terms of our project, in many cases participants were disclosing information about pregnancy and infertility that their family and close friends did not necessarily know about at the time. As such, we explore the ethical implications of the trust participants place in researchers, which may be heightened in the context of qualitative longitudinal research focused on relationship transitions.

In the context of our study, in some cases, participants mentioned that Clare was the first person outside of the couple to know about the pregnancy, or at least one of few who knew in the early stages, in some cases even prior to their own parents. This, we would suggest, demonstrates the level of trust that participants had in Clare, but also implicitly in what was a university-based study that gave a level of authority to the project. One couple had not told their parents (or potentially anyone) they were trying to have a baby due to continued pressure they received from them to have children. Similarly, one male participant told Clare that she was one of four people to know the name of their baby at the six month of pregnancy interview, and that even his parents did not yet know. When speaking about the birth at the third interview (when their baby was six months old), another male participant told Clare he had not discussed the traumatic birth with anyone aside from his partner. While this offers us as researchers an important insight into the relational dynamics that shape couples' experiences of having a child, it also means that the researcher is located in a significant relationship of trust with the participants, which brings with it considerable emotion work in terms of being a key (or potentially the only) person with whom the participants were sharing their ongoing concerns and challenges. This means there is the potential for interviewers to become treated as pseudo counsellors, as the very nature of conducting research about 'intimate' aspects of people's lives has similarities with therapeutic practice (Birch & Miller, 2000). However, for our study, it appeared that just being able to talk about some of these issues, without counselling responses, was already beneficial for several of the participants. We return to this in our reflection on participants' experiences of being involved in the study in Chapter 10.

2.6   THE PEOPLE WE INTERVIEWED

Given the relatively small sample size of our study (nine couples, comprising eighteen individuals, along with ten parents of some of these individuals), in this section, we only provide a broad overview of the people we spoke to and their experiences. We provide additional contextual details in the relevant chapters, although have avoided sharing some specific details due to confidentiality concerns. We allocated pseudonyms to the people we spoke to in order to discuss their stories. We felt that asking the people we spoke with to provide their own pseudonyms was potentially fraught in the context of this particular study, as people often choose names of people they know or which are significant to them.

The demographic data we collected at the time of the first interviews showed that the women in the couples were 25–38 years old (mean 31.9 years) and the men were 26–41 years old (mean 32.6 years). In terms of education, all of the women and five of the men had a bachelor degree or higher, and four of the men's highest qualification attained was either secondary school or a trade certificate. Most of the people we interviewed were engaged in full-time work at this stage of the study, with three being full-time students. Income varied at the time of the first interview. Paid work and study status changed throughout the study, as did income. Twelve of the people we interviewed identified as "somewhat" or "quite" religious, with their religion named as Christian or Catholic.

In terms of relationship status, at the time of the first interviews, six of the couples were married, two were engaged, and one was in a de facto relationship (i.e., living together and legally recognised as a couple but not married). The two engaged couples married prior to the second interview (and the birth of their child). At the first interview, the relationship length of the couples varied significantly. Overall, couples had been together for a time period spanning between just over a year and just over thirteen years (mean six years) and had lived together for between six weeks and over twelve years (mean 4.5 years). Of the married participants, at the first interview, couples had been married for between four months and nine years (mean four years). Most of the people we spoke to were born in Australia, though a small number were born overseas and had migrated to Australia.

In terms of the experiences of the first-time parents with regard to conception and birth, a number of them experienced challenges in conceiving. While we had initially anticipated our study would take less than four years, it stretched to five and a half years.

All of the couples were attempting to conceive in the first year of the study (some before we had interviewed them), apart from one couple who were initially waiting due to financial reasons, and then experienced a miscarriage after conceiving the first time. However, our second interviews (at the six-month mark of pregnancy) took place over a wide time span, largely due to fertility issues of some kind. Two couples were interviewed at the six-month mark of pregnancy in the first year of the study, three in the second year, two in the third year, and two in the fourth year. Some participants explored fertility treatments, with some using 'low tech' treatments (e.g., medication, including to stimulate ovulation) and one couple undertaking in vitro fertilisation after trying several other options. Another couple were considering in vitro fertilisation or possibly a donor egg but eventually conceived. A small number of participants experienced a pregnancy loss, all relatively early in the pregnancy. We explore difficulties with conception, including pregnancy loss in Chapter 3. Some of the people we spoke to had quite complicated births (some requiring emergency caesarean sections, and one requiring the newborn to spend time in a neonatal intensive care unit), as we explore in Chapter 4. All women delivered in a hospital, some using private care, and some accessed the public system. Several requested and received an epidural as part of their delivery. After the birth, a number of participants experienced challenges that approximated what might be classified as postnatal depression, and some sought professional help related to infant sleeping and feeding. We explore this further in Chapter 3.

In addition to the couple participants, we also interviewed ten parents (six mothers and four fathers). Several of the (intending) grandparent participants were soon to be grandparents for the first time, or had just become grandparents, whereas a smaller number already had grandchildren. We note that these participants spanned a broad time period, as they were born in the 1940s–1960s and had become parents in the mid-1970s to late 1980s. They also had differing family relationships (e.g., number of children, couple relationships). These participants were interviewed when it was convenient for them in the second year of the study. This meant that their children in the study were at different stages of their parenting journey (e.g., trying to conceive, pregnant, or had their child). The parents of participants are the focus of Chapter 9.

2.7   OUR APPROACH TO ANALYSING THE INTERVIEW DATA

As we noted in Chapter 1, our early analyses of primarily the first and second rounds of interviews focused on specific topics that we found to be interesting. Several publications centred on our initial key focus of the reasons for having children and the decision-making process, specifically the decision-making of couples to have a child (Riggs & Bartholomaeus, 2016b), accounts of why the participants wanted to have a child in the context of 'compulsory parenthood' (Riggs & Bartholomaeus, 2018), the desire for children framed as 'natural' (Riggs & Peel, Chapter 4), and the views of the intending fathers in relation to reasons for having children (Bartholomaeus & Riggs, 2020). We also wrote about the gendered division of labour amongst first-time parents (Riggs & Bartholomaeus, 2020), experiences of the transition to parenthood and couple relationships (Riggs, Worth, & Bartholomaeus, 2018), and pronatalist discourses amongst women and their mothers (Bartholomaeus & Riggs, 2017a). For these journal articles, we typically used the approach to thematic analysis outlined by Braun and Clarke (2006) to examine each of these topics, and in so doing highlighted the ways that the participants in our study elaborated their views. Damien also used snippets of the data in dialogue with data from other projects on diverse family forms in his book *Diverse Pathways to Parenthood* (Riggs, 2020).

For the analytic chapters in this book, we used a different approach in order to consider all four rounds of interviews. Damien read all of the interview transcripts closely, with a view to identifying potential juxtapositions (Riggs & Peel, 2016). Damien also produced summaries of each of the interviews, to provide a broader overview for each person interviewed. In the analytic chapters that follow, we draw on these summaries, alongside specific extracts from the interviews, to provide a narrative account of the juxtapositions that Damien identified. Clare added to these summaries and the narratives throughout the book, providing context from her experiences of conducting the interviews and interacting with the participants, as well as returning to the original transcripts when needed. Whilst our presentation of the analytic material in each chapter represents the broad contours of all of the interviews, our focus is primarily on using the approach to juxtaposition to share larger narratives from the participants. In other words, rather than reporting closely codified thematic analyses of the interviews, our interest is to tell something of the story of the participants, in narrative format. In places this means we include direct quotes and unpack their contents, and in other places we paraphrase the narratives provided by the participants. Even in the context of a book, it would be impossible to do justice to every word that the participants spoke, hence this narrative approach combines both the broad contours of the interviews and provides specific details about the participants' experiences. We also note that we focus on some participants more than others in these stories, but that the experiences of all of the participants helped to inform what we wrote about in each of the chapters.

2.8 CONCLUDING THOUGHTS

In this chapter, we have considered some of the key factors that we have seen play out in the context of a qualitative longitudinal research project that focuses on relationships. Specifically, we have focused on aspects to consider when planning for and establishing such a project, some of the challenges that can arise in the context of such projects, and the emotion work that can arise for both researchers and participants. A focus on relationships is nothing new in qualitative research more broadly, but a qualitative longitudinal research project has enabled us to explore this in more depth. With regard to our study, a relational focus was an obvious way to approach the topic, given that while it is individual people who are pregnant and give birth (i.e., cisgender heterosexual women in our research), and individuals who are party to that pregnancy and birth (i.e., cisgender heterosexual men), in the context of heterosexual couples planning for a first child these are both a relational phenomenon.

Qualitative longitudinal research projects in the social sciences that focus on relationships have much to offer in terms of how we understand the lifecourses of relationships, in whatever form they take. As entities in themselves, relationships are never static, and observing their changes over time is an important research agenda. The merits of qualitative longitudinal research, however, will always be determined by the extent to which researchers plan for projects that are equally able to change and grow over time, incorporating new issues as they arise, responding to challenges, and being mindful of the emotion work they are likely to produce for both researchers and participants. We also note, of course, the many positive emotions that are produced in qualitative longitudinal research, such as connections between researchers and participants, and sharing in the joy of the journey to first-time parenthood.

As we explore in the chapters to come, across all of our interviews, considerable change is evident. This might seem axiomatic, given the interviews focus on the transition to first-time parenthood. Specifically, our interest is in how their location within a norm meant that for some of the people we spoke to change was unexpected and came as a surprise. For some, reality did not match up with expectations, and for others, the reality brought with it a whole new level of joy, or alternatively, challenges. Mapping these points of change, as we do within and between chapters, again highlights the utility of qualitative longitudinal research for the study of the experiences of heterosexual first-time parents.

3   Motherhood Moralities

Ideas about what it means to be a parent do not come about in isolation. Rather, they are shaped by the messages that people receive about what it means to be a parent: messages evident in the media, in parenting books, and from friends and family. People of all genders are targeted by messages about parenting, but as we explore in this chapter, it is arguably the case that it is women who are most concertedly the target of messages about parenting. As we explore, messages about motherhood, in particular, are typically moral messages: they instruct women not only that womanhood is normatively equated with motherhood, but further that women should enact, or at least are expected to enact, a very specific way of being a mother. Women are not only expected to become mothers, but they are expected to conceive easily, to find pregnancy and birth a joy, to find breastfeeding and childcare a breeze, and to commit to all of this with gusto and without regret. Furthermore, most of this is expected to be done within the context of a committed heterosexual relationship.

Harrison (2021) refers to the normative expectations placed upon mothers, in particular, as the 'tyranny of the should'. This phrase highlights the moral dimensions of motherhood. It is not simply that the expectations placed upon women outlined earlier are treated as ideal, but rather they are treated as a moral imperative. It is not that women have a 'choice' to become mothers, rather it is widely promoted that they *should*, and moreover that they should *want* to. Women are not widely seen as 'choosing' breastfeeding, but rather it is expected that they *should* breastfeed. And women do not have a 'choice' about how they relate to their child, rather it is expected they *should* love their child and desire to spend time with them. Furthermore, women certainly should *not* regret having children (see, e.g., Donath, 2015; Garncarek, 2020). These moral imperatives persist in contemporary western societies despite significant changes to women's roles in society. Despite more women in paid work and fewer women opting to or being able to stay at home with children, there is nonetheless a moral imperative for women, where possible, to prioritise their children, even when in paid work.

Certainly, it is the case that moral imperatives are also placed on men who are fathers. Increasingly, men are expected to be actively engaged with their children, and to do more than simply be the distant breadwinning father (Hunter, Riggs, & Augoustinos, 2017). But as we outlined in Chapter 1, in many ways, there is a sense in which imperatives about fatherhood are still seen as negotiable. While it might be socially desirable that men are engaged, there are multiple ways in which fathers are excused from such moral imperatives. The same is not the case for women who are mothers. For gestational parents who are men or who have a non-binary gender, cisgenderism functions to assert both narratives of inadequacy in terms of parenting, at the same time as reinforcing normative assumptions whereby gestation equals motherhood equals moral imperatives of self-sacrifice (Fischer, 2020). The tyranny of the should, then, is both differentially felt, but centrally shaped by assumptions about gestation and birth and the 'natural' role accorded to certain bodies.

In this chapter, we focus on a small number of women we interviewed in order to explore how moralities about motherhood shaped their experiences. We use the analytic strategy of juxtaposition in a number of purposive ways. First, we juxtapose knowledge about normative motherhood expectations prior to and during pregnancy, with the reality of living with such expectations after the birth of a child. We do this by focusing on interviews with individual women across time. We also juxtapose women's moral claims across interview time periods, highlighting how women's own moral positions on motherhood changed with experience and time. We do this by focusing on three specific areas where moral claims are often made about women and motherhood. First, we focus on the idea that conceiving a child is 'natural', and should be straightforward for women, and that infertility or challenges in conception are hence a moral failing. Second, we explore the topic of breastfeeding, including the assumption that breastfeeding should again be 'natural' and straightforward for women, and that any experience otherwise represents a moral shortcoming. Finally, we explore how differences between expectations about motherhood and the reality of motherhood can be formative in women's experiences of postnatal mental health issues.

We conclude the chapter by taking up some of the arguments we made in Chapter 1, namely Ahmed's (2010) claim that 'feelings might be how structures get under our skin' (p. 216). Specifically, we consider how moral claims about motherhood, as we explore in this chapter, evoke particular emotional responses from women that further inculcate them into normative understandings of womanhood being equated with motherhood, and we consider further how this is not equally applied to men.

3.2   MORAL CLAIMS ACROSS THE EARLY INTERVIEWS

Before we turn to look at the three topic areas outlined earlier as they were discussed by some of the women we interviewed, in this section, we first provide a broad overview of some of the previous findings published from our project. Specifically, we focus on work where we have implicitly or explicitly examined moral claims, including in terms of how they are differentiated according to participant gender. This, we feel, is important, given our focus in this chapter is primarily on women. While, as we argued earlier, moral claims about parenthood are indeed primarily levelled at women, we do not want to perpetuate the idea that men are absent from being either targets of or as perpetuating moral claims about parenthood.

In this section, we specifically focus on two journal articles we have written that explored the views of the people we spoke to at the first interview time point: when they were planning to conceive. In later chapters of this book, we focus on other articles we have written looking at different time points, that are more relevant to the topics discussed in those chapters. In the first article we wrote (Riggs & Bartholomaeus, 2016b), we focused on how the people we spoke to made the decision to have a first child. Our interpretation was that in each couple, the decision to have a child was either jointly directed or primarily directed by one person. In the one couple where it was the woman who directed the decision, we found that while the woman felt that having a child was 'natural', her partner required some encouragement in that direction. Here we see a normatively gendered moral claim about having a first child: women should want a child and men will go along for the ride. By contrast, in the two couples where it was the man who was more strongly invested in having a child, both of the women voiced strong criticisms of the moral presumption that all women should want to have children. While both women wanted to try to conceive, they were also critical of the idea that women are incomplete if they do not have children. The remainder of the couples we interviewed indicated that they had jointly decided to have a child. Yet there were differences among these couples. For some, there was a moral claim made in regard to parenthood that framed it as 'instinctual', 'natural', and a normative part of a relationship (and individual) lifecourse. Couples in this group jointly decided in the sense that both members seemed equally invested in adhering to a normative lifecourse trajectory, and in so doing espoused moral claims about parenthood that they often struggled to explain, a point we take up in the following text in regard to the second article we summarise here. The other group of couples who jointly decided did so out of necessity, primarily due to the age of the woman. Certainly, these were couples who wanted a child, but the push to do so sooner rather than later reflected less such a clear investment in moral claims about parenthood being 'instinctual' or 'natural', and more that ultimately being parents was something they wanted, and they needed to act quickly before their reproductive window closed. Certainly, the idea of a 'reproductive window' is not absent of moral claims, but the difference was that some of these participants to a degree accepted the normative injunction to have children (i.e., they did not appear to problematise it), while at the same time not being so centrally invested in it.

In the second article we wrote (Riggs & Bartholomaeus, 2018), we focused more concertedly on the moral injunction to have children. Specifically, we focused on moral claims used to normalise the desire for a child. We identified three moral claims about the desire for a child. The first was canvassed earlier, and involved emphasis upon the idea that to desire having a child was 'normal' or 'natural'. Participants who used this moral claim often struggled to unpack what 'normal' or 'natural' meant, often resorting to the idea that having children was a 'biological drive' aimed at 'perpetuating the species' or a particular family line. This is clearly a strong social argument available to people that serves to warrant the desire for a child. The second argument also took a form of moral claim, in this case, one made by other people, and particularly the parents of people we spoke to. Both the women and the men we interviewed spoke about their parents talking to them from a young age about having children in the future. For some people we spoke to there was a sense in which they felt their parents indicated they 'owed' them a grandchild, which contains the implicit moral claim that not providing a grandchild represents a moral failure. Finally, some of the people we spoke to contrasted their desire for a child with the desires of others in their lives who did not want children. Such people – typically women – were depicted as unintelligible adults: as not conforming to an idealised life script. Women, in particular, were framed as 'odd' and 'selfish' for not wanting children, a clear indication of a presumed moral failing.

The emphasis on women bearing the brunt of presumed moral failings in not wanting a child had implications for the women we interviewed. Having framed other women's non-desire for children as a moral issue, this then implicitly positioned their own journey to motherhood as a moral issue. As we explore in the three topics in the following text, each of the women we include in this chapter struggled with disparities between their awareness of moral claims about womanhood and motherhood, the reality of trying to become a mother, and having to navigate discrepancies between the two.

3.3   CONCEIVING A CHILD AND STAYING PREGNANT

As we noted earlier, the normative assumption that womanhood equates to motherhood places a significant moral burden on women. Furthermore, and as Ulrich and Weatherall (2000) note, women who find it difficult to conceive a child are placed at risk of being seen as inadequate women. They argue that fertility challenges faced by women are treated as a synecdoche for their womanhood as a whole. Given the framing of motherhood as a cultural mandate, conceiving a child becomes a responsibility placed on women, the corollary being that challenges in conceiving become a moral matter of implicit *irresponsibility*. Whitehead (2016) suggests that the cultural mandate for motherhood not only positions motherhood as something woman must want, but moreover that it is something *owed* to women. This is particularly true in neoliberal contexts, where the cultural validation of, or insistence upon, one's desires translates into a right to them. As Whitehead notes, and particularly for white middle-class heterosexual women, the entitlement to motherhood is undermined when fertility challenges are experienced.

For some of the women we interviewed, challenges with conception were a common theme. This was especially the case for two women – Gina and Mary – whose experiences we explore in this section. In her first interview, Gina shared with us that from the onset of her relationship with her partner she had been insistent that she wanted a child. As she stated, 'when we first started dating I pretty much laid it on the table, I said "this is what I want in my life and if that's not something that you see wanting in your life then perhaps our relationship is not where we are going"'. As Gina said, she did not want to 'mess around' in a relationship that was not going to lead to her having a child. Gina reflected that perhaps in some ways she had coerced her partner into wanting a child, but ultimately she felt that, with time, he too had become excited about the prospect. When we asked Gina why she felt so strongly, she described having a child as a 'special privilege', echoing perhaps the work of Whitehead (2016) who suggests that for certain groups of women motherhood is seen as a privilege or entitlement. Indeed, Gina recognised that not all women were so privileged, when she noted that 'not everyone gets to do it, and I think that's really sad for some people, especially those who really want it'. Here neoliberalism and desire interact, as we argued earlier, in the idea that wanting something should make it true, and when it comes to motherhood in particular, this is especially the case for women who 'really want it'.

Later in the interview, we asked Gina how she would feel if it was more difficult to conceive than she expected, a question we asked all of the people we spoke to. Gina responded by stating that she would 'definitely go through a phase of feeling like my body has failed me, and I think I would be the kind of person who would truly be affected by that mentally'. Different in a sense to the idea that women's reproductive organs are treated as a synecdoche for the whole woman (Ulrich & Weatherall, 2000), Gina makes a distinction between her body and herself. Yet at the same time, it is *her* body that has failed, which means something very specific for the 'kind of person' she is. Here she alludes to both being someone who is very invested in having a child (perhaps the kind of person she described earlier: 'especially those who really want it') and being someone who is hard on herself when she does not achieve her goals more broadly.

As it turned out, Gina and her husband Cameron did find it difficult to conceive, or at least to stay pregnant. Initially, they were able to conceive within four months of trying; however, this first pregnancy ended in a miscarriage. For Gina, this was 'very very difficult to deal with'. Gina's account of miscarriage reflects other women's experiences in the literature. Research by Gerber-Epstein and colleagues (2008), for example, found that the women they interviewed experienced miscarriage as rendering them as 'fertility failures' and as 'inadequate wives'. Moreover, participants suggested that the loss was not just of the child-to-be, but of motherhood: miscarriage can represent the end of a dream of motherhood, a dream that, as we argued earlier, is often culturally framed as central to womanhood. For Gina, ultimately she and her partner tried again, and after some time were able to conceive and birth a child (and then conceive another child); however, the initial experience of a miscarriage represented a significant hurdle in the context of an intended lifecourse that Gina had mapped out for herself.

In many respects, Mary too shared a narrative of fertility challenges that emphasised a normative desire for motherhood and the impact of this on her journey to conception. In her first interview, Mary wondered 'what is if takes us two years [to conceive] and that that's kind of embarrassing'. Mary went on to note that she questioned herself as to why it should be 'embarrassing', but we would suggest that, given the normative equation of womanhood with motherhood, it is perhaps understandable that Mary would fear that any challenges in conceiving would be 'embarrassing' for her. Yet despite being prepared for this potential 'embarrassment', when Mary was interviewed after she and her partner had conceived, she nonetheless noted that the experience was 'very different to what we expected'. Despite, as she noted, them being 'young and so healthy and fit', it took them a long time to conceive, which she found 'definitely unexpected and very very hard, probably definitely the most challenging part of my life'.

Mary shared that after the initial months of trying to conceive she 'stopped doing pregnancy tests because they're too devastating'. While, for Gina, a miscarriage was devastating, for Mary, even a negative pregnancy test was devastating. This speaks to a considerable investment in motherhood, one that translated into significant implications for Mary's well-being as time went by and they were unable to conceive. Mary's response, however, was to shift her investment. She noted that after months of trying, which she found 'demoralising', she had started to imagine a life without children, and was 'working toward accepting it'. Yet this was paired with ongoing hope that she might indeed conceive, which, for Mary, meant that there was still the possibility that all of her work in trying to shift her dreams for a child would all be for naught. Ultimately, Mary said it was her partner who convinced her to give it 'one more go', which resulted in the conception and birth of a child after taking a drug to assist with ovulation.

For Gina and Mary, even though they were aware that conception can be difficult for some women, they both told themselves – largely due to their young age (in their 20s) – that for them conception would be relatively straightforward. Their actual experiences flew in the face of this. For both women, the experience of fertility challenges placed them outside of the normative trajectory to motherhood they had expected would happen, instead situating them within the narratives that they had feared: of sadness about being unable to conceive or embarrassment. While Gina persisted in the face of sadness, including that associated with a miscarriage, Mary by contrast tried to convince herself to accept a life without children. For both women, however, their journeys through fertility challenges were largely shaped by their own views on the cultural mandate to motherhood, and the underlying assumption that conceiving a childhood would be relatively straightforward, particularly because of their young ages.

3.4 NAVIGATING BREASTFEEDING EXPECTATIONS AND CHALLENGES

As we noted in the introduction to this chapter, becoming a mother is just the start when it comes to normative moral expectations placed on women. There are a plethora of other expectations that women face about what it means to be a 'good mother'. Key among these for new mothers is the expectation to breastfeed, and moreover, the expectation that breastfeeding should come 'naturally' and should be enjoyable. As Shakespeare and colleagues (2004) note, there is a moral imperative for women to 'succeed' at breastfeeding, when in reality the actual experience of breastfeeding is often 'devastatingly different' to expectations for many women. Challenges with breastfeeding, they note, can lead some women to feel that they have failed as mothers, which can negatively impact upon women's feelings about their baby. Yet despite awareness in healthcare sectors that breastfeeding does not come easily to many women, research by Brouwer and colleagues (2012) similarly found that women continue to be 'shocked' by breast-feeding difficulties. Nonetheless, they found that many of the women they interviewed continued to equate success in breastfeeding with good mothering, meaning that for women for whom breastfeeding is difficult, this can lead to a sense of failure. Furthermore, the strong health discourses associated with 'breast is best' disguise the frequency with which breastfeeding is not straightforward, or even possible, for a sizeable number of women (e.g., Símonardóttir & Gíslason, 2018).

A number of the women we interviewed experienced consid-erable discrepancies between their expectations about breastfeeding and the reality of breastfeeding. In her first interview, Paula stated that she felt physically ready for breastfeeding, though was not par-ticularly interested in accessing any classes about breastfeeding. She was aware of a breastfeeding information session and noted 'I might go to that, I might not'. In a later interview, Paula noted that she was asked by her midwife if she planned to breastfeed, to which Paula was surprised, as she had not even thought about doing otherwise. As she noted, 'I didn't realise there were people who actually planned not to'. Here, for Paula, breastfeeding is a normative assumption for mothers, and we might suggest, a moral imperative. Paula shared that she was aware that 'some people have trouble with [breastfeed-ing]', but presumed that she would not have any trouble with it, and indeed was pleased she planned to birth at a 'pro-breastfeeding' hos-pital that had already indicated she would be well supported to start feeding from birth. Paula noted that she planned to feed 'for as long as possible', that she assumed it 'would come naturally', and that she had no plans to supplement with bottles. Paula also noted the experiences of friends who found breastfeeding the most enjoyable of experiences, and that she could not 'wait to bond with breastfeeding'.

For Paula, however, the reality of breastfeeding was very differ-ent. From the onset, breastfeeding was difficult due to her baby being small after arriving a month early, and her newborn required being fed expressed breastmilk initially through a tube and then via bottles.

For Paula, this resulted in a 'a big sense of failure as a woman'. As it turned out, the hospital was indeed very supportive, but their continued support came to feel for Paula like insistence or a moral imperative, compounding her sense of failure. Added to this were the voices of her parents and her partner's parents, who insisted that she keep trying to breastfeed. Paula shared the arduous routine she engaged in to try and breastfeed directly and to express breastmilk. This cycle was on a perpetual loop for the early months of her baby's life, having a significant impact on sleep for Paula, and impacting on her relationship with her child and her partner.

As time went by, Paula reconciled herself to bottle-feeding using formula, yet throughout this time her parents and her partner's parents continued to encourage her to try to breastfeed, which Paula experienced as pressure for her to continue to pursue breastfeeding in the face of substantial challenges. For Paula, switching to fully formula feeding when her baby was about four months old was a source of tension. Not only did she feel like she had failed in the face of her family members, but she too was torn between 'loving' formula feeding, and feeling like she had 'let her child down'. Paula had taken on the injunction to breastfeed as her own, saying she 'was planning to breastfeed her for two years; you know, I was going to be the breastfeeding mum because "breast is best" and all that'. For Paula, however, what helped her turn a corner was sharing her experiences with other people. Once she started telling people that she had struggled with breastfeeding, 'it seemed like everyone had one problem or another'. This helped her to realise that she had presumed 'the majority of mums just do it perfectly, but [in reality] they don't'. Hearing that breastfeeding difficulties had a negative impact on other women's experiences of motherhood helped Paula to reconcile her own feelings, and to recognise and resist the considerable pressures she faced to breastfeed.

Lara too had a shifting view on, and experience with, breastfeeding. In her first interview, Lara stated that she had 'thoughts on breastfeeding'. She noted that she thought it was 'really important to breastfeed if you can, that it is nutritionally important'. Lara also had very clear views on how long it was 'appropriate' to breastfeed, planning to feed only for the first year. Lara had a less-than-positive view of women who fed longer, especially if it was done just to 'calm the baby down', though she noted that it was hard to know what it will be like 'until you become a mum and you're faced with the situation'. Despite feeling the moral imperative to breastfeed, however, Lara struggled with the idea of breastfeeding in public, noting that she would likely cover herself if feeding in public. Here Lara draws attention to tensions between the cultural mandate to see 'breast as best', and the stigma often experienced by women who feed in public (Bresnahan et al., 2020).

The reality for Lara was somewhat different to her expectations, even taking into account that she was aware that she could not know exactly what breastfeeding would be like until it started. Notably, in her first interview, Lara seemed aware of a diversity of positions about breastfeeding, while still holding her own moral position about its worth and duration. Yet in the first interview, Lara did not raise the possibility that breastfeeding might be difficult, nor had she heard of such experiences from other people. In her third interview, however, after the birth of her child, Lara reported that 'breastfeeding initially was painful' for the first month. While Lara indicated that this was later rectified, she also noted that her child at times continued to refuse to be breastfed, instead preferring a bottle. For Lara this was 'really upsetting actually, I felt rejected'. In the end, however, her child started biting during feeding, so for Lara 'that was the end of it' and she stopped when he was around six or seven months old, which also coincided with her returning to paid work. While biting became a justification to switch entirely to bottle feeding, for Lara, the challenges she faced with breastfeeding nonetheless remained a 'distressing memory'. Notably, in talking about her breastfeeding experiences, Lara did not return to the topic of feeding in public in her later interviews. It is potentially the case that her challenging experiences with breastfeeding overrode her concerns about stigma in public, emphasising her own point that you cannot know the reality of breastfeeding until it occurs.

For both Paula and Lara, their relatively rosy initial views about breastfeeding were strongly tempered by the reality of breast-feeding. Part of the issue, it would seem, related to the lack of discussion about the realities of breastfeeding before birth, at least as far as Paula and Lara were concerned. For Paula, later conversations with other women about difficulties with breastfeeding were a panacea to her feelings of failure. Yet for both women, a feeling of failure or rejection stayed with them well after they had stopped breastfeeding, highlighting the power of moral claims about what 'good mothering' means in terms of breastfeeding.

3.5   POSTNATAL MENTAL HEALTH ISSUES AS MISMATCH BETWEEN EXPECTATION AND REALITY

In this final section, we explore the topic of postnatal mental health issues. Research on women and postnatal depression specifically suggests that for many women their experiences of depression after birth result from having an unrealistic expectation of what motherhood would be like, which is sharply contrasted with the reality (Mauthner, 1999). For many women, this occurs on multiple fronts, and can include discrepancies between expectations about, and the reality of, conception, pregnancy, birth, partner support, breastfeeding, sleep, and attachment. For women who see motherhood as the 'pinnacle' of their lives, conflicts between expectations and reality can be especially distressing. Postnatal depression can often thus include a moral dimension: ideals about motherhood are brought into conflict with the reality of being a mother, yet letting go of ideals that are so firmly entrenched as cultural imperatives can understandably be difficult for some women. Indeed, research suggests that for some women letting go of idealised images of motherhood is part of the journey to recovery from postnatal depression (Edhborg et al., 2005).

A number of the women we interviewed shared experiences that could potentially be grouped under the banner of postnatal depression or other postnatal mental health issues. This included conversations about negative affect after the birth of their child, or a general sense of feeling 'down' during early motherhood, and a small number of women had sought help from a psychologist. For example, Gina, who we introduced earlier in this chapter, had experienced fertility challenges and then a miscarriage before she then conceived again and gave birth to her first child. After the arrival of her child, Gina found motherhood especially challenging. Her newborn struggled to sleep, and spent much of his time awake crying and would not settle. Gina reached out to a maternal health nurse who ran a mothers' group she was a part of, as she found the experiences with her child very upsetting. However, in the face of her distress, the nurse she approached was dismissive, stating 'oh we're going to have to deal with this again'. This left Gina feeling that she did not have anyone to talk to about her feelings, which was exacerbated by the sense that no one else in her mothers' group spoke about negative feelings. Gina wondered if in fact other women did have similar experiences, but that 'people don't like to talk about these feelings because it makes them appear to be a bad mother'. Whatever the reason, Gina felt isolated in her experiences, potentially exacerbated by the idea that talking about her experiences would position her as a 'bad mother'.

A large part of the issue was sleep, but Gina said it was also that 'perhaps there was a disconnect on what my expectations of parenting would be like and what my enjoyment would be out of it and how it actually was'. As Gina noted, 'I thought it would be a lot easier than it was and that I would be able to go and do things with my child'. Instead, Gina had to constantly hold her child, she could not really go out and see people and socialise, and she was surrounded by people who did not seem to be having the same challenges. Echoing the work of Ulrich and Weatherall (2000), which suggests that women who experience a mismatch between expectations and the reality of motherhood might be particularly susceptible to postnatal depression, Gina appeared particularly burdened by discrepancies between an idealised experience of motherhood and her own experiences.

As we noted earlier in this chapter, Gina had stated from the beginning of the relationship with her husband Cameron that she wanted children. Gina's desire for a child was paired with her expectations of what having a child would be like. While, as we noted earlier, Cameron had come around to the idea of having a child and was quite excited about it, for Gina the reality of Cameron's involvement was different, exacerbating her distress. Gina shared that when she was the person at home with their baby, all of the challenges mentioned earlier occurred. Gina and the baby spent time in a special unit designed to help mothers with children who had sleep issues, which Cameron also spent time in, as much as his paid work would allow (although notably while he mentioned this experience in his interview, he did not mention Gina's significant distress). Putting in all of this work meant that the child eventually was able to sleep, and with the support of the psychologist, Gina was able to cope better. However, she noted that 'the psychologist never really described it as postnatal depression; she mostly used the term "adjustment disorder"'. Elaborating on this, Gina noted that (the psychologist said) 'I don't think your mood is depressed; I think you have a realistic understanding of what should have happened and what is going on.' Gina went on to note that 'perhaps [the psychologist] thought that my expectation, my mental expectation, was different to what was actually happening and that was perhaps what was causing this [adjustment disorder]'. Having put in the work to help her child sleep, Gina then returned to part-time paid work, and Cameron stayed at home full time to care for their child for twelve weeks, with primary carer leave provided by his employer. It was by this time that their child had started to settle and sleep. As Gina noted, 'I just felt like I'd battled through ten months of hell and then Cameron was home and he got all this really good time with my child'. Following this, when their child turned one, Gina continued to work part-time, Cameron returned to full-time work, and their child attended childcare for two days a week.

Not only did Gina experience a mismatch between expectations about, and the reality of, motherhood, but just when she started to achieve something closer to the expectation, she returned to paid work and her partner appeared to benefit from the 'ten months of hell' she had been through. While Gina, with the support of the psychologist, was able to address the 'adjustment disorder' she experienced, it is notable that Gina in many ways felt like she was dealing with this in isolation. Gina was isolated by the actions of the maternal health nurse, alienated from other mothers who seemingly did not have such negative experiences, and resentful of her husband who appeared to have more positive experiences. While Gina worked hard to achieve the image of motherhood she had hoped for, there was a sense in which this came at a significant cost to her, especially in terms of her mental health.

3.6   CONCLUSIONS

In this chapter, we have highlighted some of the tensions between the perception that motherhood is a category privileged by many women in the context of pronatalism (Whitehead, 2016) and the moral expectations that come with this privileging, expectations that can negatively impact upon women in the context of the lived reality of motherhood. As Ulrich and Weatherall (2000) note, motherhood is often believed to give women privileged access to a dimension of gendered being that is unavailable to women who are not mothers. This includes occupying a reified position in societies that privilege motherhood, as well as access to social spaces for mothers. Yet for some women, including the women we focused on in this chapter, access to the reified space of motherhood can be fraught. When the reality of motherhood does not live up to the expectation, women are granted access to a privileged space previously unavailable, whilst at the same time feeling that their place within this space is tenuous. Moral claims about motherhood, then, both promote motherhood as an exalted space, and create barriers to women feeling that they are included within the space.

As we noted earlier in this chapter, there is a sense in which moral claims about motherhood function to 'get structures under the skin' (Ahmed, 2010). The positioning of motherhood as a desirable, and indeed essential, part of womanhood serves to insert social structures that emphasise pronatalist understandings of a normative adult life-course into the affective lives of many people. In other words, prona-talist social policy is implemented and taken up by people through the affective dimensions of parenthood imperatives. Furthermore, that it is primarily women who are the target of such imperatives means that the insertion of feelings into moral imperatives about reproduction creates a specifically gendered dimension to pronatalism. The reifica-tion of motherhood serves to normalise the injunction to feel a par-ticular way about becoming a mother, and to have certain normative expectations about what motherhood will feel and be like.

For the women whose experiences we included in this chapter, however, the structures that women internalise about motherhood can become barriers to their engagement with the reality of mother-hood. When motherhood is not simply reified, but treated as a sphere of affect bound by joy, positivity, and attachment, for women whom this is not the reality, there is a corollary experience of isolation. When one internalises a norm, only for that norm not to be expe-rienced as a reality, this creates a disjuncture between the impetus of the social structure and its lived reality. Following Beasley and Bacchi (2007), then, we might suggest that the social flesh of mother-hood can differ from the embodied reality of motherhood. Normative discourses about motherhood give flesh to social structures, and in so doing invite women into an idealised affective relationship with what motherhood is expected to be like. This flesh further invites women to invest in motherhood as symbolic of womanhood. Yet challenges such as those outlined in this chapter with regard to con-ception, breastfeeding, and postnatal mental health, serve to high-light that the social flesh of motherhood often does not align with the embodied reality. Yet the strength of social structures too often means that, rather than questioning the social structures themselves, women are left feeling inadequate.

Moral claims and expectations about motherhood, then, invite women into the normative social flesh of motherhood, as much as they set women up to feel inadequate. What is left at the margins, however, is the inadequacy of the social flesh of motherhood itself. As we explore in the final chapter of this book, needed are other ways of thinking about the social flesh of motherhood (and parenthood more broadly), ways of thinking that focus on the agency of people to critique social structures, to refuse their internalisation, and to enact their own moral claims that centre their own experiences, rather than being reliant on normative moral claims about parenthood. As the women's experiences shared in this chapter would suggest, to do otherwise is to perpetuate the myth of an idealised motherhood experience, and thus to set women up to feel that they have failed.

It is also important to reflect on why it was women who so often focused on moral expectations about parenthood. Certainly, it was the case that men spoke about moral expectations, as we summarised earlier in this chapter in regard to our previous publications from this project. Some of the men were aware of, and drew upon, the marginalisation of people who do not wish to be parents to justify their own decision to become parents. Men were aware of expectations from their own parents that they themselves should become parents. Yet at the same time, the men we interviewed did not appear to feel subjected to the equation of manhood with fatherhood. Certainly, there was a sense in which some men felt that reproduction was a way to share their genes, a normative hallmark of masculinity, given the import given to sperm (Moore, 2008). And certainly several of the men we spoke to were passionate about becoming fathers. Yet at the same time, fatherhood was often viewed as an *additional* aspect of their identity, rather than necessarily being central.

In a sense, then, the men we interviewed applied moral claims about parenthood to *other people,* but they less often applied them to *themselves.* As we highlight in some of the chapters to come, women often bore the brunt of normative moral expectations about parenthood, both as instantiated by themselves, by other people in their lives, and by their partners (see, e.g., Chapter 5). What this meant for men, as we explore in the following chapter, is that they were often shocked when the affective dimensions of new parenthood forcibly inserted social structures under their skin. Given their relative lack of engagement with the application of moral expectations to their own experiences at the point of conception and during pregnancy, the birth of a child often resulted in unexpected feelings about new parenthood, feelings that confronted men with the social structures to which they were now subjected. The topic of differences between men's and women's experiences of first-time parenthood thus remains a focus in most of the chapters that follow (Chapter 5 being an exception as it focuses on women), as much as we also try to draw attention to the similarities in experiences between men and women.

As such, and as we outlined in the first chapter in this book, first-time parenthood has uniquely gendered dimensions that can both bring together and separate women and men. As has been the case in this chapter, we feel it is important to focus on instances where particular normative assumptions impact more on people of one gender. But as we argue in this book more broadly, our focus in any given chapter on people of one gender does not outweigh a broader focus on how normative expectations about parenthood impact on all people. Indeed, as we explore in the final chapter of this book, it is such normative expectations that require ongoing attention, so as to better align the social flesh of parenthood with the lived reality of all parents.

In Chapter 4, we take up in more detail some of the points we have introduced already in this chapter with regard to what is classified as 'natural' when it comes to first-time parenthood (i.e., that both conception and breastfeeding should come 'naturally' to women). We specifically focus on experiences of giving birth, exploring how such experiences were recounted to us by the women and men we interviewed, including a focus on what was classified by some as a 'natural' birth, and how expectations about such a birth often contrasted starkly with the reality of birthing for some of the couples.

4 Birthing Experiences

4.1 INTRODUCTION

In Chapter 3, we explored how depictions of conception and breastfeeding as 'natural' can serve to marginalise women's experiences. Specifically, the idea that conception should be straightforward and breastfeeding should come 'naturally' often contrasts sharply with the lived reality of many women. In this chapter, we apply the critique of naturalisation rhetoric first introduced in Chapter 3 to the topic of birthing. As Símonardóttir and Rúdólfsdóttir (2021) outline, the 'natural childbirth' movement was intended to counter the hyper-medicalisation of birth. As a prominent strand of feminist thought, criticisms of medicalisation have been central to challenging how women are 'managed' in medical settings (Ussher, 2006). Pushing back against the medical regulation of women's bodies, the natural birthing movement sought to assert that women should be in control of their bodies and of birthing, emphasising women's right to make decisions about how they gave birth, and the capacity of women's bodies to 'know' how to give birth.

Yet as Símonardóttir and Rúdólfsdóttir (2021) note, while the feminist focus on women's autonomy emphasised within natural birth movements has been vital to countering the medicalisation of women's bodies, the emphasis on childbirth as 'natural' is nonetheless problematic. First, there is the reification of women's bodies as 'naturally' predisposed to childbirth. Such reification is not only essentialist, but ignores that for many women childbirth is extremely difficult (and indeed historically, significant numbers of women died during childbirth). Second, and as Brubaker and Dillaway (2009) note, rhetoric surrounding 'natural' childbirth equates the category of 'good mother' with 'natural childbirth'. This means that women will often strive to give birth vaginally even when it is not medically indicated, and that for women who are unable to give birth vaginally there can be a sense of failure. And third, rhetoric surrounding 'natural' childbirth ignores the multiple ways in which the broader cultural context is inserted into childbirth. From having ultrasounds to taking vitamin supplements during pregnancy, and from having access to foetal monitoring to the provision of drugs to alleviate pain, what is in fact 'natural' in contemporary western childbirthing practices is highly questionable.

Indeed, childbirth is a highly mediated experience, for all people. So much so, we might argue that there was a sense that it was often difficult for the people we interviewed to speak about the affective dimensions of childbirth. Certainly, some of the participants spoke in highly emotive terms. But for other people we interviewed, their accounts of childbirth were primarily focused on blow-by-blow descriptions of moments of childbirth, sometimes absent of a discussion of the affective dimensions. This, we would argue, highlights how experiences of childbirth (in hospitals, which was the setting for all of the people we interviewed) are mediated by the medical context, even if some of the participants framed their birthing experiences as 'natural'. Indeed, and again following Ahmed (2010), we are interested to explore in this chapter how feelings get institutions 'under the skin'. Specifically in this chapter, we are interested in how the institutional space of the hospital becomes part of the emotional experience of childbirth, shaping and mediating what is felt and how it is felt. Of course, our suggestion is not that outside of hospitals people somehow have access to an unmediated (i.e., more 'natural') experience of childbirth. Rather, given that all of the people we interviewed gave birth in a hospital, we are interested in how the institutional space shapes feelings about childbirth, and how the institution itself becomes part of the affective experience.

In the following sections, we first provide a broad outline of the birthing experiences of the people we interviewed. We then turn to consider women's and men's experiences of childbirth. In one sense, the focus on birth was often a relatively small part of the third interviews we conducted. With the passage of time (i.e., six months since the birth), memories of the birth were often intense yet fleeting. In another sense, the accounts given were often very rich, and for some highly emotive. We consider women's and men's accounts separately given the different standpoints and experiences that were evident. Yet at the same time, in some places, we situate the accounts of both partners in a couple alongside one another, to either highlight points of overlap or emphasise differences. In terms of juxtaposition, in places in this chapter, we juxtapose accounts of 'natural' childbirth with the reality of childbirth (and indeed discrepancies with regard to what counts as 'natural'), and we also juxtapose experiences between and within couples.

4.2   SUMMARY OF BIRTHING EXPERIENCES

Before we turn to examine the birthing narratives of some of the people we interviewed, we first provide an overview of the birthing experiences of the nine couples. Of the women, only three described having a 'natural birth', what Lara (whose story we explore in the following text) referred to as a 'pretty textbook [vaginal birth]'. Yet even for these three women, what constituted 'textbook' differed from that which might be described as 'natural' according to the idealised image of 'natural childbirth' introduced earlier, where this variously involved for different women the induction of labour, an episiotomy (and significant blood loss), and an epidural. An additional participant spoke about her birthing experience in a similar way and described going into labour 'naturally', after having planned an induction, but did not use the term 'natural birth'. As we explore more in the following text, then, what is classified as 'textbook' or 'straightforward' depends largely on how women classify 'natural' childbirth.

Two of the women shared that they had an unplanned caesarean section. For Catherine, whose story we share in the following text, this was an emergency caesarean, deemed necessary after slow progress with labour and concerns about her and her baby. For Catherine, her birthing team was concerned that she was past her due date, but she pushed not to be induced. The eventual labour was 'horrendous', with her ultimately requesting an epidural as 'the pain went on so long'. She shared that while she opted for an epidural it 'wasn't really what I wanted', and that the emergency caesarean was also something she had very much not hoped for from her birthing experience.

In addition to these caesarean births which could easily be classified as traumatic, an additional three women experienced birthing as traumatic. In particular, Mary, whose story we share in the following text, was overdue and had to be induced, and found the hospital staff far from helpful. She experienced high levels of pain, struggled to access an epidural, and largely found herself delivering with the help of her husband Max given the absence of hospital staff. When staff eventually intervened, the baby showed signs of distress, and at birth required resuscitation. As we also explore in the following text, Jemma reported that her labour was 'all-consuming entire body kind of pain', for which she coped with by having an epidural. The birth resulted in some tearing that required stitches, and overall left her with a largely negative memory of her birthing experience. Another woman delivered her baby four weeks early in a different hospital to the one they had planned to go to. She told us she did not think it would be possible for her to give birth and she told the delivery staff 'you're going to have to actually just stop and give me a Caesarean because I actually can't'. While she was able to deliver vaginally after an episiotomy, she was much traumatised by the experience and told us that if it was not for her strong desire to have another child, would not give birth again.

4.3   WOMEN'S ACCOUNTS OF CHILDBIRTH

4.3.1   Discrepancies in Accounts of 'Natural' Birth

Previous research has suggested that rhetoric around 'natural' birth may take specific forms in the dominant cultural narrative in the Australian context. Callister, Holt, and Kuhre (2010), for example, found that the predominantly white women they interviewed described themselves as 'Aussies' who valued control in decision-making. Their participants widely reported eschewing 'interventions', instead viewing pain and challenges in childbirth as 'symbolic' or as a rite of passage. These types of claims about childbirth echo broader Australian rhetoric about 'hard work' being emblematic of 'Australian values' (Younane, 2008). Of the women we interviewed, Lara was the person who seemed most invested in the narrative of a 'natural' birth. As she noted, her birthing experience was 'pretty textbook actually'. Lara positioned her birthing experience as 'lucky' in comparison to 'women having to be induced or having the stretch and sweeps or caesareans'. This type of comparing and contrasting allowed Lara to position her birthing experience as idealised and indeed as 'natural'.

Lara continued with this comparative approach by stating that she had a 'wonderful natural birth', different to 'the problems or complications afterwards that a lot of women have'. Indeed, Lara made repeated claims that her birthing experience was 'really straightforward', 'a positive beautiful experience', and indeed so relaxed that she directed her partner to watch a cricket match on television while she was in labour as she 'just didn't mind'. We must wonder, however, if this use of superlatives in describing her birthing experience was intended to make up for the fact that by her own definition, the birth was not 'natural'. Further in the interview, Lara noted that she 'had an epidural towards the end which was wonderful' as it gave her a 'couple of hours of rest'. She also noted that as her contractions came closer together she 'basically felt like she couldn't breathe'. So not only did Lara view an epidural as part of a 'natural birth', but the end stages of the labour were quite difficult. That Lara emphasised the ease of the birth and the lack of interventions (despite having one) potentially speaks to an investment in the rhetoric of 'natural birth'.

Jemma also had what could be considered a 'natural' birth, but, by contrast, was highly critical of this concept. As she noted, in '[birthing] class they really, really, really push natural birth, [but that's a] problem with the language of the entire thing: its vaginal birth as opposed to caesarean birth, [not] one is somehow natural and one is unnatural'. Jemma was also critical of the 'natural birth' push-back against epidurals. As she noted, 'I got to the point where I was completely non-verbal. I had thrown up from pain, I would pretty much say that for part of it I dissociated because of the pain'. For Jemma, an epidural was a welcome relief, one that allowed respite from the pain, and when the epidural wore off, Jemma was able to engage with the pain differently: 'The pain changes. It goes from an all-consuming, entire body kind of pain, to searing, burning, but it's different. From every single atom, being sort of wave after wave of agony, to a very concentrated, searing kind of thing.' Different to Lara, then, rather than focusing on (positive) generalities and largely avoiding the affective dimensions, Jemma was explicit in her focus on the emotional aspects of childbirth, including the negative ones.

Jemma also did not minimise the interventions she had, even at the same time as her account of her birthing experience was of a vaginal birth that could have been depicted as largely 'natural'. Not only did she speak about wanting and receiving an epidural, but she spoke about needing stitches, something that itself was challenging. As she noted, at first, she was told she would need a 'few stiches', but in the end it was more serious, and she shared that she could see the procedure reflected in the surgeon's glasses, and that she had 'seen things that I wish I could un-see'. Again, then, Jemma's account of giving birth was quite detailed, emotive, and visceral, eschewing the type of idealised 'natural' birth account provided by Lara.

4.3.2 'Down a Rabbit Hole' with no Direction or Support

Despite their different orientations to normative understandings of an idealised 'natural' birth, Lara and Jemma were similar in terms of reporting high levels of support and care from hospital staff, reflecting some of the other participants in our study and other studies (e.g., Karlström et al., 2015). This, however, was not the case for all of the women we interviewed. Accounts of less-than-positive experiences with hospital staff have been widely reported in previous research. Nilsson (2014), for example, reports that for many of the participants in her study, 'negative birth experiences' were associated with unresponsive hospital staff, particularly when staff treated women as bodies to be administered to, often talking as though the women themselves were not present. This left women feeling like they were 'passive participants' in the birth, rather than being seen as active agents capable of making decisions. In the Australian context, researchers such as Dahlen, Barclay, and Homer (2010) too have found that lack of communication from hospital staff meant that women had less-than-positive birthing experiences, and that lack of communication can be especially fraught for women birthing a first child, leaving them feeling like they had little control. Eliasson, Kainz, and Von Post (2008) further report from their research that unresponsive hospital staff are those who ignore women's accounts of pain during birth, leaving women to endure high levels of pain whilst also feeling that they are being implicitly told that their pain is not valid. Others have highlighted the impacts of contextual issues around hospital staffing, including staff numbers, impacting on the level of care able to be provided (Larkin et al., 2012; Reiger & Lane, 2013).

Many of the negative experiences mentioned earlier were encountered by Mary, as was evident in her account of labour and birthing. In recounting her experience, Mary started by noting that she 'wanted as little involvement as possible', potentially emphasising assumptions about an idealised 'natural' birth. However, she quickly turned to share how this was not the reality. She ended up having to be induced, and felt that the care she received was both unclear and unresponsive. For example, she shared that she asked hospital staff whether the level of pain she felt was normal, only to be told to try to sleep. Not only did Mary find this advice unrealistic, but it left her worried that the level of pain she was experiencing meant something was wrong. Mary also repeatedly asked if the pain meant she was in labour, only to be left without a response. Mary was concerned that if the pain *was not* labour, she would be unable to cope with the pain of labour itself. Due to the lack of support she received, Mary and her partner opted to get in the shower to try to alleviate some of the pain, and to facilitate labour. But this was also a concern for Mary, as the induction occurred because of foetal distress, and in the shower, there was no monitoring of the baby. As she said, 'I felt like I was down a rabbit hole; like I was just in incredible amounts of pain and I'd been so distressed because I hadn't known what was going on by that point'. For Mary, then, not only was it the significant pain that worried her, but this was compounded by the lack of direction or responses from hospital staff, leaving Mary, with her first pregnancy, feeling entirely unsure (and thus worried) about what was to come.

Mary's husband Max too expressed concerns about these aspects of the delivery. When asked about the birth, Max's first response was 'I sort of thought for the whole time it was happening I didn't really know what was going on'. Max went on to note that 'I guess it sort of felt like a bit of a sausage factory at the hospital', something which Mary also said in her interview. This was because the couple 'didn't speak to the same person twice', leaving them feeling alone and without direction. This left Max feeling 'sort of out of control'. After labouring in the shower, Mary was eventually moved to a delivery suite, where there were multiple staff members and a high level of intervention in the birth, as we explore further in Section 4.3.3. In retrospect, Max could see the questions they could have asked, but at the time 'it was confusing' and the couple 'didn't have anything explained properly'. Both Mary and Max repeatedly noted that they could never get an answer at the hospital as to whether or not Mary was in labour, something they felt should have been an easy question to answer. However, Mary noted that she found out more details later: 'I was reading my discharge notes that they give to the GP afterwards and they said on there "Confirmed labour 10.30." And I was like "What? Like no-one ever told me that."'

4.3.3 Traumatic Birthing Experiences

Despite the competing rhetorics of medicalisation and 'natural' birth – both of which claim to know what is best for women and to offer a birth that is idealised – many women have birthing experiences that are not simply fraught, but which can be life-threatening for both woman and child. While caesarean sections are not inherently life-threatening, emergency caesareans often occur in cases where there is risk to the woman, the child, or both. As a medical intervention, caesarean sections can leave women feeling even more overlooked, as mere vessels to the delivery of a baby. Women interviewed by Bayes, Fenwick, and Hauck (2012), for example, reported that during caesarean delivery they felt 'off everybody's radar', and that they were just another surgery on a list. Further, the women noted that often a caesarean was treated as routine, indeed 'like a conveyor belt' of surgeries, but that for the women themselves caesareans were distressing. Research by Elmir and colleagues (2010) found that women who had traumatic births, including involving caesarean sections, felt that they had no control over the birth, leaving them feeling scared and alone. A lack of focus on their needs during the birth, including a lack of information, left women with highly negative birth experiences.

For Catherine, when asked to describe her birthing experience she started with the words 'horrendous' and 'traumatic'. While Catherine noted that ultimately what was important was that her child was born, this did not entirely mitigate how distressing the birth was, as highlighted in the level of detail that Catherine provided. A large part of what made the birth traumatic was the length of the labour, totalling to almost two days. While in her account Catherine was repeatedly pragmatic in her focus (i.e., the child arrived safely and that is what should matter most), her account was replete with examples of distress. Given the length of the labour, Catherine was eventually told that she would require an emergency caesarean, as she was preeclamptic and the baby's heart rate had increased. While Catherine was ultimately willing to have a caesarean if it meant her baby was okay, she nonetheless stated that it was 'absolutely everything I didn't want'. While the hospital staff were responsive to Catherine's needs, there was also a sense in which she felt left to suffer through long bouts of intense pain across the two days of labour, leaving her with an overall account of a traumatic birth.

Mary, whose narrative we introduced in Section 4.3.2, also provided an account of a traumatic birth. Not only were the hospital staff largely unresponsive throughout her labour, but following the birth further concerns arose. Given the pain Mary experienced, the duration of the labour, and the baby's distress, a vacuum delivery was required, after which the baby required resuscitation. This compounded Mary's sense of not knowing what was going on, as the birth happened and the baby was immediately taken away. Max was able to go with the birthing team during resuscitation, but Mary was left without information, waiting to find out if her baby was okay. Not only did these aspects of the delivery make it traumatic for Mary, but all of the unanswered questions compounded her sense of distress, which continued long after the birth. Mary was left wondering if being induced caused all of the experiences she faced. She also wondered if her questions had been answered throughout her labour or closer support had been provided by staff, the baby's distress and need for resuscitation could have been avoided. As she said, 'there were lots of questions as to whether that was avoidable or whether it was just going to happen anyway because she was overdue. So, a lot of that's still unanswered'. We could suggest that Mary's desire for a birth without intervention may have meant that the level of intervention was even more distressing. But even absent of such a desire, it is reasonable to suggest that there were multiple factors that, when combined, resulted in a birth that would likely be distressing for many people.

4.4   MEN'S ACCOUNTS OF CHILDBIRTH

4.4.1   Differing Engagements with Birthing

In many ways, a key point of difference between the women and men we interviewed was the point of embodiment when it came to first-time parenthood. As we saw in Chapter 3, breastfeeding was typically positioned as something only women can do. Similarly, in the context of this chapter, pregnancy and birth were often depicted as things that only women can do, meaning that men often felt one step removed from the process. Previous research suggests that this focus on embodiment means that cisgender heterosexual men are often unprepared for what birthing will be like, especially in terms of the pain that their partner will experience (Bäckström & Wahn, 2011). In the face of their partner's pain, men often report feeling helpless, which stands in direct contrast to the normative imperative for men to be in control. Men's experiences of being supported to be involved include being listened to as part of a 'labouring couple' and being shown how to actively support their partner. Here, we juxtapose two very different accounts of men in the birthing process, noting that for other couples, their experiences were on somewhat of a continuum between these.

For some of the couples we interviewed, the men were not particularly engaged with the birth of their child. This was most evident in our interview with Craig, for whom there seemed to already be signs of what was to come in his second interview because, although he was attending antenatal classes with his partner Catherine, his main thoughts about the birth were the repeated mentions of needing to get Catherine's bag ready and that they could not plan for any other aspects. When asked if he felt included in the birth, Craig provided a nonchalant response, noting that he had not thought much about the birth since, noting 'it just happened, just get it done and move on. It didn't happen to me or my body'. Yet even though Craig exemplifies the type of account where a focus on embodiment meant that Craig reported feeling one step removed from the birthing process, he nonetheless commented on how this left him feeling excluded. As he noted, 'I did feel a little excluded sometimes but that's only because it's not my body'. Here, Craig eschews the idea of a 'labouring couple', instead emphasising that 'it's her body, it's all going on with her'. This was despite Craig also reporting that the hospital staff were talking to his partner and then saying 'you two might want to talk it over'. It would seem that the hospital staff actively sought to elicit a sense of a labouring couple, but Craig was unable or unwilling to take this up, instead deferring to his partner.

This deferral by Craig led to his partner, Catherine, who we wrote about earlier, having a very negative account of his involvement in the birth. As she noted, 'he didn't know what to do, which was bitterly disappointing. I didn't have any encouragement or support from him'. Catherine shared that as the labour went on for a considerable period of time (two days), Craig went home to sleep, leaving her on her own, which she was 'furious about after. He didn't even check-in to see if I was okay'. Even when Catherine challenged Craig about this after the birth, she said his response was nonchalant: 'Oh, well your Mum would have called me'. As Catherine noted, Craig's lack of involvement was a 'bone of contention' for some time after the birth, leaving Catherine with memories of a 'hard and too stressful' birth in which she largely felt alone. While Catherine's mother came to the hospital after Craig left, Catherine ultimately wanted her partner there to support her and share the birthing experience, as much as she was appreciative of the support provided by her mother.

By contrast, Max, who we introduced earlier in this chapter, shared his experience of being actively involved in his child's birth. As we shared earlier, when the labour become acutely painful for Mary and the hospital staff were being unresponsive, Max got into the shower with Mary to help her cope with the contractions. As he noted, 'I was just showering her down and rubbing her back, trying to help make her more comfortable'. In his interview, Max provided multiple examples of doing all he could to step in and provide support to Mary, in addition to being actively involved where possible in the birth. This included trying to get answers to questions from staff, and doing all he could to reassure Mary in the face of staff unresponsiveness despite, as we noted earlier, the fact that Max too felt anxious about what was happening and the lack of support the couple was receiving. Yet despite being actively involved, after the birth, when their child was taken away for resuscitation, Max reported that he 'felt pretty useless, just sort of standing there watching'. The challenges that the couple experienced during labour and delivery meant that even though for his own part Max did his best to be involved, the lack of interaction with hospital staff meant that he felt there was not much he could do.

4.4.2 Men's Accounts of Cord Cutting

It is often perceived that one of the ways in which men may be actively involved in the birth of their child is through cutting the umbilical cord. A small number of studies have explored what it means for men to be involved in this way. Johnson (2002), for example, interviewed men who had cut the umbilical cord, with some providing highly emotive accounts of the experience, often including accounts that were symbolic of men's active role in the child's birth. Some men noted that cutting the cord 'was like me breaking [child] free', and 'I broke the connection between [baby] and [mother] and that meant for the first time my relationship with [baby] was on his own' (p. 172). Here, the umbilical cord seems highly symbolic of the embodied relationship between mother and baby, with men cutting the cord symbolising their active insertion into the embodied relationship. By contrast, research by Dolan and Coe (2011) suggests that some men have less-than-positive experiences with cord cutting. One of their participants, for example, noted that cord cutting was a 'duty', but that they were nonetheless 'dubious' about doing it (p. 1028). Dolan and Coe suggest less of an emotional experience for the men they interviewed, and more of an instrumentalised account of cord cutting, one in which men are able to assert control and mastery in a context where they may otherwise feel out of control.

Most of the men we interviewed reported experiences of cord cutting more similar to the accounts provided by Dolan and Coe's (2011) participants, rather than the more emotional or symbolic accounts provided by Johnson's (2002) participants. Nathan, for example, stated that 'I didn't want to do it, I felt weird about cutting human flesh'. For Nathan, it would seem, cord cutting was an instrumental act that did not speak to bonding or connection, but rather to an action that would otherwise be unappealing. As he went on to note, 'it felt like I was cutting through calamari'. Interestingly, Nathan noted that he was 'forced' to do it, in the sense that he was strongly encouraged by hospital staff. Although he found it unpleasant, however, he did note that had he not cut the cord, he might have regretted it. This might suggest an emotional layer sitting behind the more instrumentalising layer: to have regretted not doing it would suggest that there was something to be gained by having done it. Obviously, these comments were provided in retrospect, such that Nathan noted that 'I really couldn't wrap my head around it at the start. But it wasn't as bad, you know it's a split-second thing, it's not as bad as I thought it would be'. In the interview, Nathan thus had the benefit of looking back on the experience and knowing it was not as bad as expected, so the potential emotional layer may only have become more evident after the event, and could not be accounted for or factored in prior to cutting the cord.

By contrast, Adam shared that he also felt that cord cutting would be unpleasant, leading him to opt not to cut the cord. Adam was mindful and appreciative that the offer to cut the cord was an initiative by hospital staff to make him feel included in the birth, but as he said 'I didn't particularly want to do those things', referring to 'catching the baby and cutting the cord'. Different to Nathan, Adam reported that he did not feel any pressure from hospital staff, but rather that it was simply an offer, and he preferred to 'stand back and observe', noting he trusted the expertise of the hospital staff. Adam was nonetheless aware that culturally speaking, cutting the cord is a 'big thing that everyone wants to do and is doing', but he felt confident that he would not regret foregoing it. Similar to Nathan, Adam noted that 'I don't want to cut parts of flesh. That just seems like it would be gross'. While Nathan overcame those feelings and wondered in retrospect if he might have regretted not cutting the cord, Adam was very confident in his decision at the time we interviewed him.

We would note here the difference between women's account of the naturalisation of certain birthing practices and 'natural' birth, and men's accounts of cord cutting. While there could certainly be an argument made that historically people of a diversity of genders have played a role in cord cutting, the rise of midwifery and the turn away from the medicalisation of childbirth (in which men played a primary role as medical staff) means that in the contemporary cultural moment in Australia, cord cutting is not necessarily seen as a 'natural' rite of passage for men. If anything, responses from men such as Nathan and Adam imply that there is something unnatural about a desire to cut the cord, and that when men do cut the cord, it is with reticence or out of a concern about regret, or at least it is an underwhelming event. What is actually perceived as 'natural' for men in the context of childbirth thus seems to be a somewhat fraught topic, one we explore further in Section 4.4.3.

4.4.3   *Men's Emotional Responses to Childbirth*

As we mentioned briefly in Chapter 3, while the affective dimensions of new parenthood are a normative expectation placed on women, men's emotional responses to new parenthood are often overlooked. As we also noted, the relative lack of moral expectations placed upon men in regard to parenthood can mean that men are unprepared for the emotional aspects of new parenthood, and birth in particular. One study that has focused on men's emotions during childbirth did so through a focus on traumatic births: framing men's emotional responses to extreme situations. Herrera (2020) reports that in the face of a traumatic birth, and in particular one in which they felt out of control, the men interviewed tried to assert a more traditional account of their emotional responses. Specifically, while they acknowledged the fear and anxiety they experienced, they also sought to emphasise how they asserted control after the event, presenting themselves as brave. Some men shared that they had been scared about fainting during the birth, and that this would represent a failure in terms of a normative masculinity. Herrera suggests that this allowed little space for men to have a mixture of emotions, and certainly foreclosed any sense that men could speak about negative emotions, including distress.

Some of the participants, such as Nathan, appeared to minimise the emotional aspects of childbirth, in many ways side stepping a focus on affect in his response to interview questions. Yet at the same time, the affective dimensions were always lurking beneath the surface. As he noted, 'when you're actually in a delivery room, it's a whole different experience' to videos or books about intending parenthood. There was a sense in which Nathan felt he was prepared for what childbirth would be like, but the embodied reality of birth stood in stark contrast, such as with cord cutting mentioned earlier. Indeed, based on his previous reading, Nathan had planned to stay near his partner's shoulders, well away from the delivery (perhaps due to a fear of fainting or feeling sick), but in reality, he had to actively assist in the delivery. As he noted, 'I didn't plan on being down the business end but unfortunately I had to'. Here, Nathan was confronted with the reality of childbirth in ways he had not planned for. Ultimately, Nathan attempted to minimise this confrontation, through a discourse of naturalisation: 'I guess it's one of those natural things that most women go through to have a child', emphasising that 'I was lucky enough to experience it I guess'. Yet despite naturalising vaginal birth and emphasising that he was 'lucky', Nathan still concluded by sharing that 'if we have another one I'll still happily be down the head and arm side than the business end'. This instrumentalising of his partner's body as 'the head and arm side' or the 'business end' potentially speaks to Nathan's attempts at distancing himself from the affective, visceral, and embodied aspects of childbirth.

By contrast, Adam was much more actively engaged with the affective dimensions of his experience of childbirth. As he noted, after a rather sudden and unexpected commencement of labour, when his partner started to experience considerable pain during contractions 'it made me very emotional because I don't think I'd seen her in that much pain before'. Similar to Nathan, Adam had been engaged with information about childbirth prior to the birth, but was unprepared for how emotional it would be. As he went on to share, 'it was very difficult to watch and not be able to do anything'. Nonetheless, Adam actively sought to support his partner throughout the pain, never turning away from the affective dimensions of the experience. By the time their child was born, Adam found himself overwhelmed by emotions. As he noted, 'all of a sudden I was very faint, and I had seen on TV and other things, that partners often faint during these things'. Here, while acknowledging feelings of being overcome, Adam nonetheless makes recourse to other men who have felt faint during childbirth, thus normalising this emotional response. Importantly, however, this does not minimise the impact of the childbirth nor his emotional response to it. This was evident when he went on to say that 'I was just very lightheaded for a minute. Not from it being grue-some or anything, just the overwhelmingness of "holy crap, there's a baby and it's ours, and it's here"'. Here, the light-headedness is asso-ciated with the joy of being overwhelmed by the arrival of their baby, thus indicating that it was positive affect that ultimately shaped Adam's emotional response, different to Nathan's attempts to try to remain more emotionally neutral during the birth, or at least when he later recounted it to us.

4.5   CONCLUSIONS

In this chapter, in a host of different ways, we have explored how childbirth is alternately naturalised or rendered as fraught in ways that challenge the idea of 'natural' childbirth. Both the women and the men we interviewed often seemed to try to reconcile expectations of childbirth with the reality of childbirth, but ultimately seemed to be left with the fact that public narratives of childbirth – in which it is positioned as natural and easy – stand in stark contrast to the chal-lenges, risks, and messiness of childbirth. In Chapter 5, we again take up discourses of naturalisation in terms of women's emotion work associated with having a first child, but it is important to note here that in many ways the naturalisation of childbirth often stands in the way of women and men being adequately prepared for, or indeed being able to cope with, the reality of childbirth.

Further in terms of naturalisation, in this chapter, we have raised the question of what exactly is 'natural' for men in terms of childbirth. It would seem that despite the increased 'naturalisation' of men's presence at their child's birth, for many of the participants, this did not easily translate into a clearly identified role within the birthing space. Indeed, and to return to Ahmed's (2010) work, while for women, the hospital space often appeared to insert normative institutionalised emotions about childbirth 'under the skin', for men there was very much a sense in which the hospital space often served to reinforce their separation from childbirth. This was even the case when men were invited into being part of the labouring couple, such as with regard to cord cutting. For the men we interviewed, cord cutting did not easily translate into them feeling included in the birth. Rather, it confronted them with the embodied aspects of childbirth, and indeed also the affective dimensions of childbirth. Certainly, some of the men we interviewed willingly shared the positive affective aspects of childbirth. But more of the men seemed to struggle with how to situate themselves within an emotional relationship to the birth of their child, instead deferring to childbirth as women's experience.

We might ask, then, how does the social flesh (Beasley & Bacchi, 2007) of childbirth cut both women and men off from the reality of childbirth? For women (and men), how do discourses of 'natural' birth leave them ill prepared for the realities of birth? How do books or classes or conversations with other gestational parents leave them ill prepared for how the hospital space (in the context of hospital births) will shape their experiences for better or worse? This is not to naively suggest that anyone can truly be prepared for a first birth. Rather, it is to suggest that naturalisation rhetoric further compounds challenges with regard to being prepared. Attempts at naturalising men's involvement may well fall short of preparing men for how they might be involved in the birth of their child, and the visceral and emotional aspects of childbirth. Certainly, we would not want to be complicit with normative gendered accounts in the context of childbirth. But for the participants, it certainly appeared that normative gendered understandings shaped men's experiences of childbirth, and required ways of engaging men that take such understandings into account, while also allowing and indeed creating space for men to engage with the affective dimensions of childbirth.

As we explore in Chapter 5, the lion's share of emotion work when it comes to new parenthood often falls to women, including in terms of facilitating men's involvement with children. Yet what might this look like if men are supported to engage in the emotion work of childbirth? How might a focus on the 'labouring couple', and one that takes into account men's involvement and potential needs, ultimately result in men feeling able to be actively involved, to allow themselves to experience a diversity and depth of feelings associated with childbirth, and how might this translate into men's active engagement with the emotion work of raising children? Indeed, research suggests that men who are encouraged to be involved in their child's birth are more likely to be involved in their child's life in general (Bäckström & Wahn, 2011). The materials we presented in this chapter hint at avenues for engaging men, and in the later chapters of this book, we will explore in closer detail how men's affective responses to new parenthood provide additional avenues for thinking about how men might be better invited to contribute to the affective work of new parenthood. While some men will embrace these and others may be resistant to such invitations, it would seem important to explore how such invitations might be extended through the social flesh of parenthood so that both women and men are equally able to actively engage with, and indeed shape, what it means to be a first-time parent, both as individual experience and as public narrative.

5 Emotion Work in the Transition to Motherhood

In Chapter 3, we explored some of the specific moral claims that women enact, negotiate with, and often ultimately reject in their journeys into motherhood. In that chapter, we argued that while men are located inside of moral claims about parenthood to some extent, ultimately the lion's share of moral weight about parenthood falls on women, given the normative association between womanhood and motherhood. In the previous chapter, we focused on both women's and men's accounts of the birth of a first child, whereas in this chapter we return again to focus specifically on women's accounts, this time focusing on the emotion work that women engage in through the early months following the birth of a child.

As we outlined in Chapter 1, the concept of emotion work was first developed by Hochschild (1979), in which she argued that emotion work involves a person trying to change the depth or form of an emotion. Such change attempts are driven by what Hochschild calls 'feeling rules', which are normative expectations about how a person should feel in a specific situation. For example, it is a culturally normative expectation to cry at a funeral, or to laugh at a joke. It is not normative to laugh at a funeral or to cry (in sadness) at a joke. Awareness of feeling rules means that people may feel compelled to engage in emotion work that ensures the emotions they display normatively align with those expected in a given situation. Given that, at least culturally in western countries, women are so often framed as emotional (as compared to men), and are expected to play the role of emotional manager in social situations, it should be readily apparent why women may be particularly affected by feeling rules, and thus heavily engaged in emotion work.

Importantly, Hochschild (1979) went to great lengths to emphasise that emotion work is not a performance, in that it is not fake. Rather, we might suggest that emotion work is performative in the sense that Butler (2002) uses the term in regard to gender. Just as Butler suggested that gender is performative in that it achieves a semblance of truth through its constant repetition, normative emotional states bound by feeling rules achieve their semblance of truth through their constant repetition and reinforcement. When it comes to motherhood, as we argue in this chapter, there are a host of normative expectations placed upon how women express emotions about becoming and being a mother, expectations that are to an extent wrapped up with the moral claims we explored in Chapter 3. Focusing on the performance of emotions related to motherhood allows us to explore in closer detail how it is that the very expectation of performing certain feeling rules creates emotion work for new mothers. In other words, when women are expected to experience new motherhood in certain ways, but their experiences do not align with the expected feelings, the emotion work they must engage in is fraught and complex.

We acknowledge here that subsequent applications of Hochschild's (1979) work have tended to reduce the concept of emotion work to 'emotions in work' (i.e., in the workplace as emotional labour), creating an instrumentalising account of the concept that can make it appear to function as a tool for workplace compliance. As Brook (2009) argues, this is certainly an accurate depiction of how the concept of emotion work has been applied within the field of organisational studies. But such critiques do not speak to the original outline of emotion work by Hochschild, nor do they fairly encapsulate all of the possible applications of the concept of emotion work beyond being used as a neoliberal management tool. Perhaps surprisingly, however, while the concept of emotion work has indeed been used across multiple fields, often its application to parents has focused on parenting outside the norm, such as the emotion work undertaken by parents of children with disabilities (e.g., Kwok & Kwok, 2020). Our focus in this chapter on the normative, indeed mundane, experience of new motherhood highlights that emotion work is likely replete across all parenthood contexts.

Focusing on the emotion work undertaken by some of the women we interviewed also allows us to further explore how emotions get institutions under the skin (Ahmed, 2010). Similar to our arguments about moral claims in Chapter 3, in this chapter, we explore how the performance, or critique, of normative feeling rules potentially binds women to the sphere of affect, framing their experiences not only in terms of normative expectations about emotions, but relegating their experiences in general to the sphere of affect. In other words, while it is likely unsurprising that new parenthood is wrapped up in affect, it is the expectation of particular emotional performances, and their mismatch with the reality of new motherhood, that is our focus in this chapter. Even if women are critical of, or resistant to, normative feeling rules, they are nonetheless compelled to engage with social structures that equate womanhood with motherhood, and both with emotions.

It is for this reason that we focus on women in this chapter. This is not to say that men do not experience emotions about new parenthood, nor that men do not engage in emotion work. Rather it is to suggest that it would seem to be the case that men's emotion work is episodic and specific when it comes to parenthood, as compared to women's which is sustained. As we argued in Chapter 4, men navigate emotions in specific contexts, such as birth. Women also navigate emotions in specific contexts such as birth, as well as being responsible more broadly for managing emotions in the family context, particularly within heterosexual couples. Emotion work is thus specifically gendered work, for which women bear the greatest burden. We demonstrate this burden by again juxtaposing expectations and realities of new motherhood, and by juxtaposing women's awareness of normative feeling rules with the feelings they actually experienced. We also juxtapose women's accounts of their own feelings with the work involved in engaging men in carework in general, and emotion work specifically. As we explore in the conclusion to this chapter, focusing on these specific points of juxtaposition allows us to further demonstrate how the social flesh (Beasley & Bacchi, 2007) of parenthood is both gender differentiated and intimately enmeshed with normative expectations in regard to how the affective dimensions of new parenthood are situated within both the individual and the social body.

5.2   GENDERED DIFFERENCES IN EMOTION WORK ACROSS THE INTERVIEWS

Before turning to consider some of the interviews we conducted with women, in this section, we first briefly overview some of the findings we have previously published from our study as they broadly pertain to emotion work. In one article (Riggs & Bartholomaeus, 2020), we focused on four of the couples, in order to explore how they accounted for the division of household and carework. From this we found that both forms of work were often not positioned as work proper, especially by men. As an extension of this, some of the women suggested they were 'lucky' if their male partner was 'helpful' when it came to household labour and carework. This left women with the burden of providing care for their children in addition to, in many cases, taking primary responsibility for household labour. Indeed, in many cases, because women were taking extended time off from paid work to care for an infant, there was a normative expectation that during this time 'at home' they would also undertake most of the housework. This collapsing of housework and caring for infants positioned them as automatic corollaries, but also functioned to conflate the two such that both were the 'natural' work of women at home. Certainly, in a small number of couples, men did a significant amount of housework, but this was treated as separate from the general running of the house and care of an infant.

Much of the above-mentioned points may be framed as emotion work, in that the women were often not satisfied with the unequal distribution of labour, but appeared compelled in many cases to legitimate their partner's contribution to the family via paid work. For some women, paid work and work within the home were each viewed as part of a complementary whole within a normative understanding of family. But other women were mindful that their majority contribution to unpaid work at home came at a cost to their career, a cost not similarly born by their partner. In the interviews themselves, men less often tended to engage in emotion work to justify their household contribution, whereas many of the women engaged in complex emotion work involving expressing frustration about their partner's contribution, and frustration with the expectations placed upon them as women, while also juggling these frustrations with gratitude for having a child and being able to be at home with them. There was a sense in which women felt they had to be grateful for being able to be a mother, gratitude that often made it harder for women to speak about the challenges they faced.

Gender differences in emotion work were also evident when the participants spoke about fertility-related challenges, as Damien has explored elsewhere (Riggs, 2020). As we noted in Chapter 3, some of the participants experienced difficulties conceiving. When accounting for this, women spoke about fertility-related challenges as impacting upon their sense of self as a woman, involving considerable emotion work to juggle grief associated with pregnancy loss and joy associated with subsequent pregnancies. Finding fertility specialists, attending appointments, and taking fertility medications were all an additional burden faced by some of the women we interviewed, a burden that came with specific emotional costs given the moral claims about motherhood we explored in Chapter 3. For men, by comparison, while some expressed concerns about the challenges the couple faced in conceiving, often these concerns were minimised through either an optimistic view (i.e., 'it will happen when it happens') or a pragmatic view (i.e., 'if it doesn't work out that's okay'). Again, this is not to say that men were not impacted by pregnancy loss or fertility-related challenges, but the emotion work required of them to 'stay positive' was different, or at least differently voiced, within the context of the interviews. Indeed, most of the men emphasised playing a supporting role for their partner, rather than being equally affected by fertility-related challenges.

Finally, in one publication, we focused specifically on men's views on what it would mean to become a father (Bartholomaeus & Riggs, 2020). In this article, we reported two differing motivations or beliefs that men may hold about what it means to have a child. In the first grouping, some of the men appeared self-motivated. This included wanting a child to continue their bloodline or to contribute to the gene pool. In the second grouping, some men were focused more on wanting to have a relationship with a child. This included wanting to teach a child or to watch a child grow. Yet even in this second grouping, which focused more on the affective dimensions of new fatherhood, men seldom spoke about the potential feeling rules or emotion work that might govern their experiences as first-time fathers. This was markedly different to women's accounts, or men's accounts of their female partners, in which feeling rules were clearly evident (as we explored in Chapter 3 and consider in more detail in this chapter). Again, this is not to say that men do not engage in emotion work, but rather to suggest that for the men we interviewed the affective dimensions of future parenthood seemed somewhat less salient – or at least less able to be expressed – than it did for the women we interviewed.

5.3   FEELING LOST IN THE FACE OF THE INJUNCTION TO BREASTFEED

In Chapter 3, we explored how some of the women we interviewed negotiated challenges associated with breastfeeding, and how some framed breastfeeding as a moral imperative during pregnancy, only to revisit this moral claim when they found the reality of breastfeeding different to their expectations. In this section, we return to the topic of breastfeeding and explore how some of the women we interviewed spoke about breastfeeding as work, and moreover as emotion work involving the complex negotiation of feeling rules about how women are expected to talk about and experience breastfeeding. The significance placed on breastfeeding reflects both institutional and cultural imperatives in many countries, including Australia (e.g., Balint et al., 2017; Fenwick et al., 2013; Sheehan & Schmied, 2011).

Previous research on breastfeeding has documented the challenges that women commonly face when it comes to breastfeeding. In the Chinese context, for example, Hanser and Li (2017) write about the considerable physical and emotional work associated with using breast pumps. Not only do breast pumps require a considerable time commitment from women, often negotiated in the context of paid work, but the use of breast pumps also elicits emotion work, such that women are expected to display a desire to produce milk 'for the good of their child' in the face of what is often considerable emotional distress associated with not being able to breastfeed (or having a low milk supply). Furthermore, women who utilise breast pumps are often expected to show a high level of commitment to this practice, despite many women finding it emotionally and physically draining. Here, there is a mismatch between the emotions that women are expected to display in regard to feeding their child, and the emotions they may experience with using breast pumps, requiring complex negotiations with feeling rules about new motherhood and infant feeding. Finally, when it comes to breast pumps, many women in the study by Hanser and Li reported that they would otherwise wish to stop providing breast milk to their child, but the injunction that 'breast is best' kept many women continuing to use a breast pump for extended periods of time.

Writing about her own experience of breastfeeding in the United Kingdom, Crossley (2009) draws attention to the tension between the idea that breastfeeding represents resistance to the medicalisation of women's experiences of caring for an infant (i.e., women's agency and bodies being paramount, as compared to formula feeding), and the increased injunction upon women to breastfeed at all costs. For Crossley, her experience of low milk production was at odds with advice from medical professionals who naturalised breastfeeding. Despite all evidence that her infant was not receiving enough milk, Crossley persisted with breastfeeding as she was told by professionals that her body would always produce enough milk. As Stearns (2009) similarly notes in the US context, the naturalisation of breastfeeding

marginalises the reality of breastfeeding. Women engage in considerable work to make breastfeeding happen, and this includes emotion
work related to managing discrepancies between the expectation that
breastfeeding will 'happen naturally' and the challenges that many
women experience with breastfeeding. The naturalisation of breastfeeding is compounded by the emphasis upon it being something that
only women can do (which is incorrect, given that some trans masculine and non-binary gestational parents chestfeed). Not only does
such an account of breastfeeding absolve men of responsibility for
supporting breastfeeding, but it also places an additional emotional
burden on women to take primary responsibility for their infant.

In our study, when asked to speak about her experiences of
breastfeeding, Lucy shared her experience of having mastitis, noting that 'I guess I panicked a bit when it started to be more painful
for so long'. Lucy felt that she should see a doctor about the pain
she was experiencing during breastfeeding, but also reported feeling
'confused' because two of her friends who were also breastfeeding
'didn't seem to complain about breastfeeding', and while one of the
friends seemed to find breastfeeding challenging, she 'didn't go into
details ... so I didn't know it can be a common thing [to experience
mastitis]'. Here Lucy would seem to be negotiating with feeling rules
about breastfeeding. She saw her friends 'not complain' about breastfeeding, from which Lucy took the message that 'complaining' was
not a normative behaviour when it came to breastfeeding challenges,
meaning that her desire to see her doctor was placed in question.

Absent of professional advice and with only the experiences of
her two friends to go on, a feeling rule that appeared to centre stoicism in the face of breastfeeding challenges left Lucy feeling 'so lost'
and wondering 'what's wrong with me'. Reflecting on this time, Lucy
noted that 'if I knew that [mastitis] is fine, then maybe I wouldn't
have come across as so stressed about it'. Lucy asked her husband
John what she should do, and he suggested the use of a pump, and
bought one for her. While Lucy shared that his advice was 'really
good for me', it meant that she continued to feed from one breast and

express from the breast with mastitis, meaning that her pain continued. Similar to the literature summarised earlier, then, the purchase
of a breast pump ensured that Lucy continued to adhere to the idea
that 'breast is best', rather than, for example, considering switching
to formula feeding while she had treatment for mastitis.

Despite these challenges, in her interview, Lucy appeared to
struggle to accept that mastitis is common, as are other breastfeeding
challenges. Lucy noted that even when she spoke with her midwife
she still asked herself 'did I do something wrong?'. The naturalisation
of breastfeeding creates a feeling rule where women who experience
challenges in breastfeeding may default to feeling that any challenges
they experience are their own fault, rather than being common to
breastfeeding for many women (and thus that breastfeeding 'success'
is not a natural or automatic outcome). Lucy did provide a rationalisation for the challenges that she faced: 'maybe my nipples weren't used
to this constant feeding every two hours'. Yet even with such a reasonable rationalisation, the feeling rules associated with breastfeeding
appeared to override this rationalisation, leaving Lucy to default to the
idea that she was somehow to blame. While her husband John showed
awareness of the stigma around mastitis and the emotional toll this
had had on Lucy (but not him), he also did not challenge the idea of
'breast is best': 'It turns out that pretty much all of our female friends
who have had kids suffered from mastitis at one stage or another. It's
weird. It seems like the untalked about – not illness – it's not really a
disease – but maybe a dis–ease. She really had a hard time with that.
"What's wrong with me?" kind of thing. "I want to be the perfect
mum." I think that's why a lot of mums don't talk about mastitis,
because they feel like they've failed or something like that.' Here John
appears mindful of the normative expectation while not explicitly
challenging the expectation itself (i.e., to breastfeed in the face of pain).

Ana too had a challenging experience with breastfeeding. Ana
shared that she had previously had breast reduction surgery, and had
been told that this might affect her milk supply. After the birth of her
child, however, Ana found it difficult to access information when she

experienced challenges with milk supply. Without adequate support or information, and facing challenges with breastfeeding, Ana turned to expressing milk, which as she noted 'took a lot out of me, it added a lot more stress to my day'. Again there is a sense in which the naturalisation of breastfeeding meant that Ana was largely left to her own devices, the expectation being that the challenges she faced would sort themselves out. Despite repeatedly emphasising to her birthing team that she had previously had a breast reduction, she received no clear information about how to manage this in the context of breastfeeding and milk production. It was only subsequent to Ana joining online groups that she learned how common her experience was.

For Ana, issues about milk supply were compounded when she was told soon after the birth of her child that 'because the milk hadn't come in and we were still wondering whether or not I was going to have enough milk, the obstetrician said that he respected the fact that I wanted to breastfeed but Daisy was born under the expected range for weight so needed to put on weight quickly, so definitely needed to do formula until my milk, if my milk was going to come in'. While this might have been a reasonable suggestion to make, for Ana it compounded the emotion work she was already facing in regard to managing her low milk supply in the face of the naturalisation of breastfeeding and the assumption that she should just know what to do. While the obstetrician 'respected' her desire to breastfeed, Ana was left with no clarity about 'if her milk was going to come in'.

In the face of this uncertainty and lack of information, Ana persisted for many months in expressing milk from the breast that was producing supply. As she noted, she was 'hopeful' that her other breast would start producing milk and that her supply would increase overall, a hope that led her to expressing throughout the day with the aim of increasing milk production. Despite this strong commitment to breastfeeding, Ana reported that she was often left disheartened when people continuously asked her how breastfeeding was going, the presumption being that it was fine. Ana shared that she resorted to telling people that she was bottle-feeding just so that the questions would stop, but that this ultimately made her 'feel less worthy'. This was despite Ana knowing that 'I'm doing a lot more than a lot of people would do, or would've done, just by waking up twice in the middle of the night to go and pump for an hour, so eight hours of my day I was basically sitting on a chair, on a couch there, expressing to get sometimes 100 mls a day, that's how much I would be getting from one boob alone, you know, eight hours of my day doing that'. Similar to Lucy, Ana's account demonstrates the emotion work that women undertake when breastfeeding. For Ana she felt 'less worthy', but to others felt compelled to display a stoic face of persistence with expressing breastmilk for bottle-feeding regardless of the challenges she experienced. The challenges were 'very frustrating and disheartening' for Ana, but displaying these feelings was at odds with Ana's feeling that she had to show to others a desire to persist, and to do so willingly and happily.

Given her persistence, Ana was mostly able to express enough milk to feed her child, but this meant bottle-feeding. Ana shared that she 'cried plenty' because of all the work required of her, especially in the face of seeing 'a friend breastfeeding and all she takes with her is a set of nappies and wipes'. Ana's physical and emotion work in expressing milk just brought with it more work in terms of taking all of the paraphernalia required of going out in public and bottle-feeding expressed milk. Indeed, as Ana noted even with all of the paraphernalia, getting out of the house was hard because so much of her time was taken up with expressing milk, given as she noted 'I was paranoid that my milk supply was going to go down if I didn't express at the right times'. But even with all of these challenges Ana persisted. She ended up buying a breast pump she could take out with her, so that she could leave the house more and continue her commitment to expressing milk. In the final interview, Ana shared that she had stopped expressing milk when her baby was seven months old, with the encouragement of a maternal health nurse who visited her regularly, and that this was a 'turning point' in her life. She tearfully told us 'I actually needed someone to say that to me and that it was okay for me [to stop expressing], that I had done my best, that it was okay, that Daisy had, I did everything that I could to breastfeed [via expressing] Daisy for as long as I could but that I would be happier and I would be a better mum to Daisy as well if I made that transition, and I think that really sunk in, and if it wasn't for her support I wouldn't have a clue how to do it.'

As we can see from the stories of Lucy and Ana, breastfeeding produces considerable emotion work for some women. When women experience breastfeeding challenges, they do so in a context that naturalises breastfeeding, does not always provide women with adequate information, and leaves women feeling compelled to express milk at the same time as feeling that they are somehow at fault. The naturalisation of breastfeeding means that the feeling rules associated with it do not readily include feelings of distress or failure, leaving women to find ways to persist in the face of these feelings, and indeed to present an image of breastfeeding (or expressing breast-milk) that emphasises stoicism and persistence. Further, and as we explore in Section 5.4, the naturalisation of breastfeeding means that women experience the primary burden of infant care, yet may often also need to undertake additional work to recruit their male partners to contribute to other aspects of infant care.

5.4   ENGAGING MEN IN CAREWORK

As we noted earlier, the naturalisation of breastfeeding often meant that the women we interviewed were expected to automatically know how to breastfeed, which for many of the women meant that they received minimal support after that initially provided in the hospital. This occurred for women who experienced challenges with breastfeeding, such as Lucy and Ana, as well as for many of the other women. This naturalisation of breastfeeding is part of a wider discourse about motherhood, which frames mothering as 'natural' for women. By contrast, men are often expected to have to 'learn' how to parent, as they are presumed not to have the same 'natural' inclinations or skills as is presumed of women. The literature we have summarised in this chapter consistently notes that the narrative that men must 'learn' how to parent means that men are given considerable leeway when it comes to knowing what to do with an infant, and indeed it can mean that some heterosexual men eschew ever 'knowing what to do', instead deferring to their female partners.

From the early work of Oakley (1974) onwards, feminist scholars have highlighted that the naturalisation of women's parenting work serves to ignore both that motherhood is not 'natural' for women and that it is indeed work. Not only are there the physical aspects of housework and carework, but there is the wider work of managing the household, including for heterosexually coupled women managing their male partner's involvement. As Seery and Crowley (2000) note, discourses of 'maternal gatekeeping' are often used to legitimate men's lack of involvement with their children, yet this discourse in fact is a form of mother blame in the face of some men's relative lack of involvement. As we noted earlier, some women feel that they are 'lucky' if their male partner makes any contribution, so challenging broader inequities in the division of labour can be difficult. Even when women do challenge inequities, as Seery and Crowley note, they may focus on ensuring that their male partner is more 'involved' with their children, without necessarily also being involved more broadly with the running of the household and broader decision-making about the family. Again, this does not constitute a fault on the part of women, but rather likely reflects power dynamics within heterosexual relationships wrought by the naturalisation of motherhood.

Morison and MacLeod (2015) suggest that normative understandings of masculinity can act as barriers to men being actively involved in running the household and in decision-making about the family (as opposed to being passively involved on instruction from their female partners). While it has been noted that there are contemporary shifts in men's involvement in household and childcare labour (e.g., Hunter, Riggs, & Augoustinos, 2017), often, as we noted earlier, this is led by women and directed towards children. As Miller (2011) notes, while men often suggest that there are no differences between their parenting and that of their female partner other than in regard to breastfeeding, in reality men often justify their differential involvement. Again, this typically involves recourse to women's 'natural' propensity to motherhood, meaning that men either have to be 'taught' or left to make a secondary contribution. As Sevón (2012) notes, for many of the heterosexual women she interviewed before and after having a baby with a male partner, before the birth there was a lot of 'we talk' (talking about what they and their partner will do), while after the birth there was much more 'I talk', reflecting the greater share of work that women undertook, a share that they had not expected based on conversations with their partner prior to the birth.

Given the challenges she faced with breastfeeding and expressing and the intensive work she put into it, it is not surprising that Ana ended up taking the lead in most aspects of caring for her newborn. At the same time, however, Ana was surprised at the extent to which she had to scaffold things for her partner so that he could be involved. Ana was surprised, as prior to the birth her husband Daniel had been strongly committed to having a child (more so than Ana), and was excited about the birth and becoming a father. As Ana noted, while Daniel does 'certain' things for their child, such as bathing her, anything that requires him to provide primary care requires considerable input from Ana: 'I've been out a couple of times but I have to pre-programme these things, I cannot just say "I am going out now"'. Here Ana reports having to engage in a broader form of emotion work, namely scaffolding the emotions and interactions of other people, particularly her husband.

Ana went on to share that 'I always have to ask and say, "okay, this day I want to book this, are you able to finish work or stop working at this time so I can [go] and have my things done?"'. This idea of having to 'book in' with a partner in order to have time away from their child highlights the primary responsibility accorded to women to care for children. Yet even when this was possible, Ana reported 'feeling guilty going out and I do not allow myself to enjoy being out as I don't know how he's dealing with' their child. Here Ana is potentially adhering to the feeling rules associated with intensive mothering, such that she is expected to prioritise her child, and that any instance of not doing this results in feelings of guilt. This is exacerbated by the lack of hands-on interaction that her husband has with their child on a day-to-day basis, leaving Ana feeling unsure about his capacity to care for their child alone.

Yet contrary to the naturalisation of her role as a mother, Ana spoke about a considerable adjustment period where she had to be 'patient' and learn what certain cries meant, and how to respond to them. By contrast, Ana reported that Daniel had not taken the time to undertake similar learning, meaning that at the time of the third interview, Ana said she 'doesn't have a lot of patience for him these days'. Here Ana highlights that mothering was not automatic for her, and instead that she had to actively learn to understand her child's needs, something that she felt Daniel should have done but did not. At the time of the third interview when their child was six months old, Ana was actively working on stepping out of the space and leaving Daniel to learn what to do. Ana was concerned that this would cause undue distress for her child, again highlighting the emotion work that women such as Ana feel compelled to perform for the sake of the family, but at the same time, she had gotten to a point where she felt Daniel was not working towards learning, and that as a result, she had to step back where possible so that he had no choice but to learn. A key area where Ana was doing this was in regard to sleep. While the couple notionally had an agreement where they would take turns in getting up to their child during the night, often Ana felt it fell to her, although Daniel suggested at the third interview it was 'half-half'. Ana spoke about instances where even if Daniel was the one who got up when the child cried, he would wake Ana to ask her what to do. At the time of the final interview, Ana was being more insistent that when it was his turn to wake up, he had to manage on his own, rather than turning to Ana for a solution. During the first nine months of their baby's life, they also had support from Ana's mother who was temporarily living with them to help them during this early stage of parenting, but Ana was preparing for her mother to return home. For Ana, this was a turning point, where she was forced to speak more openly with Daniel about caring for their child as she realised there would be no one nearby to help them and it was up to the two of them to support each other.

Paula's experiences provide an interesting juxtaposition to those of Ana. Prior to the birth of their child, Paula and her partner Isaac were what Paula referred to as 'besotted' with one another, with both very committed to, and excited about, having a first child together. Paula shared that this feeling continued after the birth, with Isaac 'constantly saying he was so proud of me, that I'd done such a good job, and we were so happy we had produced this healthy baby, and we were kind of very lovey-dovey'. Paula shared that over time Isaac had continued to do 'anything I ask him to do', but it would appear that the very fact of having to 'ask' was beginning to be an issue for Paula. As she noted, 'there's the feeling of resentment that I have that whenever there's a problem it will come down to me'. Different to Ana, then, Paula had a partner who was actively involved in caring for their child, yet there was still a sense in which Paula was expected to run the show. We might argue that this is reflected in Isaac's 'pride' in Paula, an emotion that it might be suggested serves to naturalise her role in childbirth and subsequent motherhood, the effect being that Paula is positioned as in the driving seat, and Isaac requires 'asking' in order to take charge in a particular situation.

Paula also shared that she felt increasing 'resentment' and 'frustration' because Isaac had the 'freedom' to go to (paid) work and generally leave the house easily, while she was stuck at home most of the time. Paula was mindful that Isaac had to make adaptations too, especially in regard to the time she had for him, but this again emphasises the normative expectation that women will be available for their partner, and that if they are unable to do that following the birth of a child it has a negative impact on men, ignoring that it also impacts on women (e.g., having less time for themselves). The normative expectation that women guide and shape families constitutes itself a form of emotion work that can leave women feeling left out if their partners do not make a similar contribution to feeling rules. For Paula, this occurred when Mother's Day passed by and Isaac did nothing to celebrate it for her and their child. Paula noted that 'for him he didn't realise it was a big deal', indicating that, at least in this instance, being mindful of the emotions of other people in the house in terms of parenthood was not as salient for Isaac.

Yet even in the face of this disappointment, Paula was again quick to explain away Isaac's actions, providing rationalisations such as his busy paid work schedule, and that 'he cooks a couple of nights a week, he makes me coffee every single morning and brings it to me in bed, he does all the nappies when he's at home, he does Emily's bath, he does the night-feed at 10 o'clock every night with a bottle'. We would suggest that these are not exceptional actions, but rather they are the actions of a parent making a contribution to their child's life. Yet for Paula, it appeared difficult for her to break the feeling rules of gratitude or 'luck' in having a supportive partner to equally emphasise how weighty she felt the responsibility was for providing primary care for their child. Certainly, we are not intending to dismiss the fact that Isaac may have been doing more than men in some of the other couples, such as Ana and Daniel, but at the same time, we would emphasise that Paula was positioned as the arbiter of key decisions, and having to 'ask' for additional contributions from her partner. This constitutes emotion work whereby not only did Paula have to manage her own conflicting emotions and their relationship to feeling rules about what mothers should normatively do, but it also involved work associated with requesting her partner's contribution, which even at times did not come to fruition (such as Isaac overlooking Mother's Day).

5.5 'EATING YOUR FEELINGS' AND BEING 'BORED'

In Sections 5.3 and 5.4, we highlighted how motherhood is expected to come 'naturally' to women, especially as compared to men who are expected to have to 'learn' how to care for a child. This naturalisation of motherhood comes wrapped up with the assumption that women will automatically feel love for their child, and will take great joy in becoming a mother. For many of the women we interviewed, however, this was not the case. In this section, we explore how for some of the women there were considerable discrepancies between what they expected of the affective dimensions of new motherhood and the reality of their experiences. Such discrepancies created additional emotion work for women, requiring them to navigate normative feeling rules about how women are meant to feel about motherhood, and what this meant for their adjustment to motherhood.

Previous research has consistently emphasised the idea that heterosexual women are expected to be selfless in their commitment to motherhood, including forfeiting much of their life in their commitment to their child (e.g., Weaver & Ussher, 1997). This contrasts with the greater latitude that men have in regard to deciding how much of their time and life they will give over to their child. Yet even for women who do report selflessness in regard to their commitment to their child, previous research suggests that many women are often unprepared for the extent to which they must sacrifice their own needs for those of their child. Choi and colleagues (2005) in their research conducted in the United Kingdom, for example, report that through the early months of motherhood many women in heterosexual couples come to realise the considerable cost of motherhood, a cost not born by their male partners.

Part and parcel with the idea of selflessness is the idea of intensive mothering. Many of the Australian women interviewed by Lupton (2000), for example, reported being committed to the idea of being available to their newborn child, yet the reality of this was much harder than expected. Lupton's participants found childcare 'all consuming', often with little reward. A constant merry-go-round of feeding and nappy changing, all on little sleep, stood in stark contrast to the rosy image of motherhood that many of the women held prior to the birth of a first child. The monotony of motherhood was again a sticking point for many of the women interviewed by Lupton when compared to the relative freedom that the women's male partners appeared to enjoy, with many of the women's partners positioning themselves as 'helpers', rather than as actively involved co-parents. In their focus on 'master narratives' of motherhood, Kerrick and Henry's (2017) US study found that most of the women they interviewed held a 'master narrative' involving motherhood as overwhelmingly positive, involving an instant bond with newborns. The reality of new motherhood, however, was quite different, resulting in ambivalence for many of the women. In response, many of the women in Kerrick and Henry's study were forced to renegotiate their expectations of what motherhood looked like.

For some of the women we interviewed, such as Gina, there was indeed a discrepancy between their expectations and reality of new motherhood, resulting in considerable emotion work required in order to navigate the normative feeling rules associated with selflessness, joy, and instant connection. Gina shared that women can 'naively think that you are totally ready', and that women will 'innately know what to do', whereas the reality is that 'nobody has any clue what they're doing'. Different to the joy that she expected to experience, Gina described 'lots of emotion and lots of exhaustion and lots of eating your feelings'. We would suggest that such affective consumption speaks to an active engagement with feeling rules, with women such as Gina being mindful of the normative assumption that motherhood should be easy and a joy, and that by contrast women such as Gina must 'eat' negative feelings so as to navigate a path that is bearable.

As a way to manage the tensions she experienced, Gina made recourse to a narrative of new motherhood that served in some ways to naturalise the challenges she faced. Talking about knowing what to do in the face of uncertainty, Gina emphasised that 'probably the only thing that would have come naturally is your gut instinct with your child. I think everything else you kind of learn, but it's still a very little bomb, a mine field'. Here, Gina employs contrasting accounts to manage the feeling rules she was faced with. As indicated earlier, Gina realised that she was unprepared for the challenges of new motherhood, and in response she emphasised the utility of 'going with your gut'. Yet at the same time, working out how to mother was a 'mine field'. What was exploded by her child were the assumptions that motherhood would be easy, yet Gina attempted to mitigate this bomb by 'going with her gut'. Here, then, Gina both challenges normative feeling rules (that motherhood should be easy) *and* draws on a normative account of motherhood (that women can trust their 'gut instinct' to know what to do). Nonetheless, Gina went on to note that 'I expected it to be this beautiful, I don't know, fully instinctual journey where you would automatically feel like a mother and automatically bond with your child'. So while Gina makes recourse to her 'gut instinct', her expectation that motherhood would be 'fully instinctual' was not realised.

For Paula, the reality of new motherhood was different to her expectations in terms of the repetitious nature of infant care. For example, she had the expectation that having a baby would involve walking around with them on her hip. By contrast, infant care involved for Paula a lot of holding (because newborns do not just sit on the hip), meaning that Paula found herself wondering 'how to fill the hours', ultimately finding herself 'kind of bored' and that her child was 'kind of boring'. This boredom was largely a product of the routinised nature of infant care. Paula expected that she would enjoy the routines, when in reality she found herself just biding time in between feeding and sleeping. This discrepancy between expectation and reality forced Paula to confront the feeling rules associated with new motherhood, particularly the discrepancy between the joyful image she held before her child was born and the monotonous nature of infant care.

Yet even as Paula's child grew and became more aware of her surroundings and more engaged, Paula did not find this to be immediately positive. As she noted, 'I don't live for the moment Emily wakes up. I think some people want to cuddle their baby all the time but I'd rather not and I don't want her clinging to me all the time and I don't want to feel that she needs me constantly'. Despite waiting so long to be able to have a child, and previously looking forward to being at home with her child, the reality for Paula was 'not her cup of tea'. Different to Gina in a sense, Paula did not seem particularly worried that she was not more interested in or engaged by her child. Yet at the same time, during her interview, Paula spent a considerable amount of time justifying why she found the routines boring, or why she did not want her child 'clinging' to her all the time. These justifications, we would argue, highlight Paula's awareness of what she thought she *should* be feeling, and that the interview was an instance of emotion work where she sought to acknowledge the feelings she thought were expected of her, and which required a justification for why she did not hold those feelings. By the fourth interview, Paula had a second baby and, while it was challenging juggling two small children, she no longer spoke about being 'bored', and instead spoke about being enthralled by watching Emily learn and play.

In a similar way to Paula, Ana too provided justifications for feelings about her child that differed from those expected based on normative feeling rules about new motherhood. Ana noted that she was 'beyond grateful, beyond, beyond grateful' for her child (who had come after unanticipated fertility challenges), yet this extreme formulation belies her experience of motherhood being 'demanding'. As she noted, 'it's been very hard, a lot harder than I was expecting, maybe because I had expectations that I based on the image that I had in mind of what it would be having a newborn'. Ana had expected that there would not be much crying unless the child was hungry or needed a nappy change, yet the reality was that the child 'wanted to hear their voice and they just kept screaming and screaming'.

Feeling rules were evident when Ana attempted to reconcile her expectations with the reality of new motherhood. As she noted, 'it is an adjustment for me, for my expectations. If I'd had the opportunity to have a child a lot younger, I wonder if it would've been this way in terms of expectations, maybe it's because I've had a lot of time doing things for myself when I wanted, how I wanted, spur of the moment, and things are not like that anymore'. There is a sense here in which Ana attributes her unrealistic expectations to the relative freedoms she had prior to motherhood, conjecturing that if she had a child when she was younger this might have been different. Rather than resisting normative feeling rules, then, Ana instead potentially blames herself for finding new motherhood difficult. Ana could, for example, have situated the expectation that motherhood would be easy or joyful as a problematic discourse, one that leaves many women unprepared for the reality of motherhood. Such an account, however, is fundamentally at odds with the feelings Ana hoped to experience as a mother, leaving her with little recourse other than to blame herself. The question of blame when it comes to normative feeling rules is a topic we now take up in the conclusion to this chapter.

5.6   CONCLUSIONS

In this chapter, we have explored the emotion work that women engage with in the transition to motherhood. This emotion work takes multiple forms. It can involve complex negotiations with normative feeling rules about motherhood. Women are expected to take joy from motherhood, to find it easy, and to commit themselves to motherhood at the expense of themselves. For the women we interviewed, however, many found new motherhood exceptionally challenging, something they were not prepared for. Some of the women tried to find ways to resist or speak back to normative feeling rules, while other women blamed themselves for unrealistic expectations. Additionally, several of the women we interviewed had to engage in the emotion work associated with involving their male partners, which included helping them to navigate carework, though ultimately, for most of the women, they still undertook the majority of the carework. We take these points up again in Chapter 8 when exploring couple relationships.

Similar to Chapter 3, then, in this chapter, we have highlighted how the affective dimensions of motherhood work to insert institutions under the skin (Ahmed, 2010). Not only do social institutions insist upon motherhood for certain women (i.e., middle-class, predominantly white heterosexual women, such as those people we interviewed), but such institutions assert that motherhood should be associated with a specific normative set of feelings. Women are expected to feel immediate love for their newborn, to bond with them, and to enjoy all aspects of infant care. These normative affective dimensions of motherhood are internalised by many women, and even for women who seek to resist normative expectations, their experiences are framed in a relationship to such expectations. Importantly, and following Ahmed, our point here is not to pose a simplistic receptive model of affect, whereby women passively internalise the norms set by social institutions. Rather, our point here is that the affective dimensions of all people's lives are framed by what is rendered intelligible in the world they live in. Certainly, it is possible to envisage and enact alternate affective dimensions beyond those rendered intelligible by others. But this must be done in the face of strong social discourses that assert often singular hegemonic accounts of people's affective lives, including in this case in terms of the affective dimensions of motherhood.

As we noted earlier, the question of blame is especially complex. While we might suggest that women, based on their experience of motherhood, can create new feeling rules, ultimately this is likely to be difficult for many women, given the weight of normative feeling rules. We must ask, then, what is it about the social flesh of motherhood that so strongly shapes women's experiences, to the extent that it becomes difficult to speak freely about their experiences absent of a sense of blame? Centrally, we would argue, the issue is one associated with social flesh, and in particular the normative association of womanhood with motherhood. Women who are open about not wanting to have children face considerable social prohibitions on their decisions (Morison et al., 2016). By contrast, the default presumption is that women who do desire to have children and are able to have them will be warmly embraced by motherhood, both in their interactions with their child and in the broader social context. Yet this is only potentially the case for women whose experiences align with the social flesh of motherhood, namely an experience encapsulated by the assumption of joy and connection.

Recent conversations about motherhood regret demonstrate some of the slow changes that are occurring around the intelligibility of speaking about motherhood as anything other than a joy (e.g., Donath, 2015; Garncarek, 2020). Certainly, none of the women we interviewed spoke explicitly about regretting that they had had their child, yet it was most certainly the case that many of the women struggled with the reality of new motherhood, and regretted aspects of their experiences. Public conversations about motherhood regret – paired as they often are with criticisms of pronatalism and the association of womanhood with motherhood – help to create spaces where a diversity of women's experiences become intelligible. At the same time, however, more attention is needed to how women conceptualise motherhood prior to having a first child. Talking with women about the reality of motherhood – as compared to the imagined rosy future held by many of the women we interviewed – may be an important intervention into the social flesh of motherhood. This would not, of course, mitigate negative or challenging experiences, but it would mean that women are more prepared for the challenges that might lie ahead, and might make it more possible for women to speak back to normative feeling rules associated with new motherhood.

6 Development of a Parental Identity

6.1 INTRODUCTION

In Chapter 3, we noted that for many of the people we spoke to, reproduction was treated as axiomatic: that it was 'natural' for heterosexual couples to want to have children, which we have also written about elsewhere (Riggs & Bartholomaeus, 2018). Yet, as we have explored in the other chapters in this book so far, the journey to parenthood was not easy for many of the people we spoke to, and the reality of parenthood was often different to the expectation. In this chapter, we take this expectation/reality contrast in a different direction by exploring how the participants came to understand themselves as parents. While many treated reproduction as axiomatic, by contrast, for many of the participants, *feeling like* a parent was *not* axiomatic. In a sense, the contrast between expectation and reality was particularly acute for the new parents we interviewed in terms of feeling like a parent, most notably when the assumption that having a first baby would automatically translate into feeling like a parent was not realised. Echoing the previous chapters, then, this chapter focuses on the affective dimensions of new parenthood, exploring the relationships between feeling, wanting, and having.

As we argue in this chapter, the assumption that feeling like a parent is a corollary of having a child ignores the fact that parent–child relationships are developed through interaction, as much as they have an imaginary component. Certainly, it was the case that the participants imagined a life with a child: they planned for having a child, were invested in becoming parents, envisaged what they would do with their child, and thus had hopes and dreams about becoming parents. Yet the imaginary component of having a child is, for many people, shaped by the social flesh (Beasley & Bacchi, 2007) of parenthood. This includes some of the assumptions that we explored in previous chapters, namely that having a child will be easy, and parents will automatically bond with their children, and that aspects of caring for a newborn, particularly breastfeeding, will be relatively straightforward. These types of public narratives about new parenthood, we would suggest, leave many people ill-prepared both for the reality of new parenthood and for the challenges in developing a parental identity specifically. In other words, when the imaginary components of parenthood are shaped by a social flesh that too often overlooks the reality of new parenthood, and when it is assumed that a parental identity will naturally flow from becoming a parent, some people may struggle to develop a sense of themselves as parents.

Furthermore, and shifting focus from the imaginary to the interactional, despite the increased push towards first-time parents (and especially women) engaging with technologies aimed at monitoring pregnancy and by so doing engaging with the unborn child (Johnson, 2014; Lupton, 2020), the interactional aspects of pregnancy are in many ways at a distance. In other words, while expectant parents are increasingly encouraged to talk or sing to their unborn child in order to promote positive outcomes (Bhamani, 2017), this does not necessarily translate into the development of a relationship with the unborn child. Certainly, some people may develop a connection to their unborn child through such practices, but it is a connection absent of many of the cues we expect of interpersonal relationships, specifically direct action-responses, visual cues, and eye contact (for those who are sighted). It is, therefore, a mediated relationship: mediated both by the imaginary and by the fact the unborn child is a sight relatively unseen (other than via ultrasound, an issue we explore in more detail in the following text).

When the child is born, then, parents are presented with increased opportunities to interact with them, and to build a relationship. Yet this sits alongside the challenges of new parenthood, as we explored in the previous chapters. Furthermore, the interactions themselves may be highly limited, given the capacity of newborns to engage in relationship building. Certainly, babies demonstrate attachment behaviours, and other interactional cues are evident from birth (Mobbs et al., 2016), and parents can engage with these to encourage bonding and to develop a relationship with their child. But for new parents, such relationship-building practices are reliant upon very different interactional cues than are used with adults and older children. Coming to know a baby, then, requires new parents to adopt new ways of looking, hearing, and interacting, skills that are not necessarily taught but rather must be learned *ad hoc*. It is perhaps no surprise, then, that for many of the people we spoke to it was challenging to not only bond with their child, but to develop from this a parental identity.

This then brings us to a necessary distinction: bonding with a child is different to having a parental identity. Many adults enjoy strong bonds with children to whom they are not parents. As such, a parental identity is not essential to bonding. Indeed, some of the people we spoke with had worked closely with children in their professional lives prior to having children of their own, or were close to the children of their siblings or friends. Yet, as we already explored in Chapter 5, the assumption that bonding would be easy and straightforward was not the reality for all of the people we spoke to. If bonding was a challenge for some, then for many more developing a parental identity was even more challenging. As we explore in detail in the following text, this was especially the case for some of the women we interviewed. The social flesh of motherhood, as we have explored in previous chapters, equates womanhood with motherhood, suggesting that women will not only automatically bond with their child, but that they will feel like a mother. This leaves little space for recognition that a parental identity does not come automatically or easily for many women. By contrast, the narratives we explored about men in previous chapters, and specifically the idea that men must 'work at' or 'learn' how to parent, potentially creates a space where it is more intelligible for men to have to work at a parental identity.

As we unpack further in this chapter, these gendered discourses were evident among the people we interviewed.

In terms of juxtapositions, in this chapter, we juxtapose the interviews we conducted when the participants were pregnant with those we conducted six months after birth. We look at how differing people had shifting experiences of a parental identity across this time period. We also juxtapose differing groups of participants: those who felt a parental identity early on and those who did not, and those who found it difficult to develop a parental identity after the birth of the child and those who did not. Finally, we juxtapose differences in the development of a parental identity across time and within couples, as well as reflecting on similarities. What we ultimately present are the complicated aspects of developing a parental identity, and we conclude the chapter by exploring what this means for Ahmed's (2010) point about feelings as a mechanism by which institutions get under the skin, specifically in terms of the affective dimensions of parental identity.

6.2 FEELINGS ABOUT PARENTAL IDENTITY DURING PREGNANCY

As we noted earlier, ultrasounds are a key means through which expectant parents can visualise their unborn child. Writing about ultrasounds, Nash (2007) suggests that such technologies are problematic as they help to foster a relationship between mother (and father) and unborn child that creates a simulacrum of interaction that is premised upon visual inspection rather than a relationship. Moreover, as Nash suggests, ultrasounds accord agency to the unborn child, inviting women in particular into a relationship with medical science in which they are subjected to what is construed as the will of the unborn child. Such constructions of unborn children sit in a broader social flesh where, worldwide, there is growing opposition to abortion, with 'children's rights' heralded through the use of ultrasound imagery (e.g., Palmer, 2009). In terms of our argument in this chapter about the complexities of parental identity development, Nash (2007) argues that the increased marketisation of ultrasounds translates into the assumption that viewing an unborn child will result in bonding between mother and child, an assumption that completely overlooks the difference between bonding and parental identity.

Schmied and Lupton (2001) too are critical of ultrasounds as ontological technologies. As they suggest, it is taken for granted that by the end of a pregnancy women must, and indeed will, come to see their unborn child as a real person, a practice that is aided and abetted by ultrasounds. For the women they interviewed, however, many found it difficult to articulate the relationship they had with their unborn child, and even more difficult to accept that after their child's birth they would automatically become mothers. For some women, this was because they could not translate ultrasound images into a 'real' person, while for other women, there was an outright rejection of any desire to foster a relationship with their unborn child before their birth. For the latter group of women, pregnancy was unpleasant, in no small part because they struggled to 'share' their body with another being. Ultrasound, while providing some comfort about the neonate's development, did little to nothing to foster any sense of a bond, let alone a sense of a parental identity.

Research with expectant fathers, by contrast, has repeatedly emphasised that ultrasounds offer a key avenue through which men come to experience a sense of reality about the impending arrival of their child, and that this brings with it an increased affective commitment to new fatherhood (Walsh et al., 2014). A smaller number of studies suggest that for some women ultrasounds do help in rendering the pregnancy 'real', and thus make the unborn child more tangible. In a study by Cunen and colleagues (2021), for example, both men and women reported that attending an ultrasound helped them to conceptualise the impending reality of having a child, and that this encouraged them to engage in bonding practices (such as deciding upon names, and using them during the pregnancy, along with other pet names). Nonetheless, even having attended ultrasounds, some of the participants continued to struggle to see their unborn child as a person, or to conceptualise what it would be like to be a parent in the future.

When we interviewed the participants during the pregnancy, we asked them 'Do you feel like a mother/father now?', and 'Do you feel like [your unborn child] is part of your family?'. A minority of the participants spoke about struggling to conceptualise their unborn child as a real person, resulting in them having little sense of themselves as parents during the pregnancy. Of note is the fact that this was almost exclusively the case for women. By comparison, a majority of the people we spoke to conceptualised their unborn child as part of the family already, with some also conceptualising themselves as a parent during the pregnancy, and others seeing the child as part of the family already but themselves not necessarily already as parents. Of note is the fact that most of these participants were men. We explore these two different accounts (unborn child as abstract and unborn child as part of the family) in turn.

6.2.1   Unborn Child as Abstract

As noted earlier, when we asked women during their pregnancy if they felt like a mother, many noted that they did not yet feel like a mother, largely because their unborn child was not yet perceived as a person to interact with and care for. Paula, for example, said 'I feel protective of what's growing but I don't feel like a mother yet'. Here her unborn child is a 'what' that is growing, rather than a person. In part, Paula noted that becoming a mother does not happen until you have done the 'hard work' of parenting, though at the same time she noted that she did not expect to feel 'maternal' even after the birth. There was a sense for Paula in which not only was she yet to do the 'hard work', but also that it was hard to conceptualise her unborn child as a person: 'it just seems like something too magical really'. When asked if she spoke to their unborn child, Paula shared that 'I feel like I'm talking to a story-book character or a doll or something'. Paula went on to note that it felt 'silly' to talk to her stomach 'because we haven't met her yet, and because we're talking to a tummy and not an actual person with a face'. When asked if her unborn child was part of the family, Paula noted that 'in an abstract way' she was, but then clarified that her unborn child is 'an object that's part of my life'. For Paula, this meant that 'we're not a mum and a dad and a baby', but the child is nonetheless 'becoming part of our family, but she's not ready to be real yet'. Here Paula both accords some agency to her unborn child (i.e., she is 'not ready to be real yet'), but at the same time positions her unborn child as an 'object' (variously referring to her unborn child as 'it' and 'she').

When asked if she felt like a mother during her pregnancy, Mary noted that she already felt like a mother to her dogs, and that she did not feel any more like a mother to her unborn child. She clarified this by noting that Mother's Day was approaching and she did not associate herself with that at all. For Mary, she felt she would not be a mother 'until there's an actual child, and probably not until there is a talking child'. Similar to Paula, then, an unborn child is not yet an 'actual child', and even after birth for Mary a child who is born is still not an actual child at first. As she went on to note, it is not until the child is able to 'interact' that she will feel like a mother: 'once you start to see the impact that you have in shaping them as a little individual, I think that's when I'll feel like a mother'. That impact, she went on to note, was about the specificities of the mother–child relationship: 'when you see a genuine response to it being you [such as making eye contact], as opposed to just anybody picking them up'. Here, Mary makes a comment that relates to the points we made in the introduction to this chapter, namely that it is in the interactions that a relationship is formed, and through which parents may come to form a parental identity. When asked if she speaks to her unborn child, Mary provided an instrumentalising account similar to Paula: 'Again it comes back to that it doesn't really feel real. It doesn't really feel like a person. It just still feels like my body. Do you talk to your foot?'. This struggle to see her unborn child as 'real' and as a 'person' meant that Mary struggled to see the purpose in talking to her unborn child. While Mary noted that other family members clearly felt her unborn child was already part of the family, for Mary this was complex. While she noted her unborn child was 'part of the family' according to other people, Mary did not 'naturally see it that way myself'.

Alice too noted that she did not feel like a mother during her pregnancy, though she did 'feel like someone who's having to consider another life'. While Alice expected that she would 'emotionally connect quickly' with the baby once it was born, she found that during the pregnancy there was no great sense of attachment, so much so that she felt that if she lost the baby during the pregnancy she would be okay. Again, this was because she did not yet feel emotionally attached to her unborn child, and that emotional connection is 'really one of the roles that I see for a mother and child'. Similar to Paula and Mary, Alice felt that she would not feel like a mother 'until the baby is born, when I'm having to do things physically for the baby and care for it'. While she acknowledged she was already caring for the baby 'in a way, it doesn't feel like the mother role that I have in my head'. While Alice shared that she did occasionally talk to her unborn child, it was more as a form of noticing activity, such as when her unborn child kicked, rather than purposively setting out to talk to them. In terms of whether her unborn child was part of the family already, Alice reiterated her point about emotional connectedness (or the lack of it), sharing that 'if this baby didn't eventuate it wouldn't feel like the family had changed. It would be a big loss but it wouldn't feel like a loss for the family'. She clarified this by saying 'you wouldn't feel like someone was missing'. Again, then, for Alice it would seem that her unborn child was not yet a 'someone', which meant that Alice did not yet feel like a mother.

6.2.2   Unborn Child as Part of the Family

Different to the people included in Section 6.2.1, those included in this section provided accounts that suggested they more clearly viewed their unborn child as part of the family, even if this did not necessarily translate for all into having a clear sense of parental identity during the pregnancy. As noted earlier, the feeling that an unborn child was already part of the family was typically more often the case for the men we interviewed. Alice's husband Josh, for example, noted that doing practical things like shopping for prams can make you feel like a father during the pregnancy, though for him feeling like a father would be cemented when he could first hold the baby: 'when it is totally dependent on me'. Yet at the same time, Josh felt that his unborn child was 'definitely' already part of the family. Josh illustrated this by noting that his unborn child 'comes up in conversation a lot', and is a physical presence between the couple: 'if you try and cuddle you've got to allow for there being something between you'. This led Josh to state that 'it is part of the family'. While Josh uses the term 'it', then, suggesting that his unborn child was still not viewed by Josh as a person proper (and/or perhaps partly due to not knowing the sex), his unborn child was still very much part of the family already. This is a different account to that provided by Josh's wife Alice, as outlined earlier. Indeed, Alice herself noted that their unborn child was actively included as part of the family by Josh, but not so much by herself. This might in part be explained by the fact that Josh's family were very excited about the impending birth, and frequently commented on their unborn child being part of the family already.

When asked whether he felt like a father, Nathan provided a mixed response, answering 'yes and no'. He shared that he was 'very much looking forward' to the baby being born, and thus was already thinking about being a father, but at the same time, similar to Josh, it would not be 'until you hold your baby for the first time' that he would really feel like a father. Nathan was, however, very focused on engaging with his unborn child in utero. As he noted, 'it's interesting to know how much they actually absorb while in utero. They're learning and they know your voice'. Different to the participants in Section 6.2.1, then, Nathan already had an image of his unborn child as a person capable of 'learning' and 'knowing'. This perception of his unborn child as a person was even clearer when Nathan noted that they are 'absolutely' already part of the family. As he shared, people had given his unborn child Christmas presents and are 'always referring to them', making the child a very clear presence for Nathan and for his extended family. Nathan's wife Lara similarly noted that 'instead of thinking about just the two of us I'm thinking about that it's going to be the three of us'. As she noted, their unborn child was already part of their family because she and Nathan talk about 'how we're going to include' their child and that as expectant parents 'I wonder if he's going to be interested in this and that and what not'.

Isaac also shared the belief that his unborn child was already part of the family. Isaac shared that he 'sits there on the couch watching little kicks and movements' and having 'silly conversations' with the child in utero. This was very different to his wife Paula, whose narrative we considered in Section 6.2.1, and who shared that talking to her unborn child felt like 'talking to a storybook character or a doll'. By contrast, Isaac planned to start reading books to their unborn child, following a similar logic to Nathan: 'they say that you should do that because they can start to hear and recognise your voice, so it's a good idea'. These comments from men relating to talking to their unborn child may also be influenced by the fact that they are not carrying their child and therefore their child is not exposed to their voice as much as the mother's. Also different to Paula, Isaac had a clearer sense of already feeling like a father. Part of that related to practical activities, such as furnishing the nursery, which gave him a sense of impending fatherhood. For Isaac, 'working on that helps it feel a bit more real and makes me feel a little bit like a dad'. Isaac also shared a shift in his understanding of himself, in preparation for the arrival of his child. As he noted, 'I've gotten a bit more conservative in my views', which for Isaac reflected a maturing of his views in line with those he expected should be held by a father.

6.3   FEELINGS ABOUT PARENTAL IDENTITY SIX MONTHS AFTER BIRTH

Research with new mothers suggests that many find it difficult to accept an identity as a mother, at least in the early months following birth. Arnold-Baker (2019), for example, suggests that for the women she interviewed in the context of the United Kingdom, many of the women found that their experience of new motherhood did not align with the images of motherhood available to them in the world around them, making it harder to reconcile their experience with these images (images similar to those we explored in previous chapters). This left the women feeling like they were not yet mothers, or that they were inadequate mothers. Focusing on women whose babies were born preterm (which was also the case for some of the participants we interviewed), Spinelli and colleagues (2016) found that many struggled to reconcile the imagined baby with the real baby, exacerbated by the physical distance enforced by neonatal units. For some of the women interviewed, the separation from their baby made it further difficult to develop a parental identity, creating a delayed effect such that it took them many months to recover once the baby was home with them, and to develop a sense of themselves as mothers.

Other studies too suggest that for women who have difficult pregnancies or births (again, as was also the case for some of the participants), the transition to motherhood can be particularly fraught. In their interpretive synthesis of five qualitative studies, Røseth and colleagues (2018) found that some women blamed themselves for the challenges they experienced, which made it hard for them to bond with their child when they were born, or to see themselves as mothers. For some of the women, however, these feelings were eventually overcome when the relationship with the child developed over time. Australian research too suggests that while many of the women interviewed came, over time, to feel like mothers, many attributed this to a sense of surrender: surrendering themselves to their child's needs (Carolan, 2005). As such, their development of a parental identity was largely ambivalent, in that their imagined future of 'perfect motherhood' had not materialised, and instead they had to reconcile themselves to a parental identity that was different to their expectations.

Research with fathers again contrasts with the experiences of mothers. A study of the experiences of Japanese fathers, for example, suggests that for many of the men interviewed, there was a 'catalyst' moment when they started seeing their child as a person, and themselves as a father (Iwata, 2009). For many of the men, the catalyst was a practical action that demonstrated to them that they were now fathers. This included the presentation of a birth certificate with their name on it, an infant looking at them and smiling, or being invited into groups with other men who were fathers. In an Australian context, Brady and colleagues (2017) suggest that men approach bonding with a child in two often interrelated ways: by being physiology-focused (e.g., as we explored in previous chapters, where women are seen as naturally predisposed to parenting and men must work at it), or by being time-focused (e.g., a relationship is developed with a child according to the time devoted to building the relationship). For men who primarily emphasised a physiology-focus, they largely sat back during the early months following birth and waited until the child was older so that there was a clearer role for them as fathers. Time-focused men, by comparison, worked on connecting with their child from birth. Unsurprisingly, men who were time-focused developed a sense of themselves as parents earlier than did men who waited until their child was older.

In many ways, the accounts provided by the people we interviewed echo the literature on women's parental identity, but present a counterpoint to the literature on men's parental identity. A majority of the participants reported that at six months after their child's birth they were still struggling to see themselves as parents or as having a clear parental identity when we again asked them 'Do you feel like a mother/father now?'. This was equally the case for both women and men. By contrast, a minority of participants had a very clear sense of a parental identity six months after the birth of their child, though similar to the literature this was more the case for men than it was for women. We explore these two narratives (complexities in parental identity and clear sense of parental identity) in turn.

6.3.1 Complexities in Parental Identity

When we interviewed the participants six months after the birth of their child, many were still coming to terms with new parenthood, in terms of developing routines, understanding their child's needs, and navigating shifts in their homelife and intimate life. As we explore in this section, many were still navigating a parental identity, balancing their role as a parent with the affective dimensions associated with being a mother or father. Paula, for example, who we noted earlier struggled to conceptualise her unborn child as a person, reported that she 'didn't know' if she felt like a mother yet. As she noted, she had a very clear sense immediately following the birth that she would 'have to be really responsible', but this sense of immediate responsibility did not translate into a clear parental identity. There were aspects of Paula's interview responses that spoke to a parental identity, such as when she stated 'never again am I not going to have something to worry about', and 'I'm just worried permanently' about her child. Certainly, narratives of worry are common in research with mothers (Mannix & Jackson, 2003). But this sense of worry and responsibility did not automatically translate for Paula into feeling like a mother. This might be explained by the fact that Paula noted she had expected to feel like a mother at this stage, to which she added 'feel like a better mum'. It was potentially the case that Paula *did* have a sense of a parental identity, but because it did not align with her own expectations or those she perceived in the world around her of what a mother should be like, she was cautious in claiming a parental identity.

Paula's husband Isaac also emphasised a sense of responsibility over having a clear sense of a parental identity. As we noted earlier in this chapter, during the pregnancy, Isaac felt like his unborn child was part of the family, and he found that doing things to prepare for the child's arrival helped him to start to feel like a father. When interviewed six months after his child was born, Isaac gave examples of moments when he felt like a father, such as when his child smiled at him. However, he also noted that he felt the weight of responsibility of raising a child, and that he expected he would feel more like a father as his child became more able to interact with him. While in many ways Isaac seemed to depict himself as a father-in-waiting in terms of his relationship to his child, by contrast he shared a much clearer narrative of himself as 'head of the family'. He shared that the sense of responsibility he felt meant he was working harder to improve his situation in his paid work so that he could provide financially for his family. He noted that financial responsibility was 'something I was thinking about during the pregnancy, but it's a lot more real when you've got a child'. Similar to Paula, there is certainly a normative sense of parental identity here, in this example, men feeling expected to be the 'breadwinner'. Yet for Isaac, this aspect of a parental identity appeared to be separate to his sense of a parental identity formed through his relationship with his child.

Of all the participants, Alice was the one who was most clear about not yet feeling like a mother when interviewed six months after her child was born. When asked if she felt like a mother, she shared that she had been talking with other women, and all agreed that they too did not feel like mothers. For Alice, this was because she had a 'rock solid' identity before the pregnancy (and even before she met her partner), and that her identity 'has nothing to do with the circumstances that happened around me'. For Alice, then, having a child (or entering into a relationship with her partner) are 'circumstances' that do not change her 'rock solid' identity (an identity related to her own personal attributes, and not to being a partner or a mother). Alice shared that when her child starts to call her 'mum' she might then feel like a mother, but she also noted that she does not know what feeling like a mother would be like: 'I suppose it's the concept that you have of that word and also what the reality is. It's not a word that I identify with readily, mother'. This was despite the fact that Alice shared she had expected to have a 'strong sense of identity' in terms of the word mother after her child was born. Perhaps it was the case that Alice had expected a particular situational context in which she would feel like a mother, and that context had not yet presented itself (specifically in terms of her child calling her 'mum').

Further in terms of situational contexts, Mary shared an interesting account of feeling like a mother. When asked whether or not she felt like a mother after the birth of her child, Mary stated that 'I've gone to work a couple of times to do just bits and bobs and it's amazing how quickly I don't feel like a mother when Sarah is not with me'.

Here, Mary presents an account of parental identity that is context specific. When her child is present, a parental identity is activated, but when Mary is away from her child it is not. As she went on to share, when away from her child 'I pretty much immediately switch back into my old self, it's pretty easy to forget that I am a mother and that Sarah is out there somewhere'. In contrast to the normative assumption that womanhood equals motherhood, for Mary it would seem that a parental identity is activated in specific contexts (i.e., interactions with her child) and does not overwrite her sense of self prior to having a child. Being a mother may well be something that Mary holds as part of her identity, but it is not an overriding aspect of her identity, nor one that she always holds at the forefront.

6.3.2 Clear Sense of Parental Identity

For a smaller number of the people we spoke to, there was a very clear sense of having a parental identity. For some of the men we interviewed, the sense of being a father was very much formed through interactions with others. Josh, for example, noted that he felt like he is part of the 'fathers' group' at work. As he shared: 'I hadn't really noticed it too much in the past like when I didn't have a kid, but now that I do have a child it's interesting, you sort of get brought into this group and if they're talking about stuff you can sort of relate to it and they're sort of interested with how you're going'. Having a shared experience of parenting appeared to translate for Josh into a parental identity that was affirmed by others around him at work. Beyond work, however, Josh also noted that he felt like a father 'straight away'. For Josh this primarily related to responsibility: 'when you don't have a child and you're holding someone else's child and they start crying, you just pass them back. You don't have responsibility. But once you realise the buck stops with you, you quickly realise that "yeah I'm the father, I'm the responsible person"'. Different to Paula's and Isaac's accounts of responsibility mentioned earlier, then, for Josh it would seem that being responsible clearly activated a parental identity.

Similar to Josh, Nathan too noted that a parental identity was activated through interactions with other fathers. For example, Nathan shared that 'I have mates with kids, and we talk about playing sports and having our children having a kick and a catch and taking them to sports games in the future'. Having a shared experience of parenting with other men – even if a normative expectation about what future parenting might look like – helped Nathan to imagine himself as a father into the future. In the present, Nathan was also very clear about feeling like a father. As he noted, 'even when I'm off at work I'm always thinking about him, and I just want to come home early and see him and play with him'. This is an interesting contrast to the normative account of sporting activities as a way to orient himself to a parenting identity: men wanting to leave work early to see their child is not a typical cultural script, but for Nathan it clearly spoke to his sense of himself as a father, and his desire to engage with his child. Furthermore, and different to Mary in Section 6.3.1, for Nathan it would appear that his parental identity was activated across contexts, rather than only through interactions with his child (e.g., he thought about his child at work, not just when he was physically present).

Of the women, Nathan's wife Lara spoke most clearly about having a parental identity, a change from the second interview where she said she felt 'an element of being maternal', but not really like a mother. As she noted, by the time of the third interview (six months after the birth of her child) parenting felt 'natural' because 'you know what you're doing and you feel very protective and you worry about them'. Different to Paula mentioned earlier, worry is framed by Lara more clearly as part of a parental identity, and indeed one that is 'natural'. Nonetheless, Lara also noted that, while at the time of the interview she framed her parental identity and actions as 'natural', this had not always been the case. As she stated, 'when we first had him [child] and we looked at him we thought "oh you're cute" but we were not sure what to do'. By contrast, Lara now felt that she was 'much more in tune' with her child, which was partly the product of having developed clear routines that worked and suited both her and Nathan. Lara's account is important, then, as it suggests that while a parental identity may not be automatic for many parents (even if it appeared to be so for some of the participants, such as Josh and Nathan), it can be intentionally developed through routine. This is, of course, dependent on the child and their willingness to engage with routine setting by parents. Nonetheless, for people such as Lara, being able to develop a parental identity (when that was desired) was an important outcome in the early months of new parenthood.

6.4   CONCLUSIONS

In this chapter, we have drawn out some contrasts between inter-view time points, but also within couples and between all partici-pants. Arguably, the most salient points of contrast pertain to gender. Among the participants, women more often saw an unborn child as an abstract object, and more often experienced complexities in the development of a parental identity. This, we would suggest, speaks strongly to the social flesh of parenthood, as we have explored in previous chapters. The presumption is often that women will enjoy pregnancy, that it will allow them to bond with their unborn child, so much so that by the time the child is born women already feel like mothers. Yet the reality, as documented in previous research and in this chapter, is often quite different. Carrying a child does not inherently create a bonding experience, and indeed pregnancy can feel alien to many women. Even for women who purposively plan for a first child, as was the case with the participants in our study, the reality of pregnancy can be foreign, and as an embodied experience can create tension with women's sense of their own identity, and their relationship to their unborn child. Cisgender men, by contrast, who do not have the embodied experience of pregnancy, are perhaps much more reliant on the imaginary aspects of pregnancy, meaning that they may more readily be able to project personhood onto the unborn child, and to see them as already part of their family. In a certain sense, then, the social flesh of pregnancy potentially limits or negatively shapes some women's experiences, while it may positively shape some men's experiences.

In a related way, feelings associated with new parenthood potentially get the institutions of motherhood and fatherhood under the skin (Ahmed, 2010) in ways that may be barriers to, or facilitators of, a parental identity. By referring to motherhood and fatherhood as institutions, we are suggesting the ways in which normative understandings of motherhood and fatherhood are institutionalised, are given credence, and are made to seem as though they are real, and thus should be experienced uniformly by all men and women. When new parents come up against the reality of parenthood, as compared to the institutionalised accounts of motherhood and fatherhood, the affective dimensions of new parenthood leverage responses that may constrain the development of a parental identity. For some of the women we interviewed, the reality of motherhood contrasted with the idealised image of motherhood, so much so that they perhaps felt unable to accord themselves the category mother. Feelings of responsibility in particular seemed to accord a weight to new parenthood for many of the women (and some of the men) in ways that further ingrained normative expectations about new parenthood, situating some participants at a further distance from the ideals of a normative parental identity. By contrast, for a smaller number of participants, the approximation of an ideal – particularly when reflected through the eyes of others such as co-workers – made it easier to adopt a parental identity.

Obviously, in focusing on two time points out of the four in our study, we have only provided a snapshot in this chapter of the development of a parental identity among the participants. Nonetheless, as we explore in Chapter 7, experiences of parental identity development, alongside experiences of parenting in general, played a role in decisions about whether or not to have more children in the future. This is not to suggest that having a clear parental identity is essential to decisions about having more children. But it is to suggest that the reality of parenthood, as compared to expectations about it, clearly helps to shape the decisions that people make about having more children. When the reality is less clearly aligned with the social flesh of parenthood, and when feelings about new parenthood bring under the skin a conflicting relationship to the institutions of motherhood and fatherhood, it is perhaps not surprising that some people feel less compelled to have more children than they expected would be the case before having a first child. The ways in which views about having more children shift or are cemented are thus our focus in Chapter 7.

7 Views about Having More Children

Given the diversity of narratives we shared in the previous chapters – some of joy, some of challenges and many of both – it is perhaps not surprising that when it came to talking about having more children, some of the participants found this to be a complex topic. This reflects the literature, which suggests that people who have decided not to have more children have much clearer reasons and make much firmer decisions than those who have yet to decide whether or not to have more children (Evans et al., 2009). We suggest that this point of difference speaks to some of the topics we have explored in the previous chapters. As we noted in Chapter 3, many of the participants treated having a first child as axiomatic. Pronatalist discourses encourage heterosexual couples to simply accept that they should want to reproduce. There is a sense, then, in which having a first child is treated almost like a non-choice by many people, instead of being something that simply must be done. By contrast, when faced with the reality of new parenthood, for many people, the decision to have additional children is very purposive, and in part informed by experiences of conceiving, birthing, and raising the first child.

As Bhrolcháin and Beaujouan (2019) have argued, demographic research focused on the topic of ideal family size has, to date, typically assumed a 'rational choice' model, one in which people weigh all of their options against their resources and experiences, and make an informed decision about whether or not to have more children. As they argue, however, this leaves little space for uncertainty about knowing whether or not having another child really is a good idea. As they note, the lack of attention to uncertainty in demographic research on ideal family size is surprising, given uncertainty is a common feature of lay accounts of reproductive decision-making. Following the thread we have unwoven in the previous chapters, we would suggest that, in part, through the process of having children, institutions (of motherhood and fatherhood, as well as government institutions such as education or healthcare) get under the skin (Ahmed, 2010), shaping people's views about parenthood. For some, this occurs in a normative sense where people take up the message via the social flesh of parenthood that having more children is important for themselves and for the nation. But for other people, having one child provides a window into the reality of parenthood, making them question the cult of parenthood.

As such, our research supports Bhrolcháin and Beaujouan (2019), who suggest that ideal family size is a process of discovery rather than being a predetermined goal, and can change over time (see also Weston et al., 2004). How couples determine what is the right number of children for them is partly dependent on their experiences of first-time parenthood, in conjunction with the normative expectations from those around them to have more children (or not). For heterosexual first-time parents, then, the task of decision-making about having more children involves reconciling heart and mind. There are both the affective dimensions of enjoying (or not) raising children and the ways in which institutional norms get under the skin and create an injunction to have more children. This competes with, or might be complemented by, the actual experiences of raising a child, which for some might be intensely challenging and for others might be relatively easy. People thus achieve the goal of knowing their ideal family size *once they achieve it*, rather than being directed towards a goal of a family of a particular size from the onset in a linear, unchanging line. Indeed, we might suggest, given the affective dimensions of decision-making about ideal family size, that knowing when you have achieved your ideal family size is based on a reconciliation of affect (or perhaps more precisely fantasy) with the experience of parenting a first (or subsequent) child(ren). In contrast, perhaps having yet to decide whether or not to have more children involves not having yet reconciled one's fantasies with the reality of parenthood (in addition to feeling beholden to institutions that encourage particular – white middle-class heterosexual – couples to have more children).

Taking up all of the issues we have raised earlier, in this chapter, we explore in closer detail how the people we interviewed navigated the decision of whether or not to have more children. At the first interview, we asked participants how many children they would like, at that stage. We then asked about decisions around more children during the third interview (when their baby was six months old) and during the final interview (when their baby was eighteen months old). As a sidenote, it is useful to reflect that it was important to reassure some of the participants that we were interested in their views at the time of each interview, rather than holding them to their earlier views at a later interview. In other words, there was space for their views to change over time. As we show, the participants had a diversity of experiences, with some experiencing a clear shift in their views between these time points, and others continuing along a path they had already determined before the arrival of their first child. To highlight these points of difference, in this chapter, we juxtapose the differing decision outcomes between our couples, and to a lesser extent, for some couples, we explore differences in decision-making within couples. Notably, participants primarily spoke about having future children in the same way as their first child, rather than via fostering or adoption. Before exploring these different narratives, we first situate this chapter by giving an overview of the literature on the topic of ideal family size, decision-making about having more children, and the role of gender in decision-making. We conclude the chapter by returning to the topic of affect, and how it shapes people's decisions about whether or not to have more children.

7.2   DECISIONS ABOUT FERTILITY PLANNING

Previous research on fertility planning suggests a host of fairly straightforward factors likely to inform whether or not people have more than one child. Some research suggests that first-time parents feel they should provide a sibling for their first born, particularly those who were 'an only child' themselves (Holton et al., 2011), and some experience a strong desire to have children of differing genders (Evans et al., 2009). Such research also suggests that people weigh up many other factors, including their health as parents, their age, the stability of their relationship, the support they have available to them from their wider family, and whether or not they feel that they have successfully balanced work and family life after the arrival of a first child. In addition, for heterosexual women specifically, additional factors may include how much support they received from their male partner in raising a first child, and how much enjoyment they experienced in becoming a mother. Much of the research on outcomes of fertility planning has focused on factors that result in people not having any more children. Some studies suggest that the experience of a difficult pregnancy can result in women not wanting to have more children (Dudová et al., 2020; Newman, 2008). For many couples, research suggests that expectations about ideal family size are often negotiated down following less-than-positive experiences with a first child (Read et al, 2012).

When it comes to gender and decision-making, there appear to be cultural variations, particularly with regard to the influence of men over women's decision-making. In the European context, for example, Dudová and colleagues (2020) found that in their Czech study men often left decision-making about having another child up to their female partners, suggesting that the desire for more children (or not) is primarily an affective space occupied by women. By contrast, Peng's (2020) research conducted in China under the two-child policy found that men and their own parents may actively seek to influence or effectively coerce female partners into having more children. This may occur through recourse to a narrative of good mothers as compared to bad mothers, such that the latter do not love their children and do not want more children, whereas good mothers are those who devote themselves to their children and desire to have more children. Paired with this is the binary of good wife and bad wife, such that the latter prioritise their own needs and hopes, whereas good wives were framed as women who accede to their husband's desires (in this case, to have a second child). Some of the women reported that their male partners also used their own parents to reinforce these negative messages, including by having parents-in-law pressure women to have more children.

Research has also explored how having children impacts on the subjective well-being of parents, and how this shapes decisions about whether or not to have more children. Australian research suggests that children are a 'costly-joy' in terms of the subjective well-being of parents (Luppi, 2016). In other words, for many people, having first child is a joyous experience, but it often brings with it significant costs in terms of well-being. Having additional children depends on whether or not parents feel that a second child will bring additional joy and thus increase well-being, or whether a second or subsequent child would bring additional strain and thus reduce well-being. When subjective well-being drops following the arrival of a first child, many parents may decide to stick with one child, rather than risking further negative impacts on their well-being (Margolis & Myrskylä, 2015). In the Australian context, Newman (2008) found that the first twelve months of life with a first child played a key determining role in decisions about having subsequent children. When those first twelve months were less positive than expected, when fatigue was high and partner support was low, women in particular were less inclined towards having another child.

Finally, a small but growing body of research has focused on regret in relation to motherhood. As we mentioned in Chapter 5, while none of the people we interviewed spoke about regretting having a first child, there are some echoes in what some of the participants said, as we explore in detail in the following text, of the limited literature on regret. This is most clear in the context of what Moore and Abetz (2019) refer to as 'circumstantial regret'. This is when a parent does not regret having a child, but they do regret the circumstances in which they became a parent. This can include having a less-than-supportive partner, feeling that one has made a considerable sacrifice in having a child (e.g., sacrifices in time, money, and/or further education), or changes in the partner relationship after the arrival of a first child. We might argue, based on the narratives we have shared in the previous chapters, that in part circumstantial regret arises from a mismatch between expectations and reality about new parenthood: when things do not turn out the way they are expected to, some parents might wish for an alternate outcome, and feel regret about the cards they have been dealt. Other research, however, suggests that for some people there are much clearer accounts of regret that are not simply circumstantial. Matley (2020), for example, in an analysis of a UK-based parenting website, suggests that some women experience such significant negative changes to their lives after the birth of a child that they regret parenthood altogether. Matley, however, frames this as 'after-the-fact agency', suggesting that while such parents would not relinquish their child (i.e., place them for adoption), acknowledging their regret helps them to process the loss and grief they experience in association with having a child. Again, while such narratives were not evident in the people we interviewed, it is important to acknowledge how regret in any form shapes decisions about having more children.

7.3   SHIFTING EXPERIENCES AND OUTCOMES

Of the couples we interviewed, there was considerable diversity in terms of decision-making about the number of children they would have. Jemma and Adam, whose story we explore in the following text, had always planned to have one child, if any. There were other couples who had initially expressed desire to have more than one child, but had revised this after having their first child. We explore this through Catherine and Craig's story in the following text, who had intended to have more than one child, but ultimately decided not to have any more, largely due to age. Another couple, Lara and Nathan, whose story we also explore in the following text, had originally intended to only have one child, but had changed their views after the birth of their first child. For the remaining couples, most had planned to have at least one more child and this was consistent through the

interviews, with the number depending on factors such as ease of conceiving and the gender of children (with the desire to have children of
differing genders being reported by a number of couples). We explore
this through the story of Paula and Isaac who had already had a second
child at the time of the fourth interview, but did not intend to have
any more. We also note that another couple (Gina and Cameron) were
pregnant with their second child at the time of the fourth interview,
and thought this may be enough children, although Gina said if they
had a second boy she might like to try for a girl.

7.3.1   Always Only One

Jemma was unsure about having children, and was very critical of
the womanhood equals motherhood discourse. However, according
to Adam, when he reassured her it was possible to have just one child
(counter to the pronatalist discourses Jemma had experienced), she
became more open to the idea. When asked about additional children
at the time of her third interview, Jemma clearly stated 'we are having
one. We're not having another one. No, no way. The plan was always
one. Nothing that has happened makes me want to change that'. Here,
Jemma alludes to the challenging journey she experienced to pregnancy (which involved undergoing in-vitro fertilisation following no
success in conceiving through intercourse), the traumatic birth which
we discussed in Chapter 4, and the all-consuming nature of parenting
a child. For Jemma, the question of having another child was salient
as she and her partner had recently received an invoice for payment
for the ongoing storage of their remaining embryos. While she was
very clear that she did not want to have another child, she nonetheless noted that 'we can probably send [the embryos] off to experiments
now, but we won't make that absolute decision now. We will give it
a year'. So even while Jemma was resolute in her decision to have one
child, the final decision to relinquish the remaining embryos was not
as straightforward. As she explained, given at the time their baby was
only six months old, it was not the right time to make the decision,
so they opted to pay the fees and give themselves some more time.

By the time of the final interview, Jemma and Adam had made the decision about the stored embryos. As she noted 'they're gone, they're off to, I don't even know what's happened to them. I'm assuming scientific experiments because that's what the paperwork said when we didn't renew them'. This is quite a different account of embryos to those we heard in our previous research on embryo donation, where stored embryos were framed as part of the family, or as the potential for someone else to start a family (Bartholomaeus & Riggs, 2019). For Jemma, by contrast, it seemed that positioning herself as not really even knowing where the embryos went served to fully evacuate them from her circle of reference. This is understandable given they were created as part of a standard process to create multiple embryos to ensure that at least one is viable, a process that did not reflect her desire to only have one child. Jemma reiterated her desire to have one child when she returned to a topic we discussed in the previous chapter in relation to Mary, namely not thinking about her child when he was away from her. Jemma reiterated how important it was for her to be able to 'compartmentalise' and focus on her work, reiterating the idea that having a second child would reduce her capacity to do this, which would have been a negative outcome for Jemma. As Jemma noted, having one child, and being able to switch off from him when at work, was 'empowering', as it allowed her to enjoy having a child and a paid work/home life balance that suited her.

Jemma's partner Adam had a similar account of having one child. As he noted, 'there is no part of the experience that would make me want to do it again'. Again, this is related to challenges in conceiving and the birth. Adam was so certain in his view that he noted that he could not 'understand why people would want more [children]'. Indeed, he went on to note that 'if someone was unsure about wanting to have kids, I don't know that I would recommend it to someone else'. Here we might suggest a potential account of circumstantial regret: Adam clearly loved his child and did not regret having a child, but the circumstances of conception and birth made the experience less than positive. This was something that Jemma also spoke about in our interviews with her. On the positive side, however, Adam was very clear that having one child meant that the couple could 'enjoy the positive parts' of their child. For Adam, these positive parts weighed strongly against the negative, yet at the same time, he struggled to understand how anyone could have a negative experience and still have another child. As he noted: 'wanting another baby is madness to me, people literally don't remember. You're not sleeping much, you aren't good at forming memories, so you might just remember some of the good bits, but all of the bad bits are just gone'. For Adam, by contrast, he was very mindful of the 'bad bits'. Nonetheless, overall, Adam was very thankful to have 'one instead of none: we're already winning'.

In his final interview, Adam's position on having more children remained the same: 'I couldn't imagine having another child. It's painful and costly and traumatic so it's definitely not going to happen again'. Beyond the negative experiences associated with conception and birth, however, at the time of the final interview, Adam also reflected on other less-than-positive experiences: 'I'd like to continue to sleep, to enjoy the time that I have'. Adam had clearly weighed up what could have been gained by having another child, and felt that another child would be more of a cost than any kind of gain. As he said 'if you have more children then there's always one of them awake and complaining and wanting things and needing things from you'. These feelings made it easy for Adam to make the decision with Jemma to cease storing embryos: 'we're not going to want [more children] so we're not going to spend money on that'. In a sense, then, for Adam and Jemma not having more children was a very clear cost–benefit analysis, one that Adam felt confident resulted in the right decision. While he acknowledged that some people regret ceasing embryo storage, he noted that 'I can't see that happening with us'. Due to the fertility issues Adam and Jemma experienced, and their need to undertake IVF in order to conceive, ceasing embryo storage could be seen as offering some closure or finality to the decision of not having more children, unlike participants who conceived through intercourse and who may later revisit the decision.

7.3.2 *From More Than One to One*

At the time of her third interview, Catherine shared that she had revised her ideal family size from more than one to one child. She noted her age and the challenges in conceiving as the reason that it was 'probably never going to happen that we're going to have another one even if we wanted to anyway'. This was in addition to the fact that Catherine had a caesarean, and it had been recommended to her that she not conceive again within twelve months, meaning that she would be even older by the time she was able to try for another baby. Catherine further shared that if she were younger when she had her first child it would have been different, but as it stood having two children relatively close together (if that were possible) was not something she considered ideal: 'I just think it would be huge and your life would change a lot'. Finally, Catherine shared that she felt having two children would 'financially ruin' her and her partner Craig. As she noted, these thoughts might change with time and they were open to revisiting the decision, especially because other people had told her that they had a second child to provide a sibling for their first child. But ultimately Catherine noted that 'we'll revisit in a year but you know the clock's ticking and it's unlikely even if we decided we wanted to, you know the chances of that happening are quite slim'.

At the time of her final interview a year later, Catherine was more definitive: 'we won't be having any more children'. She shared that while previously she had been somewhat open to the idea of another child, the extent of tiredness she experienced with her first child meant she did not want to go through the experience again: 'we just want to move on. I feel like having children, you're really taking time out of your life, like everything stagnates a little bit'. For Catherine, then, the joy of having a first child was offset by the costs, leading her to decide against having any more children. As she went on to share: 'we just kind of don't want to backpedal around moving forward with our life'. Here, there is a sense in which having children is an impediment to life moving forward, quite a stark contrast to the normative narrative that many of the participants shared before conceiving, namely that having children moves life forward in a normative sense. While Catherine shared that her partner was even more definitive in not wanting to have another child, she was 'okay with it', suggesting that she had managed to reconcile the reality of parenthood with her expectations, and to situate her experience of parenthood in the context of her other life goals.

Catherine's partner Craig was certainly open to having another child when we spoke with him during his third interview; however, similar to Catherine, he noted that conceiving was a 'tough process', one he was not keen to repeat, meaning that they would 'stick at one'. He noted that having a child had been hard on their relationship, and having a second child 'doesn't bode well for a relationship. So if we're to survive this relationship I think a second child would not be helpful at all'. Again, in contrast to the narratives that the participants shared before pregnancy, narratives in which having a child was seen as cementing a relationship, for Craig having a child had been fraught in terms of its impact upon his relationship with Catherine. Craig shared that he had 'joked' about the relationship strain with Catherine, but that as much as he had made a joke about it, he nonetheless felt that another child would 'ruin' their relationship. Similar to Adam, Craig questioned how people could have a second child in the face of challenges and strains associated with a first child, noting that he had come to the conclusion that 'they forget just how tough it is or was for the first time, so they have a second'. For Craig, by contrast, no such 'forgetting' was possible.

At the time of his final interview, Craig remained certain in the decision to have one child: 'it is dead hard and it's expensive, and we're not young parents by any stretch'. He shared that having a child had 'knocked the wind out of us', meaning that 'there is no way we can do this again'. Craig did share that maybe if they had a different experience – if conception had been easier or if their child had slept more – then they might have had a second child. But Craig remained mindful

of how much the loss of sleep had impacted detrimentally on his relationship with Catherine: 'at times we just were getting on because we
were just functioning or trying to function so I don't think our relationship would cope with another child. It would destroy us'. Such strong
language captures Craig's commitment to remembering what had been
so hard, and to draw on that memory to shape his decision-making.
Rather than 'forgetting', as he suggested other people must do when
they have a second child, Craig appeared committed to remembering
why it was he felt having a second child was not a good idea. Craig felt
it had been a mutual decision with Catherine, with both noting that
the other would not cope well with a second child. For Craig, it was
'fortunate we can acknowledge that and laugh about it a little bit'.

7.3.3   *From One to More Than One*

For Lara and Nathan, after the arrival of their first child, Nathan had
some reservations about having a second child. While Lara was quite
keen to have a second child in a relatively short time period, she
noted that at the time of the third interview she and Nathan had 'an
agreement that when I'm ready to have another baby, then we'll talk
about it'. This was despite Lara noting that Nathan had previously
said he 'always wanted just one' child and she herself had suggested
she would be happy with one or two in the first interview. Lara said
she was not sure if Nathan's views had changed since the birth of
their first child, though she did feel that 'now that his friends are
having more than one, and these were men who weren't really sure
they'd want a second, maybe he's changed a little bit'. Despite these
feelings (or perhaps hopes) that Nathan had changed his mind about
another child, Lara had yet to have a concrete conversation with
Nathan, 'because we agreed we wouldn't until I was actually ready. I
wish he was a little more on the same page as me but he's not'. Lara
was aware that Nathan's reservations related primarily to having the
time and money to devote attention to more than one child, but she
nonetheless hoped that Nathan was 'more on the side of yes' when it
actually came to deciding about having another child.

At the time of his third interview, Nathan was quite clear that 'I've always wanted one and I wanted one boy and that's what we got'. Despite Lara's more equivocal account of Nathan's views, Nathan himself was much more certain that one child was enough. As he noted, a second child was 'kind of like a double-edged sword'. Their first child had been 'easy' (and the conception was straightforward), by his account, so having a second child ran the risk of this experience *not* being repeated: 'you never know whether you're going to get [an easy child], and you know it's kind of like a lucky dip in a way when it comes to having kids'. Given his ambivalence about the idea of a second child, Nathan noted that he had not given the topic any more thought, though he was aware that Lara brought the topic up now and again. He nonetheless felt that Lara was happy with how their life was going, and hoped that her return to paid work would make a difference. Nathan did acknowledge that they had agreed to return to the topic of a second child at a later point, but he was clear that this was very much guided by Lara, and he was aware that 'it's probably something that she would want maybe a second [child] because you know we've had such a good experience' with the first child. Yet as noted earlier, this 'good experience' did not mean that Nathan was leaning towards having a second child. Rather, he was concerned that they would not have such a good experience a second time.

When asked in her final interview about the topic of another child, Lara noted that 'we'd love to have another baby', going on to share that 'it's addictive, I can see why people keep wanting to have children'. Lara shared multiple examples of the joys of motherhood, such as interacting with her child and sharing special moments with him. Lara emphasised repeatedly that it was these joys that disposed her towards having another child. Indeed, she noted that were it not for her age, she would have three children or more. The emphasis on *'we'd* love to have another baby', however, required some explaining on Lara's behalf. As she noted, 'I talked him around. He came around. It was good, it wasn't very hard', though she nonetheless noted that 'he's definitely said that's it, that's it at two, and that's fine'. From

Lara's comment here it is unclear if she feels she 'talked him around', or if 'he came around' by himself or as a result of her encouragement.

When Nathan was interviewed for the final time, however, his account was not as definitive. He maintained his focus on the fact that their first child had been very easy, and he noted that while he had been 'reluctant' when his first child was six months old to consider a second child, he was at the time of the final interview 'leaning' towards another child, but this was not definitive. He certainly noted that he and Lara had undertaken discussions on the topic, and that 'nothing about the experience [with their first child] had made me have any second thoughts', but there is a difference between not being opposed to an action (i.e., having a second child) and being in complete support of it. One reason why Nathan was more open to the idea of a second child was that he had 'always thought I just wanted to have one child, but I do see the benefit of our child growing up with a brother or sister'. Nathan was aware that while he grew up with siblings, Lara was an only child, and they were both mindful of the differences in their experiences. While Nathan felt that their child received plenty of social interactions with peers, he felt that it might nonetheless be beneficial for him to have a sibling. Nathan, then, provides an explanation for his change of heart: not that he necessarily wants the 'lucky dip' of a second child, but that pragmatically it might be the right thing to do for his first-born child.

7.3.4 Having Two Children

Different to the experience of Lara and Nathan, across her fourth interview, Paula spoke extensively about how challenging her experience had been of first-time parenthood. As she noted, 'it was so exhausting and so all-consuming and hard and I didn't love it, I found it not that enjoyable'. Yet despite this negative experience, Paula was guided by a view similar to that expressed by Nathan in his final interview, namely wanting her child to have a sibling, and further that she wanted children of differing genders. As she shared, her idea was 'to just try again and just have them both and get it out the way as soon as we can', largely due to her age. This was despite the fact that she did not 'want another baby because babies are such hard work', and the traumatic birth experience that we discussed in Chapter 4. To her surprise, she fell pregnant again quickly, and at the time of her final interview, she was a parent to two children, both of the same gender. Paula shared that she 'was a bit disappointed' to find out she was having a second girl, but was very aware of the risks associated with pregnancy for women her age, so while 'we would still love a boy, we've both pretty much decided we're not going to have another one'. While the birth of her second child had been 'quite easy' compared to the first, worries about complications meant that 'we've pretty much decided we're stopping now'. While Paula said when she was younger she had wanted a large family (reflective of her own experience) and had been waiting for some time to have children, in her first interview she said two or three was more realistic, likely due to her age.

During her second pregnancy, Paula noted that many people had told her it was going to be 'awful' having two children under two, and indeed that she was 'crazy' for having a second child so quickly. Yet for Paula, while her second pregnancy was harder than the first, she was finding having two children 'fairly easy', though she did feel that she did not give her first child 'her best' during the second pregnancy, because she was so exhausted all the time. In terms of having children of differing genders, Paula spoke about this at length, noting that she enjoyed interacting with boys, and felt that her partner Isaac 'would make an amazing father to a boy as he is such an exceptional person that I wanted him to have the chance to role model to a boy, so that's a real shame'. Paula shared that she was 'gutted' that they did not have a boy, though she was nonetheless 'thrilled with two girls, it's not that I'm not thrilled, they'll be very close, they'll share a room and clothes'. Paula also noted that 'Isaac would've been a great role model for a boy, but he will also be a great dad to girls and show them what to look for in a guy'. Here Paula manages to reconcile her competing feelings about not having a boy by emphasising the positive outcomes still to be gained from having two girls. Yet despite this, there was a sense in which Paula felt that Isaac was missing out on something. This was so much so that in their discussions about permanent contraception, Paula had decided that she would be the one to do this, because 'if something was to happen to me and he was to remarry, it would be a real tragedy if he couldn't father again'. While perhaps surprising, this comment was likely influenced by both personal experience and Isaac's younger age.

Isaac provided a slightly different account to Paula in his final interview. He shared that after their first child he had felt that 'let's just have one, this is horrible'. But a few months after the birth things 'improved a lot', and he knew that they 'always wanted two or three', so they decided to proceed with a second pregnancy. Isaac was aware that Paula ideally wanted a large family, but similar to Paula was aware of age as a factor, in addition to 'logistics and finances'. Nonetheless, Isaac noted that 'we'd both like to have a little boy, and maybe we'd try again for that'. Yet despite appearing somewhat open to having a third child, Isaac appeared mindful of the many challenges associated with having a second child, let alone a third. He shared examples of challenges with feeding and sleep, as well as some health complications that their second child was experiencing at the time of the interview. At the same time, Isaac adhered to a narrative in which having a second child had not been as hard as he had expected, and he shared much praise for Paula in adapting to having a second child so quickly. This is perhaps why Isaac appeared less definitive about the possibility of having a third child (the much hoped for boy), whereas while Paula very much desired to have a boy, her concerns about undertaking another pregnancy at her age appeared to override this desire.

7.4   CONCLUSIONS

In this chapter, we focused on how four of the couples in our study talked about whether or not they would have more than one child. To a certain extent, the views of the couples we interviewed echo the findings of the previous research. For some couples, the desire to provide a sibling to a first-born child served as an impetus to have

a second child. For others, the desire for children of differing genders motivated having a second child (even if for Paula and Isaac this
desire had not come to fruition). For all of the couples, their experiences with their first born, their age, their economic position, and
the impact of a first child on their relationship had weighed into their
decisions about whether or not to have another child. Weighing up
these factors had led one couple to decide against having another
child, and had meant that one couple remained steadfast in their previous decision to only have one child. This couple aside, our interviews highlight the claim that ideal family size is a moving target,
only decided once it is realised, rather than necessarily being based
on a predetermined ideal that couples persist towards regardless of
their experiences with their first child (or subsequent children).

Echoing Bhrolcháin and Beaujouan (2019), then, there is a sense
in which heterosexual couples may act as though they are making
rational choices about family size, but perhaps in reality each decision
is driven by a degree of uncertainty and ambivalence, alongside experiences and normative expectations. Some couples may feel compelled,
for a variety of reasons, to have a second or additional children. This
may be in the face of positive experiences with a first child, or in the
face of less-than-positive experiences. Other couples may weigh up
their experiences with a first child, and change their thoughts about
ideal family size. This, we would suggest, is not per se a compromise.
Rather, it demonstrates adaptation to the reality of parenthood, leaving
aside previous dreams or plans, and ignoring injunctions from others to
have more children. This is not to suggest that those couples who stop
at one child are to be especially praised for a realistic assessment of
their situation and resistance to any external pressures to have another
child. Rather, it is to emphasise the point that each couple faces a mul-
titude of factors shaping their decisions about additional children, and
these factors can ultimately only be arbitrated by the couple.

Yet even within couples, the couple unit is comprised of two
individuals, and in the case of our study, two individuals of differing
genders. As we have highlighted in this chapter, at times women and

men held seemingly very similar views, and at other times women and men thought they shared the same views as their partner, but when they spoke to us, it appeared their views were somewhat different. In other cases, women and men were aware that they held quite different views to their partner. Similar to research in the European context (Dudová et al., 2020), it did appear in our interviews that men largely deferred to their female partners if there was a difference in terms of desires for additional children, but this did not mean that men did not stake out a position. Rather, deference to women often seemed to be shaped by the realities of pregnancy, and particularly the challenges that some of the women faced. While men may have had their own views about additional children, they were mindful that it is ultimately their partner who must undertake another pregnancy and, for most of the couples, do the most carework.

The topic of decision-making about ideal family size, it would seem then, is thoroughly imbricated with the affective dimensions of new parenthood. There is a sense in which we have presented the four couples as having made decisions based on practical experiences of first-time parenting as well as the affective aspects of parenting. Yet we would not wish it to seem that these decisions were easy or were unilaterally definitive. Some of the couples we interviewed were still working through their decisions and perhaps some would continue to defer decisions until the decision was made for them (e.g., until age was a barrier, or if they conceived). While for the couples we included in this chapter, there was a sense of decision-making, there was also much negotiation, a lot of hedging their bets, and this all of course being contingent on actually being able to conceive again (with two couples having done so by the time of the final interview). Given, as we have argued throughout this book, it is via feelings that institutions get under the skin, it should come as no surprise that the feelings that come with new parenthood bring with them injunctions to further children that must be negotiated. Some couples may tackle this head on, contrasting their own experiences with the expectation of more children. Other couples may feel compelled to have more children, aligning themselves with normative institutionalised views about ideal family size. And yet other couples may remain decided. Ultimately, decisions about having more children cannot be reduced to any one factor, but are instead likely shaped by many forces that coalesce through the affective dimensions of new parenthood.

As we introduced briefly in this chapter, and as we explore in more detail in the next, key to decisions about having more children is the impact of a first child on the couple relationship. Indeed, the topic of the couple relationship presents an interesting point of tension in terms of institutionalised feelings and idealised family norms. While 'finding a partner and having children' was cited by most of the participants as a guiding norm for adults, the reality of new parenthood meant that the two did not always easily sit together. In other words, for some couples, having a first child introduced conflict into the couple relationship, meaning that achieving the norm of coupledom and parenthood created tension, rather than simplistically moving the individuals in the couple into the 'next phase of their life'. For some couples, of course, their normative expectations were realised, but nonetheless, the form those expectations took still often required adjustment when a baby arrived. In Chapter 8, we thus explore these differing relationship trajectories as they were experienced by the participants following the arrival of their first child.

8 Changes in the Couple Relationship over Time

8.1 INTRODUCTION

In some of the previous chapters, we have examined both tensions and alignments within couples in terms of their experiences of having a first child. In this chapter, we focus more closely on the couple relationship itself and consider in detail accounts provided by three of the couples we interviewed (as indicative of broad themes across all of the couples) to explore their different experiences. Changes in the heterosexual couple relationship throughout the transition to first-time parenthood are often wrought by normative gendered expectations. As Sevón (2012) notes, it is increasingly argued that gender inequities in heterosexual relationships following the arrival of a first child have lessened in western countries over the past two decades. Sevón, however, argues for a more realistic appraisal, suggesting it is more likely that more traditional gender-imbalanced relationship practices coexist with more contemporary approaches to the balancing of care between partners. Indeed, following the thread we have pursued throughout this book, namely the impact of the social flesh (Beasley & Bacchi, 2007) of parenthood on first-time parents, we might argue that the normative assumption that having a child will bring a couple together fails to appreciate the impact of gender norms, and how they often function to create disharmony, rather than unity. Certainly, as we outline in this chapter, it is possible that a shift in expectations can lead to greater unity, but adherence to maintaining pre-existing expectations about new parenthood can serve as a barrier to couple cohesion, particularly when these are often unrealistic expectations, as we explored in the previous chapters.

The assumption that having a first child will bring a couple closer together illustrates again how feelings can be one mechanism through which institutions get 'under the skin' (Ahmed, 2010). Again, this is especially the case when it comes to normative gendered expectations, and the roles that each member of a couple feels they should perform. For some couples, the arrival of a child may reinforce normative gendered expectations, such as in the assumption that carework is primarily 'women's work'. For such couples, the affective dimensions of new parenthood can mean that institutional norms about motherhood and fatherhood are further internalised. Yet other couples may resist such normative injunctions. The journey into new parenthood may provide some heterosexual couples with an opportunity to rethink or rework how they understand gender roles, and in so doing resist and challenge institutional norms about motherhood and fatherhood. And as Sevón (2012) suggests, it is likely that for many couples the two coexist: both the enactment of normative gendered expectations in some aspects of new parenthood and the simultaneous reworking of gender norms.

One area where normative gendered expectations may be either further enshrined or resisted pertains to the topic of intimacy. As we explore in this chapter, and following the work of MacAdam and colleagues (2011), it is vital to take an expansive, rather than limiting, approach to understanding intimacy in the couple relationship across the transition to new parenthood. Rather than conceptualising intimacy as only pertaining to sexual intimacy, it is important to think about intimacy as encompassing a diversity of what Chonody and Gabb (2019) refer to as relationship maintenance practices. In the face of the many challenges often associated with new parenthood, how do couples maintain their affective bonds with one another, and how are these bonds shaped or pushed in new directions by the arrival of a child? Thinking about intimacy as a 'series of small things', as MacAdam and colleagues (2011) suggest, rather than discrete sexual acts, provides us with important analytic leverage for thinking differently about the affective dimensions of the couple relationship throughout the transition to first-time parenthood.

As we indicated earlier, in this chapter, we specifically juxtapose experiences within three of the couples we interviewed, examining how women and men differently or similarly speak about the couple relationship. Across the couples we interviewed, accounts of relationships across the transition to new parenthood shared several similarities, and all of the couples were still together when we interviewed them for a final time when their baby was eighteen months old. However, the transition to parenthood was smoother for some couples than others. Certainly, for some couples, there were more bumps than was the case for other couples, but the three couples we included in this chapter speak in many ways to the gamut of experiences across our sample. In terms of our focus in this chapter, we home in on the second, third, and fourth interviews (i.e., six months into the pregnancy, when the child was six months old, and when the child was eighteen months old). We have not focused in detail on the first interviews in this chapter, partly because we have explored these elsewhere (as we outline in the following text), but also because accounts of the couple relationship at the time of the first interview were highly uniform, with all couples providing positive accounts with relatively little detail about the nature of the couple relationship. It is important to note that we did not ask couples specifically about intimacy, but rather at each of the interview time points we asked about how the couple relationship was going. It is this interview question that we focus on in this chapter, highlighting in places how intimacy in all its forms was either an implicit or an explicit topic of conversation.

8.2 THE COUPLE RELATIONSHIP, GENDER, COMMUNICATION, AND INTIMACY

Perhaps unsurprisingly, and as we indicated earlier, much of the literature on heterosexual first-time parents and the couple relationship has focused on gender and the distribution of childcare. Sevón (2012), for example, interviewed Finnish women about their relationship with a male partner across the transition to first-time parenthood. When interviewed during their pregnancy, the women talked positively about their partner, expecting that their partner would be closely involved in childcare once the child was born. When interviewed after the birth of their child, however, while many of the women noted that their partner was involved in childcare, this involvement required work from them to encourage their partners to be involved, an issue we explored in Chapter 5. Finally, when the women were interviewed when the child was twelve months old, a number of the women reported highly negative accounts of their partners, who they felt were not at all involved in childcare. These experiences, which differed markedly from the women's expectations prior to the arrival of the child, had a negative impact on the couple relationship.

In a number of studies about the couple relationship and first-time parenthood, a consistent theme is that of communication being central to the maintenance of a positive relationship. Ahlborg and Strandmark (2001), for example, note that for the heterosexual couples they interviewed in their Swedish study, the arrival of a baby had a significant impact on the amount of time they had to spend together, meaning that they were more focused on being mother and father, rather than wife and husband. To counteract this, the couples reported that focusing on maintaining a good line of communication was vital to both couple and individual happiness. This included ensuring that each other had opportunities to talk about the affective dimensions of new parenthood: both the joys and the challenges. This was especially salient for couples whose child experienced difficulties in sleeping. Lack of sleep for the entire family often led to short tempers and outbursts that were not reflective of the couple relationship, but rather were reflective of sleep deprivation. Being able to talk about any outbursts, and in so doing repair the couple relationship, provided couples with an important mechanism through which to engage in relationship maintenance.

Another key focus in the literature on heterosexual first-time parents is the topic of intimacy, particularly sexual intimacy. Much of this literature has focused specifically on men. MacAdam and colleagues (2011), for example, report that the Swedish men they interviewed viewed the time after the birth of a child as a period of 'survival', the presumption being that sexual intimacy would return at a later date. Many of the men noted that even when sexual intimacy started to return to their relationships, it took a different form, due to time limitations and fatigue. For some men, this necessitated a focus on 'small things' that helped to maintain the relationship, such as contributing to housework and small acts of care such as making a cup of tea. Some men, however, reported being dissatisfied with changes to sexual intimacy, feeling that the child had become their partner's first priority. Men interviewed in a study by Olsson and colleagues (2010), also in Sweden, too shared that they often felt they were competing with their baby for their partner's attention, while also acknowledging that this was a product of gender imbalances, such that for their female partners having a child appeared all encompassing, whereas for the men they were able to compartmentalise childcare, paid work, and the couple relationship. This awareness led some of the men to shift their understandings of intimacy, moving away from hegemonic understandings of men's sexuality, and towards a focus on closeness and care. In some respect, this shift reflects what Faircloth (2015) talks about as a type of 'companionate marriage' valued by some women after the birth of a child. Certainly, for some of the women Faircloth interviewed in her UK study, sexual intimacy was an important marker of relationship happiness, but for other women, a shift in understandings of intimacy marked a broader shift towards an understanding of 'family intimacy' under which couple intimacy (in its many forms) sat, rather than (sexual) couple intimacy being paramount. As Olsson and colleagues (2005) noted from their focus group data with women in Sweden, a focus on family intimacy does not mean time spent with a partner is not important, but rather that when physical energy is limited, some women may prefer time to relax rather than engage in physical intimacy after the arrival of a child.

In one of the articles we have written from our data (Riggs, Worth, & Bartholomaeus, 2018), we focused on the couple relationship, looking at interviews undertaken at the second and third time points. We mapped interpersonal changes across these time points and found that there were a variety of changes evident. In particular, we noted two patterns when it came to the couple relationship across the transition to new parenthood. For some couples, there was a sense that conceiving a child demonstrated the couple's commitment to one another. After the arrival of the child, these couples reported that having a child had indeed cemented the couple relationship and that challenges were relatively easy to negotiate through open communication and being mutually supportive. By contrast, other couples, including those where there were some tensions evident in the couple relationship prior to conception, at the time of the pregnancy felt confident that having a baby would help to mitigate further challenges in the relationship. Yet, for these couples, when the baby arrived, any existing challenges in the relationship were further exacerbated by the stressors of new parenthood.

As important context for the stories mentioned in the following text, we note the differing lengths of time the couples had been together when we first interviewed them, although we do not want to solely attribute these to the strengths, challenges, and changes in the couple relationships. Jemma and Adam had been together for over a decade, since their late teens. Alice and Josh had been together for about five years, and Catherine and Craig had been together for about eighteen months, but had moved more quickly in trying to conceive a child due to their ages.

8.3   JEMMA AND ADAM

When interviewed during the pregnancy, Jemma shared that being pregnant had made her relationship with Adam 'stronger', though she noted that the idea of a relationship becoming stronger during pregnancy was a bit of a cliché, instead opting to frame the relationship changes during pregnancy as 'resiliency'. As a result of using in vitro fertilisation to conceive, and the many challenges in conceiving that had preceded this, Jemma felt that the pregnancy was symbolic of all that she and Adam had gone through in terms of becoming parents, leading her to share in the second interview that she was 'as confident as I can be in our relationship's capacity to cope'. Here there is a sense in which the relationship functions as a third entity or an umbrella that sits over Jemma and Adam as individuals: it is Jemma and Adam who together have become resilient, but it is the relationship in which she has confidence. In terms of sexual intimacy, Jemma was one of the few people to, at least implicitly, orient to this topic. When asked if the pregnancy had changed how she relates to Adam, Jemma shared that 'some things aren't happening as often as they used to because somebody doesn't feel like doing anything ever because I feel gross all the time'. Here Jemma alludes to sexual intimacy, referring to a 'somebody' before then clarifying that the somebody is her. The challenges in talking about sexual intimacy meant that Jemma did not go into any greater detail about the 'some things that aren't happening', but what she did share highlights how the embodiment of pregnancy can, for some women, impact at least one aspect of the couple relationship.

While Jemma was focused on both the couple relationship and her own feelings, Adam by contrast was much more focused primarily on Jemma when it came to talking about the couple relationship during the pregnancy. He felt that the relationship 'hasn't really changed much', though then noted that he was 'looking after' Jemma more, such as when she gets sick. Adam shared that he had not previously had to look after Jemma so much, and that 'even if it is annoying', it was 'nice looking after her'. When asking to clarify why 'looking after' Jemma was annoying, Adam shared that it was because he had to do a lot more, 'sort of do everything', though then went on to say that 'it made me feel good that I was helping'. While a relatively simple claim, as we have explored in other chapters the idea that men 'help' women, and that they otherwise do not expect to do 'everything', is a hallmark of the forms that gender inequality can take in heterosexual relationships: that the relationship is primarily one between two equal partners, but that nonetheless the default assumption (often made by men, but sometimes also by women) is that women will undertake the lion's share of emotion work and care for their partner. Indeed, in regard to the latter, Adam noted that he was 'being nicer to her at the moment', suggesting that previously he had not seen emotion work as his role, but that during the pregnancy he was cognisant of the need to be 'nice' to Jemma.

When interviewed after the birth of their child, Jemma maintained the claim that her relationship with Adam was 'stronger', but she clarified this by stating that the relationship was also 'heavily compromised'. Specifically, the relationship was compromised by the baby: by the constancy of his needs. As Jemma noted, previously the relationship had been 'very good, comfortable, easy, and that we were intertwined'. The arrival of the baby had considerably reduced opportunities for 'moments of actual connection' with Adam that were not about the baby. Indeed, in many ways, Jemma appeared to frame the arrival of the baby as an imposition on the relationship, rather than necessarily being an imposition on them as individuals. This reflects the idea that Jemma was 'confident' in the relationship: the relationship had lived up to the confidence placed in it, but nonetheless it was 'compromised' by the needs of the baby. By comparison to the 'compromised' state of the relationship, when it came to Adam, Jemma was clear that all of the challenges of having a baby had made her appreciate Adam 'immeasurably in a way that I didn't before'. This new appreciation for Adam meant that Jemma was committed to putting 'conscious effort into maintaining a kind of adult relationship, rather than just a day-to-day functioning relationship'.

Again by contrast, Adam did not appear to view the relationship as 'compromised' due to the arrival of their child. If anything, Adam felt that the relationship was 'better', primarily due to the fact that while the couple might have had less time for each other after the arrival of their child, 'we are around each other more and see each other more and we talk more'. While Jemma was concerned that the arrival of the baby had led to a 'day-to-day functioning relationship' rather than a 'kind of adult relationship', Adam appeared to be enjoying the 'day-to-day functioning' that allowed them to see each other more and interact more. As he shared, this was a positive change for him given that previously they had each been 'off working on our separate things', so the arrival of the baby had brought them together in a focused way. This shared focus appeared to have created a shift for Adam, such that his suggestion in the second interview that he was not used to doing emotion work in the relationship had changed to what seemed to be a genuine investment in the emotional aspects of the relationship. As he shared, 'we are having this shared experience of this difficult but loving time', a time he described as 'a sort of hell-scape of joy'.

At the time of her final interview, Jemma shared that the relationship was 'probably in a good place', but nonetheless noted that things had been hard for Adam who had spent the past year at home with their child after Jemma had returned to paid work, a year in which the COVID-19 pandemic began to have a significant impact in Australia, placing considerable restrictions on Adam's movement. Jemma was also mindful of the challenges that Adam might have faced, based on her own experiences of returning to work. Jemma reported being annoyed at co-workers who had asked her who was at home with the baby, challenging them to think whether they would ask the same question of a man. Jemma reported examples of childcare ringing her at work rather than Adam, and other examples that highlighted normative gendered assumptions about primary responsibility for a child. In terms of the couple relationship itself, Jemma shared that while the relationship was 'probably in a good place', there had nonetheless been a few 'major runs-ins'. One of these involved Jemma being angry upon returning from work one day to find that the house had not been cleaned, which Adam had agreed to do. This led to Adam feeling that his work in the home (including caring for their child) was not appreciated, for which Jemma was 'immediately sorry'. This example provided by Jemma highlights how childcare and housework are so easily rendered invisible in comparison to paid work outside the home. While this type of invisibilisation is typically directed towards women, for Jemma it was a reminder that while she might be critical of those at her paid workplace who made normative assumptions about carework (e.g., asking who was at home with the baby), she herself slipped into making assumptions about Adam's contribution to the household.

Adam echoed Jemma's concerns about the impact of COVID-19 restrictions, sharing that they had not been able to have other people come over to care for the baby, meaning that 'there hasn't really been a great deal of time for us to spend time just together by ourselves or to do anything too special'. In another turn in the couple's account of the relationship, and compared to his last interview, here it is Adam who is concerned that there is not enough time for a focus on a 'kind of adult relationship' (although it is unclear if he was alluding to sexual intimacy here) as compared to 'day-to-day functioning relationship'. Adam was hopeful that they would soon enough be able to start spending time together as a couple rather than as two parents, and Adam also noted the importance of having time for himself, which at the time of the interview was at the bottom of the list in terms of time availability. Adam was mindful that Jemma likely had even less time for herself due to working outside of the home, and was hopeful that sooner rather than later each of them would get more time for themselves and for each other as a couple.

Overall, for Jemma and Adam, there appeared to have been many shifts in the couple relationship. For Jemma, the couple had gone from strong and resilient to strong and compromised. This included intimacy being reduced to time together (which was greatly increased, even if that was not specifically 'couple time'), and from Jemma being increasingly appreciative of Adam to Jemma being concerned about the impact on Adam of being restricted at home due to COVID-19. For Adam, there was very much a sense of a through line in terms of consistently seeing the relationship as solid, but nonetheless, there were shifts in terms of feeling he had to 'be nice' to Jemma during the pregnancy, to enjoying the increased time together after the birth, and shifts from not seeking emotion work as his province to seemingly enjoying emotion work and other aspects of being at home, to the extent that he balked when he felt his household contributions were questioned. Throughout the interviews, both Jemma and Adam appeared mindful that relationships take work, and that while their primary focus might at the time be their baby, this would shift in the near future to a more balanced focus. Their plans to have one child, as discussed in Chapter 7, also meant that this shift may have been a more realistic expectation than if they had opted to have additional children.

8.4 ALICE AND JOSH

For Alice, being pregnant had definitely helped to 'cement' her relationship with her husband Josh, more so than had buying a house together or getting married. Having a baby meant that Josh would be in her life 'forever no matter what happens'. At the same time, being pregnant had led Alice to 'reassess everything in a positive and a negative way, but overall positive'. For Alice, the positives about being pregnant were that she now really looked forward to a future with Josh, and to seeing him as a parent. Interestingly, Alice did not elaborate on any negative reassessments of the relationship at the time of her second interview. In a way similar to Adam, Alice noted that Josh was being more attentive to her and paying close attention to her needs during the pregnancy, but other than that she did not feel the relationship had changed during the pregnancy.

Josh provided a broadly similar account of the relationship during the pregnancy. He noted that the pregnancy meant the relationship had 'naturally evolved into that next step'. Given the pregnancy was purposive, with a planned rather than 'natural' evolution, Josh may have been making a normative claim to a baby being a natural part of the lifecourse of a heterosexual relationship. As he went on to say, 'we both eventually wanted a child as the relationship grows and you sort of know that down the track sometime you will have children'. Indeed, both spoke in their first interview about early conversations where they both made sure the other person wanted children, as a way of making sure the relationship was right for them. Here, the growth of a relationship hinges on having a child to a certain extent. Similar to Jemma, Josh was one of the few people who spoke about physical intimacy, albeit also in ways that were subtle. Having noted that during the pregnancy he was much more 'conscious' of Alice and her needs, he went on to note that 'physically you have to be careful, you can't just sort of spontaneously give a cuddle or something like that'. Here, already it would appear that for Josh there was a sense in which the pregnancy (and thus baby) created an extra layer to the relationship, though perhaps not in quite the same way as his suggestion that it is a 'natural evolution'. Instead, the extra care required represents something of a limitation to physical intimacy, or at least an extra consideration required.

When interviewed six months after the birth of their child, Alice shared that while the relationship was 'largely the same', 'the higher are higher and the lows are lower'. Alice attributed these extremes to expectations that were unrealised. Alice had expected that Josh would be highly involved, yet as it turned out she had to encourage Josh to play an active role with their child. This was exacerbated by Josh's significant work-related travel, meaning the burden of carework was placed on Alice, and they found it difficult to adjust when Josh was at home. Given how much Josh wanted to be a father (according to Alice and as appeared in our first interview with him), Alice had expected that he would be 'intimately involved', and when this did not come to fruition Alice was left feeling 'disappointed'. This disappointment pertained not only to the present but also to the future, in terms of having more children, as Alice was at first concerned that a lack of involvement from Josh would limit whether or not they would have more children. But at the same time as these disappointments, Alice shared that the couple had 'really opened up those communication lines'. This was vital, as Josh's relative lack of engagement had left Alice feeling 'unloved and worried that he doesn't love or care for' the child, but through communicating Alice was able to see that these were not Josh's feelings, and in return Josh had become more involved and outwardly loving. As Alice shared, the relationship had been in a 'pressure cooker' since the birth of their child, but she felt they had managed to overcome some fairly significant challenges quite quickly, meaning that Alice now felt more confident about having more children in the future.

Continuing on with his comments during the second interview, at the time of the third interview, Josh shared that the arrival of their child had further curtailed spontaneity, with any activities for the couple now requiring consideration and planning. This was the case both for things that the couple wanted to do and for things that Josh wanted to do by himself, echoing Adam's points about the importance of individuals in a couple having time for themselves after the arrival of a baby. Yet despite these limitations, Josh shared that he felt the arrival of their child had strengthened the relationship, though the effect of this strengthening was primarily a product of the 'respect' that Josh felt for Alice as a 'brilliant mother'. Clare then carefully questioned Josh about what this meant, and Josh shared that he felt having a baby had strengthened the relationship because Alice 'had been able to achieve something she wanted to do'. By contrast, Josh framed having a baby as 'getting it out the way', meaning that he framed having a child as doing something for Alice, rather than for himself *per se*, a different account than the 'natural evolution' claim he made in the first and second interviews. Josh went on to share that the 'maternal instinct' was strong for Alice, but that the 'paternal instinct' was not so strong for him (running somewhat counter to how they both discussed their sense of parental identity, as we explored in Chapter 6). Perhaps this might explain Alice's feeling of disappointment that Josh was less involved at first, but also suggests a marked shift from the idea that a child was a 'natural evolution' to the idea that Josh became a father to support Alice in her desire for a child.

In her final interview, Alice maintained a similar narrative to her third interview, in suggesting that the relationship is 'definitely stronger in some ways and definitely different in other ways'. Alice felt there was a 'deeper purpose' to the relationship, one that 'binds you and you can talk about every waking moment', but also that there had been 'harder times' in the relationship since the birth of their child. These harder times related to physical and time demands, which Alice explicitly noted had impacted on the couple's sexual relationship. As she shared, sexual intimacy had always been challenging because Josh travels a lot for work, but now it is definitely not a 'top priority'. However, Alice noted she was mindful that while it is 'easy for me to ignore it that often leads to us feeling a lack of connectedness, so it's something I've just had to make a priority over the last 18 months to help Josh'. Alice's comments here are interesting. Perhaps in some ways similar to Josh viewing having a child as helping Alice achieve her desire to be a mother, Alice appears to concede that making sexual intimacy a priority is important to 'help Josh'. Yet at the same time, we would emphasise that these actions are not commensurate: one relates to partners feeling that they are supporting one another to achieve a goal in life, and the other relates to intimacy as something that is mutually negotiated and agreed to, rather than being directed by the needs of one partner. This is an issue we explore more in the conclusion to this chapter.

Josh's account of parenthood as something done to help Alice achieve her desire was further evident in his final interview. As he said, the relationship has not really changed, 'we're sort of used to the fact that we're parents'. This very pragmatic account sounds something like reconciliation to a new reality, rather than necessarily joy with that reality. Certainly, not all parents have to feel joy about having a child, but the relative lack of emotion in Josh's talk about fatherhood may again speak to his differential investment in parenthood as compared to Alice, and his view of parenthood as 'natural evolution'. For Josh, the meaning of parenthood appeared to be symbolised by the cultural capital he had accrued by becoming a father. As he noted, 'I feel like we're now not just a married couple, it feels like we're part of a family now, a legitimate family'. Here, having a baby serves to accord status to a couple, something that appears to give meaning to parenthood for Josh, perhaps relatively absent of other meanings that parenthood might have accorded to the couple relationship.

Josh and Alice are an interesting couple to include in this chapter for a number of reasons. For Alice, the arrival of their child rendered visible the gap that some women experience between expectations about, and the reality of, a couple having a child, especially when it becomes apparent that their commitment to a child is different. For Josh, while the normative idealisation as a 'natural evolution' appeared to hold true (e.g., in his statement that a child accords legitimacy), there was a sense that there was something of a mismatch between his thoughts about what having a baby might be like and the reality of having a child. This might explain the narrative shift from a form of desire as part of a 'natural evolution' to a narrative of 'helping' Alice to achieve her desires. Nonetheless, as he noted in his final interview, Josh was open to the idea of having a second child, albeit again driven by the desire of Alice, although, as mentioned earlier, she had expressed doubts about this due to the lack of Josh's involvement in carework.

8.5   CATHERINE AND CRAIG

Similar to the other couples, when interviewed during her pregnancy, Catherine noted that having a child bonds a couple, but for Catherine, there was also a sense of being in it on her own. In part, Catherine attributed this to Craig not being 'overly expressive', even if at the same time Craig had been very supportive when Catherine was feeling unwell or when she was feeling anxious about the pregnancy. Ultimately, Catherine appeared to view the pregnancy as a team-building exercise and felt happy with the level of support she had received from Craig during this time. At the same time, and similar in a way to Alice, Catherine shared that she had to 'teach' Craig how to be supportive. As she noted, 'he doesn't know how to get it right all the time, and sometimes I have to get some support from girlfriends about my insecurities over Craig not always giving everything I need'. For Catherine, these insecurities related to a gap between the practical and the emotional: Craig was very good at providing for Catherine's practical needs, but he sometimes struggled to recognise, understand, and respond to her emotional needs.

For Craig, there was a clear sense that for him the relationship with Catherine had not changed during the pregnancy, but there was also a concern that it might change for the worse after the birth. As he noted in the second interview, 'we might disagree on things and it might push us apart'. That said, Craig felt that during the pregnancy they were good at communicating as a couple in regard to baby-related things, and he felt like 'nine times out of ten we completely agree, which is positive'. Similar to Adam and Josh, Craig appeared to equate any changes in the couple relationship during pregnancy with his increased attention to Catherine, such as getting up during the night if she needed something or making sure she was physically comfortable during the day. These types of everyday acts of intimacy, or relationship maintenance practices, thus seemed to be a common way that the men we interviewed framed not only their role in the pregnancy but also how they sought to maintain a connection with their female partners during the pregnancy. While the men did not often frame their actions in this specific or explicit way, the net effect was that when asked about any changes to the relationship, men such as Craig responded by commenting on their actions in regard to the perceived needs of their partner.

At the time of her third interview, and in contrast to the second, Catherine had a somewhat less rosy account of the relationship with Craig. As she shared, the relationship had been 'rocky' with Craig since the birth of their child and indeed, the birth itself where Catherine was disappointed in Craig's lack of support, as we explored in Chapter 4. While she noted that in some respects they had been more connected in regard to the baby, there had also been many challenges. For Catherine, these challenges required 'constant work at being present and checking in and making sure everything is okay with each other'. In part, these challenges were due to the fact that the couple were 'no longer just Craig and Catherine, you know, we've added another role into our lives, and that really takes some adjustment'. Further, Catherine felt that this period of adjustment was especially acute for Craig, though she was also aware that Craig did not agree with her perception of this.

Where Craig differed in his account at the time of the third interview was not that the adjustment period had been difficult for him in regard to having a baby, but rather that the adjustment was in his view a matter of whether the couple were functioning as a team. At the time of the second interview, as we noted earlier, Craig felt the couple agreed on most things baby-related. But at the time of the third interview, when their baby was six months old, Craig felt that things had defaulted to a situation where Catherine made all the decisions. As he noted, 'she takes more control and makes more of the decisions and I just have to go along with it'. This meant that Craig felt less involved in decision-making when it came to their baby, leaving Craig feeling that he had to accept this new status quo, rather than arguing all the time. As he noted, 'there has been a change in dynamics'. Craig shared that he had not expected this outcome at all, believing instead that the couple would continue to make decisions jointly. He was hopeful, however, that things would change as their child grew older, as their daughter could make decisions for herself, rather than Catherine making all the decisions. Indeed, Craig was not particularly optimistic that things would change in the near future in terms of the couple relationship dynamic, instead hoping that their daughter's increased agency would force a change to happen.

In her final interview, Catherine shared that she felt the couple had to a certain degree moved beyond the 'rocky' place they had been in after the birth of their child. She felt that they had 'come out the other end of it stronger, we communicate better, we're more patient in listening to each other'. Upon reflection Catherine could see that at the time of the third interview, she had been really struggling with her mental health, compounded by sleep deprivation. This combined with Craig also being exhausted had meant they 'almost retreated into our own camps, and when we did come together we were clashing'. This got to the point where, as Catherine noted, they had a 'kind of blow out one weekend', which led them to recognise that they could not go on as they had been, and that they needed to actually sit down and talk about the issues they were having. The couple went out to dinner on their own, and had a 'really good chat which was really good because we were really honest, open and candid'. As she said, the relationship was still hard work, but she believed all relationships are hard work. What was different now was that they were both aware they needed to do the work, even when they are tired.

At the time of the final interview, Craig was in a much more positive place as compared to his third interview, sharing that his relationship with his child was much better now that she was a toddler and was more engaged with him, but also that the relationship with Catherine was 'reasonably good most of the time'. Part of things being 'reasonably good' related to a perception by Craig that what they now had was primarily a 'family relationship' rather than solely a couple relationship. While Craig shared that as a couple they still try and make time for themselves to spend together, he was happier in the relationship as a result of his growing appreciation of the family relationship. In other words, rather than parenthood being seen as a cost to the relationship, Craig had come to see it as a benefit. While Craig maintained the position that he had stated in his third interview, that if anyone was planning to have a child he would advise against it, he had come to appreciate the changes that having a child had brought for his relationship with Catherine and life more broadly.

Overall, Catherine and Craig had a somewhat fraught journey into parenthood. It was not necessarily fraught due to unmet expectations, as was the case for Alice, for example. Catherine had a reasonably realistic appraisal of Craig as a partner, and what support he could provide. Perhaps the gap, however, was that Catherine could not have been prepared for how hard motherhood would be, and her default was to try to control the situation to manage her own mental health and as a response to how reliable she viewed Craig as being, a response that left Craig feeling shut out. As a couple with a fairly pragmatic approach to their relationship, however, Catherine and Craig were able to talk through the challenges they faced, and to come to a place where they could see that the couple relationship needed a concerted focus, as much as the couple relationship could be put in its own place in regard to the broader family relationship. While the tensions that Craig and Catherine experienced were some of the more significant ones reported within our sample, their own approaches to relationships and the nature of the relationship itself meant that they were able to navigate the 'rocky' parts of the relationship through the transition to parenthood.

8.6   CONCLUSIONS

In this chapter, we have explored how the arrival of a first child impacted on or changed the couple relationship. To a certain degree, we found that the arrival of a baby had neither an inherently positive nor negative impact on the couple relationship. Rather, the impact of the arrival of a baby depended on how couples adapted to change, and also represented for some couples a continuation of the kind of relationship they had prior to having a child together. It would seem that the arrival of a baby does not constitute the simple insertion of the baby into the existing couple relationship. Instead, the arrival of a baby changes the meaning of the relationship and the relationship practices within it, shifting from a couple relationship to a family relationship. There was obviously a gendered dimension to these changes, one that to a certain extent mirrored broader social narratives about gender and the distribution of care. Women expected men to be involved with their child, and men expected to have to care for their partner, particularly during pregnancy. These are both potentially complementary (if normative) accounts, and accounts that potentially place couples at odds, such as if men are not involved or if men feel that their own care needs are not met in return.

For all of the couples in this chapter, the ability to be able to communicate with their partner and reach a mutual understanding seemed key to positive relationship experiences. Jemma and Adam appeared to have strong lines of communication with each other before having a baby, which continued during the pregnancy and after the birth. Adam even reflected that he thought that spending more time together after the arrival of their child meant they were able to talk more than previously. Communication appeared to be more of an issue for the other two couples. Josh's significant travel for work and the positioning of having a baby as doing something for his wife Alice seemed to create tensions in the relationship, something which the couple did not mention the two of them having openly discussed. In contrast, after initial tensions during and following the birth, Catherine and Craig were able to openly talk about the issues they were having, meaning that they spoke more positively about their relationship in our final interview with them eighteen months after the birth of their child.

Another specific area that pertains to the topic of care needs is sexual intimacy. As we saw for two of the couples, the form that such intimacy took displayed marked change during the pregnancy and after the birth. There was an extent to which this was naturalised and treated as understandable by both women and men. And there was most certainly a shift toward intimacy being constituted by small acts of kindness, rather than necessarily physical intimacy. But this did not mean that some women, such as Alice, did not feel a form of pressure to engage in sexual intimacy for their partners. While we did not have a sense that Alice's husband was requesting or demanding this, we are nonetheless concerned about broader social narratives in which women are expected to provide for their male partners in all senses, including sexually. Certainly, there is a sense in which the literature on couple intimacy after the birth of a child reinforces this expectation, in its emphasis on (1) how quickly (or not) hetero-sexual couples resume intercourse, (2) that men may feel 'left out' if intimacy does not recommence after birth, and (3) that women are often left carrying yet another expectation within the relationship. This speaks more broadly to ideas about the existence of a 'male sex drive' that often serve to naturalise women's acquiescence to their male partners (Hollway, 1989). Again, we raise these issues not to suggest that these were explicitly focused on by participants, but rather to suggest the importance of an ongoing focus on how hetero-sexual couples talk about intimacy following the birth of a child, and to signal that the equation of sexual desire with other desires (such as to have a child) fails to understand their differential impact and gendered dimensions.

As we can see from this chapter, having a child is most certainly a mechanism by which feelings get institutions under the skin (Ahmed, 2010). Couples or the individuals within them may feel compelled to act in certain ways, or to engage in certain behaviours, because such behaviours are constituted as normative within the social flesh of parenthood. Loving one's partner and child may compel couples to adhere to social norms about parenthood, and more specifically gendered norms that place particular expectations on women and men. As we explore in Chapter 9, the reification of the social flesh of parenthood is likely to be intergenerational, with parents helping to shape their children's experiences of what it means to be a parent. Equally, parents may use the opportunity of becoming a grandparent to revisit or revise their parenting behaviours, thus potentially contributing to change in the social flesh of parenthood.

9 Grandparents Navigating Shifts in Relationships and Identity

9.1 INTRODUCTION

Even when people become adults, they remain their parents' children, often relying on them for advice and support in a number of ways, sometimes both emotionally and financially. While not all adults have relationships with their parents (or have living parents), they are likely to be important in many adult children's lives. This importance can take on a particular significance if adult children start to think about becoming parents themselves. One experience that can mark a significant turning point in an adult child–parent relationship is when a child themselves becomes a parent. Dun (2010) suggests that the arrival of a first child constitutes a first 'big bang' in the adult child–parent relationship for people who have children. Dun suggests as much because the birth of a first child marks a significant moment in the adult child's life, because it invites both the adult child and their parent to enter into new types of relationships (i.e., as parent and grandparent, respectively), and because it may require a renegotiation of the adult child–parent relationship itself. As Dun notes, new grandparents must navigate the desire to continue to provide support to their child, while respecting that their child is now a parent themselves. This heralds a shift in the adult child–parent relationship, potentially engendering more of a peer relationship than a didactic adult–child relationship.

In this chapter, we explore interviews we conducted with some of the parents of the first-time parent participants who have been the focus of the book so far. Many of the parents of the participants we interviewed were soon to become grandparents for the first time, while a few were already grandparents many times over. While the social flesh (Beasley & Bacchi, 2007) of parenthood creates particular norms to which new parents are expected to adhere (as we have explored in the preceding chapters), the social flesh of grandparenthood is even more sedimented in some respects, while in other respects it is nebulous and unbounded. In some ways, grandparenthood is sedimented by the popular tropes that exist in relation to grandparents: that becoming a grandparent means someone is 'old', that being 'old' equates with reductions in capacity or slowing down in general, and that such changes are largely negative (Caldas-Coulthard & Moon, 2016). Conversely, there are a growing number of grandparents actively involved in parenting their grandchildren, whether due to parental poor health, incarceration, or work demands. For such grandparents, the tropes of grandparenthood are rendered redundant, as much as parenting grandchildren can indeed constitute a considerable strain on both grandparents and their relationships with their own children (Orb & Davey, 2005). Grandparents may also continue to be involved in paid work, impacting on the time they can spend with their grandchildren. How grandparents navigate their role as grandparents, and what this means for their sense of self and their relationships with their own children, is thus a focus of this chapter.

Also a focus in this chapter is the through line of this book, namely how feelings get institutions under the skin (Ahmed, 2010). As we explore in the following sections, for many grandparents, the experience of grandparenthood is one of new or heightened emotions that are often framed through normative institutionalised accounts of grandparenthood, such as those mentioned earlier. Indeed, in many ways, the accounts we explore in the following text suggest something of a tension between expectations about the grandparent role and what this role means for grandparents' sense of self. With specific gendered dimensions to these tensions, as is also evident in the previous literature we outline in the following text, grandparents may find themselves pushed towards taking up normative institutionalised accounts of their affective responses to new grandparenthood, as much as they may try to rework what the category 'grandparent' means in the context of their own lives and family relationships. As such, grandparenthood in many ways invites people into new relationships with the state and its institutions, as much as for some it may offer opportunities to resist or rework what it means to have a relationship to norms of parenthood and grandparenthood.

In this chapter, we have opted to focus solely on our interviews with grandparents, but we note in the following text who each of the grandparents are related to in terms of our first-time parent participants so that the reader can take the previous chapters into account. We have done this for a number of reasons. First, we only interviewed the grandparents at one time point, as compared to interviewing the first-time parents at four time points, and thus it is seemed unfair to compare the interviews as the grandparents' views may have also shifted. Second, most of the grandparents we interviewed were women, so pairing these women with their female children would again repeat our emphasis earlier in this book on mothers, and our previous writing on daughters and their mothers in relation to pronatalism, which we outline in the following text. Finally, we would also suggest that research solely on grandparents is still a relatively marginal topic in the fields of both parenting and ageing, and thus a focus on grandparents is important. Our work of juxtaposition in this chapter then pertains primarily to comparisons between individual grandparents, with a major focus on differing gendered experiences and a minor focus on differences between the parents (who were soon to be grandparents) of one of our couples.

Ten grandparents (or soon to be grandparents) participated in interviews – six grandmothers and four grandfathers. We asked the first-time parents to invite their parents to participate in interviews if they were comfortable with their involvement. In some ways, then, the participating grandparents were those that may have had closer relationships with their children, although this was not always the case, as we explore in the following text. We also note that for one couple, due to receiving such intense pressure to have a child from the female partner's parents, the couple had not told their parents they were intending to have a child, let alone were actively attempting to conceive. This clearly removed the possibility of inviting them to participate in interviews. Finally, we note that the grandparents had become parents in different time periods (mid-1970s to late 1980s) and also had differing family relationships (e.g., number of children, couple relationships). For ease of reference, we refer to these participants as grandparents, although some were not yet grandparents at the time we interviewed them.

9.2 OUR PREVIOUS EXPLORATIONS OF GENERATIONAL VIEWS ON PARENTHOOD

As noted earlier, we have previously written about the views of daughters and their mothers in regard to reproduction, with a specific focus on accounts of pronatalism (Bartholomaeus & Riggs, 2017a). In that article, we directly considered five of the intending mothers we interviewed at time points one and two (before conception and during the pregnancy) in relation to the single interview undertaken with their mothers. We were particularly interested in the transmission of views about the importance of having children and found that the intending mothers reported numerous examples of the normative expectation from their mothers that they should want to have children, with the mothers seeing motherhood as a time of joy that they wished their daughters to share. We also looked at advice giving, a topic we take up in more detail in the following text. We found that while many of the grandmothers felt that giving advice, where sought, was an important part of their role as parents, most of the women reported that they would sometimes seek advice from their mothers, but would more often turn to the internet or medical professionals. Finally, we looked at differing views about what it means to be a mother between the cohorts. The most prominent point of difference pertained to paid work, with most (but not all) of the grandmothers being out of the paid workforce during or after their pregnancy, while all of the daughters planned to (and did) engage in paid work through their pregnancy with many intending to return to paid work within a year of the birth of their child.

Damien (Riggs, 2020) has also looked at the interviews with the grandparents. In that chapter, Damien looked at the experiences of becoming a parent in a previous generation, alongside views about becoming a grandparent. There was an interesting juxtaposition between these two experiences for most of the participants. For many of the participants, and particularly for the women, becoming a mother was hard work. For some it was hard to conceive, with some experiencing multiple pregnancy losses. For many participants, new motherhood had been very hard to adjust to, even if for most there was also the suggestion that motherhood had been a pinnacle of their lives, bringing to them a sense of fulfilment. Yet by contrast, when it came to their views on becoming grandmothers and their daughters becoming mothers, positive accounts dominated. In other words, while their own experiences had been complex and often fraught, they viewed parenthood for their daughters as not only desirable but largely positive. For the men we interviewed, by comparison, becoming a grandfather was often viewed as a way to 'right the wrongs' of their own actions as a parent, a finding we explore in more detail in the following section.

9.3   SHIFTS IN RELATIONSHIP WITH THEIR OWN CHILD

Returning again to the work of Dun (2010), research on adult child–parent relationships in the transition to new parenthood for adult children suggests that this significant life event often heralds a shift in the relationship. Parents may come to see their child in a new light, with parents moving from being a spectator in their adult child's life to being an involved peer and collaborator through grandparenting. Dun and Sears (2017) further suggest that such intergenerational relationships may create more satisfying ties between parents and their children, even if the initial transition period to grandparenthood and parenthood can be turbulent for some. Perhaps key to any turbulence are the views of the new parents, and whether or not they wish to parent mostly similar to, or different from, their own parents. As Munz (2017) suggests, where similarity is desired, the accord between parent and adult child can increase proximity between the two, and foster further closeness. Where the adult child seeks to parent their own child in markedly different ways to how they were parented, by contrast, this can leave new grandparents feeling that their own parenting was lacking.

For the participants in our study, these differing positions were somewhat evident. Gina's father Joseph, for example, suggested that there might be disagreements between Gina and Theresa, her mother, due to it being 'the old way or the new way' of parenting. While he ultimately felt that Theresa would be likely to 'let it go' in favour of harmonious relationships, he still also worried that there would be an underpinning current of 'you should have done it this way'. Indeed, Joseph noted that this same issue had been in play when Gina was little, and when Theresa's own mother had often sought to impose her own view of parenting on the new family of Joseph, Theresa, and their children. Nonetheless, Joseph hoped that the arrival of a child for Gina would bring him and Gina closer, in part by him 'helping her out' once the baby was born. At the same time, Joseph was concerned that he too might be the type of grandparent who says 'you should have done it this way'. In her interview, Theresa did not speak about the concerns that Joseph raised in his interview. Rather, she focused on the affective dimensions of seeing her daughter become a mother. As she said, 'something you wish for your daughter [is to become a mother] because it's a very special moment to deliver a child and to be given that gift to help this child to live as full a life as possible'. For Theresa, then, it would appear that her primary focus was on the arrival of a child to Gina benefiting their relationship as mother and daughter through a shared joy in children. Interestingly, however, Theresa expressed worry that Gina's husband Cameron could start to 'all of a sudden became very single minded about certain things' (i.e., become stronger or more vocal in his views), thus impacting on her ability to continue to give advice to her daughter. We also interviewed Cameron's mother Dianne, who had a somewhat different view on the matter on any change to the relationship, as she lived in a different state to the couple. Dianne noted that since the couple had married, she felt that there had been an increased emotional distance between her and Cameron, noting specifically that Gina's parents were now closer to the couple emotionally. In response, Dianne felt that the arrival of a grandchild might encourage her to visit more, and that this might help to re-establish the relationship with Cameron and Gina.

Lucy's parents Tania and Stan were interviewed a few months after the birth of their first grandchild. They similarly mentioned the relationship between themselves and Lucy and her partner John had improved after the arrival of the baby. Both highlighted that they met more often, and Tania noted that 'Our relationship has improved. We have more of a reason to visit them now. We love our grandchild and miss him if we don't see him for a while'. Stan described their relationship as 'more intense', due to more frequent meetings. This closeness meant that they often looked after the baby when Lucy was studying or going to classes for a hobby.

At the time of our interview with Paula's mother Lynette, Paula had already given birth to her child, and Lynette was already a grandmother to other child born to Paula's siblings. In terms of her relationship with Paula, Lynette felt that it had 'developed' since the birth of the child, because watching Paula be a mother had helped Lynette to appreciate her 'development' as a woman. She was careful to clarify that it had not changed the relationship per se, but rather that she had gained greater enjoyment from watching Paula as a mother. By contrast, Paula's father Eric stated that the relationship had 'definitely shifted a little'. He shared that years earlier Paula had distanced herself from Eric, as a result of 'not wanting to be under my authority'. More recently, however, Paula had come to live on the same property as her parents, creating a positive shift in their relationship. Whilst this resulted in another series of adjustments to the relationship, ultimately it had meant that Eric was closer to Paula, which was especially salient with the arrival of the baby. As Eric noted, 'it's been enriching because Paula has learned to relax more with me and not fear I was going to push her'. For Eric, then, Paula having a child was part of a broader set of shifts in the adult child–parent relationship, shifts that required both a change in Paula's thinking and a change in Eric's actions towards Paula.

By contrast, in our interview with Lara's mother Judith, Judith shared that she 'already has a very close relationship with Lara', but that when Lara becomes a mother the relationship will continue to grow and the baby will bring them closer. Their closeness was in part evident in the support and care Judith received from Lara in relation to health issues she had been experiencing. Indeed, as Judith noted, 'she's taking on more of a parent role. It's interesting to see that role reversal and she's making suggestions and things that she thinks will be helpful'. Interestingly, through this experience of 'role reversal', Judith noted that she can sometimes 'hear myself come back from her', suggesting something of a similarity between how the two women approach caring for another. Nonetheless, Judith felt that when Lara becomes a mother she would still ask Judith for her advice, or reflect on the arrival of the child in terms of her own experiences of being parented by Judith. Lara's father Ian too shared that he felt he was already very close to Lara, and felt confident that she would trust him to care for her child when it was born. As such, Ian did not offer the same level of reflection as did Judith, instead simply stating 'we are very close, she will talk to me about all sorts of things'. Judith and Ian also spoke warmly about their son-in-law Nathan, noting that this was already a close relationship.

For these four families, then, some felt the relationship would change very little because it was already very close, even if at the same time they had noted recent shifts in the adult child–parent relationship preceding the impending birth of a grandchild. For some, there had been significant previous shifts in the adult child–parent relationship, meaning that the arrival of a grandchild was likely to create further positive shifts in the relationship. For some, there was a sense that the arrival of a grandchild might help to repair adult child–parent relationships, as much as for some there was the potential that the arrival of a grandchild could introduce new tensions in terms of views about parenting and advice giving. We now turn to focus on the topic of advice giving more closely, through a broader focus on the role that the grandparents expected to play in their grandchild's life.

9.4   NAVIGATING THE GRANDPARENT ROLE

Research on the role that grandparents expect to take, and indeed do take, has indicated significant gender differences in terms of the role of grandmothers as compared to grandfathers. For grandmothers, it is more often the case that not only are they asked (or expected) to provide childcare when needed, but they may also be asked to engage in other forms of domestic labour to support their children (Horsfall & Dempsey, 2015). Yet despite often making a significant contribution to the care of their grandchildren and the running of their children's house, grandmothers report that they often have to take great care to not give unsolicited advice to their children. While many grandmothers may feel that they have a lot to offer in terms of knowledge about raising children, many feel compelled to eschew the sharing of this knowledge (unless asked) for fear of jeopardising their relationship with their children, and with daughters (as new mothers) specifically (Reid et al., 2010). Nonetheless, some grandmothers seek to adopt a fairly 'traditional' approach to grandparenting, playing the role of the 'spoiling' grandmother (Charpentier et al., 2013). By contrast, research with grandfathers suggest that many see grandfathering as an opportunity to pass on skills to the next generation, to be a 'source of wisdom', and to engage in physical activities with grandchildren (Horsfall & Dempsey, 2015). Grandfathers commonly emphasise the benefits of being able to spend time with grandchildren, while also not having the overall responsibility for them (StGeorge & Fletcher, 2014). In a sense, then, some of the existing research on grandfathers suggest that many adhere to a normative account of masculinity (e.g., Horsfall & Dempsey 2015); however, a smaller number of studies suggest that some men focus on rethinking their understanding of what it means to care for a child through their experience of grandfathering (Sorensen & Cooper, 2010), at least in part due to the interweaving of gender and age (Bartholomaeus & Tarrant, 2016).

Turning again first to Joseph, Theresa, and Dianne, parents of Gina and Cameron, Joseph spoke about living nearby and always being available to 'babysit' or to 'help build something' or to 'lend money'. As he said, 'we'll always be there for them, anything they need we'll be there'. In addition to this role of supporting Gina and Cameron, Joseph also envisaged a specific role with his grandchild, albeit a role that involved juggling competing desires. On one side, Joseph wanted to 'spoil them', to take them to engage in physical activities, and to comfort them. But on the other side, Joseph appeared very mindful that 'we don't want to take away from the parents: they bring the upbringing, we are just there to help'. Theresa too appeared mindful of the tension between wanting to support Gina and Cameron, but to not be seen as overstepping the mark, though for Theresa this related more to advice giving, rather than to being too involved with the grandchild, as was Joseph's concern. Indeed, Theresa wanted to be involved as much as possible, and was somewhat saddened by the fact that, due to her full-time paid work, she would not be as available as she would have liked (compared to Joseph who described himself as 'semi-retired'). Yet at the same time, Theresa was mindful that she might have to 'restrain' herself from giving unsolicited advice, and that she would be mindful not to 'impose my own beliefs'. These beliefs related to Theresa's views about child development, and at the time of the interview, which was prior to Gina and Cameron conceiving, she was already thinking ahead to ways she might gently offer suggestions without being seen as making an imposition. Dianne too was mindful of not wanting to be an 'overbearing grandmother', and indeed appeared thankful that her own mother and Cameron's father's mother were not particularly involved in her own parenting. As we noted previously, Dianne lived in a different state to Gina and Cameron, but she nonetheless hoped to visit often, even though she recognised that 'Gina is quite close to her mother and family so I think that they will probably get a lot of help anyway without me being around the corner'.

Lucy's parents Tania and Stan described wanting to support Lucy and John in their parenting, but also being mindful of following their lead. Tania was clear that while she wanted to see her grand-child often and for him to want to see her, she would respect and follow Lucy and John in their parenting decisions, such as whether or not they allowed him to eat sweets. Lucy's father Stan saw himself as an 'observer' while his grandchild was a baby, looking on at what Lucy, John, and Tania did, while also being happy to hold the baby. He hoped his grandson would be able to 'learn something useful from me in life or social behaviour', although did not elaborate on what this might look like. Tania and Stan both noted that they had not dis-cussed the role they would play in their grandchild's life with Lucy and John, but seemed to view it as not needing to be spoken about. As Stan elaborated, 'I think it's natural that grandfather and grand-mother have some obligation towards their grandchild'.

Paula's parents Lynette and Eric both appeared very mindful that because they had been 'quite disciplinarian parents', as Lynette described it, they would be more likely to 'pull back' from offering advice to Paula. Yet at the same time, given they lived on the same property, Lynette had already offered to care for her new grandchild so that Paula could go shopping, an offer that Paula readily accepted. Into the future, Lynette was looking forward to being an 'adoring grand-mother' to Paula and Isaac's child, and expected that if Paula returned to paid work, Lynette would be the one to care for her grandchild. Lynette acknowledged again that she had 'perhaps been a bit tough' on her own children, including in terms of disciplining, which led her to be open to having a different relationship with her grandchil-dren, which for Lynette included spoiling them and having fun. For Lynette, given she was a grandmother many times over already, there was great 'joy and delight' in caring for her grandchildren. Eric too shared that he was very focused on the affective dimensions of grand-parenting, though was mindful 'not to let the discipline slip entirely'. Nonetheless, he wanted to be someone who could 'put an arm around them, make sure they know they'll always be loved, and be someone they can go to when stressed or troubled'. Eric too used the language of 'joy' to describe grandparenting, albeit a joy that was fostered by the fact that 'you can give them back at the end of the day', and that 'you don't always have to be on guard about their development and upbringing'. For Eric, this more positive approach to grandparenting was something of a counter to his perception that he was 'too hard' on his children. Eric wanted both to be kinder to his grandchildren and to play a role in his grandchildren's lives that allowed him to show a different side to his own children. This different side, however, was quite gendered in the account that Eric provided, based on his perception that Paula would be unlikely to come to him for advice about children, but would be more likely to turn to him for help with other practical things. Indeed, Eric noted that Paula had been 'surprised' at how capable he was of doing domestic things around the home, and Eric welcomed the idea that his children's perceptions of him might be slowly changing through his role as a grandparent.

Alice's mother Christine, who was looking forward to becoming a grandparent for the first time when we interviewed her, offered a somewhat different account to the other grandparents mentioned previously. While those mentioned earlier were somewhat cautious about advice giving, Christine felt that she would be 'the advice person, the supportive advice person'. Christine was mindful that breastfeeding practices change, and that she would have to 'educate' herself on current best practice, but she nonetheless saw herself as playing an important role in supporting Alice to breastfeed. Christine also had strong views about disciplining, noting that she had strongly disciplined her own children, and that she had expectations about how Alice would discipline her child, and this extended to strong views about using profanities in the household. While Christine appeared mindful that ultimately these decisions would be Alice's to make, Christine nonetheless appeared strongly invested in making a contribution to the decisions, or at least having her voice heard. As she noted, 'I will be guided by their decisions and I won't impose my ideals as that would confuse the child', yet she noted that she had 'huge issues' with profanity and was waiting to see how decisions about that would 'unfold over time' with Alice, noting that 'maybe the child will just learn that at Nana's house we don't use that sort of language'. In terms of her involvement with a grandchild, Christine was 'really looking forward to spoiling them with lots of love and laughter', but she was also glad that she would be able to send them home. As she noted, 'I look forward to lots of fun and only a moderate amount of responsibility: let mum and dad put up with an overtired child, just put them in the car and say good-bye'. Indeed, despite her concerns about discipline, this appeared to be largely directed towards the decisions that Alice would make, rather than what Christine herself would do. As she noted, 'I'm really looking forward to just being the one they can't wait to go and see because I'm so much fun and will stop and do anything they want to do'.

Again, for the participants whose stories we considered in this section, there was a diversity of views. Some were quite focused on not overstepping the mark in terms of advice giving, while Christine by comparison appeared quite confident in giving advice, and had very firm views on how children should be raised. Yet at the same time, most of the participants viewed the role of grandparents as being one that involved spoiling children, while not having a high level of respon-sibility, and indeed some found it appealing that they could just 'hand them back'. While most of the men and women we interviewed spoke about the joys of interacting with grandchildren, there was still a sense of a gendered dimension to their anticipated or previous experiences. Women spoke more commonly about making an active contribution to supporting both their adult child and grandchildren physically and emotionally, whereas men somewhat more often spoke about the prac-tical contributions they could make. Yet as we saw with Eric, there was a sense in which grandparenting opened up new ways of thinking about oneself, a topic we explore in more detail in the next section.

9.5   THE RELATIONSHIP BETWEEN GRANDPARENTHOOD AND THE SELF

Like any significant life event, becoming a grandparent can provide the opportunity for self-reflection and growth. To a certain extent, the literature to date has emphasised gender differences in terms of what grandparenthood can mean for sense of self. Mann and colleagues (2016) suggest that for the grandfathers they interviewed, there was a strong sense that the men saw grandfatherhood as a means of transmitting their own understanding of masculinity across generations, including in terms of how they engaged with their grandchildren and the interests they shared. Mann and colleagues suggest that this might in part be a product of resistance by grandfathers to the image of older men 'sitting back with a pipe in a chair', instead positioning grandfathers as active and engaged. Roberto and colleagues (2001) also emphasise that the grandfathers they interviewed often relied upon normatively masculinist accounts of how they would support their children and grandchildren, though notably some of the men went beyond the practical and instrumental, and instead sought to engage in close, loving relationships with their grandchildren. This is similar to the work of StGeorge and Fletcher (2014), who found that men used grandfatherhood as a way to rework what it meant to be a man, with many seeing grandfatherhood as offering a new lease on life, one in which joy and happiness were emphasised. Sorensen and Cooper (2010) too found that grandfatherhood allowed men to access dimensions of affect they had previously not experienced with their own children.

The story as documented in the previous research on grandmothers is equally complex and contradictory. Research with young grandmothers, for example, has found that for many such grandmothers the early (and for many unexpected) transition to grandmotherhood was not particularly welcomed (Spencer, 2016). Some of the women interviewed reported that being a young grandmother aged them unnecessarily in the eyes of others, with many also reporting other losses in terms of sense of self, particularly with regard to providing high levels of care to grandchildren to support their young daughters. Interestingly, however, research with older grandmothers also emphasises resistance to grandmothering as equated with ageing. For women interviewed in some studies, grandmotherhood is welcomed for its capacity to generate new relationships, ones that are 'playful and beautiful' (Charpentier et al., 2013). Some women, however, actively resist any expectation that grandmothers should be automatically available to support their children. Marhankova (2019), for example, suggests that some of the women she interviewed were opposed to available cultural scripts about what grandmothers should be, instead emphasising their own activities and interests over caring for grandchildren. This did not mean that the women interviewed did not sometimes enjoy spending time with their grandchildren, but rather that they had worked hard to build a life for themselves during their retirement that did not involve giving all their time over to caring for grandchildren.

To a certain extent, some of the people we interviewed echoed the more normative accounts of grandparenthood identified in the literature mentioned previously. Lara's mother Judith, for example, believed that, based on what she had been told by her friends, a new relationship with a grandchild would change her, though as she noted, 'you have to work at a relationship for it to blossom and be a good thing. I'm sure my life will be enriched enormously as a grandma'. Being able to sit back and watch a grandchild's development was something Judith saw as a 'privilege'. Lara's father Ian too saw watching a new generation grow and develop to be a 'pleasure', and something that would add 'fulfilment' to his life. Indeed, Ian already had an image of that fulfilment: 'between the four of us [Ian, Judith, Lara, and Nathan], and then five [the baby], we will hop in the car as a family and it will be wonderful'.

Alice's mother Christine echoed the idea that grandparenthood offered an opportunity to reflect and sit back and enjoy the developing relationship with a new grandchild, rather than always being busy. As she noted, 'when you're a parent your life is busy with the functioning of making things happen, as a grandparent the huge busyness of life can be shelved when they are visiting and then when they go home you can do all your things'. Here, Christine provides an interesting take on the involved grandmother, similar to that found in some of the previous research. While Christine was looking forward to having time to develop a relationship with a new grandchild, this was not the be-all and end-all. As she said, 'I am very content with my current life', impending grandparenthood was an additional bonus, rather than necessarily something she intended to become central to her life. Gina's mother Theresa also indicated that grandmotherhood would not necessarily change her, but would rather 'add a dimension to who I am and it would give me an opportunity to share the growth of a young person'. Cameron's mother Dianne too stated that she did not think becoming a grandmother would change her, 'probably only a little bit'. She was clear that 'I don't want to be like other grandmothers that talk nonstop about their grandchildren'. Finally, Tania and Stan had differing views when asked this question. Tania did not think that being a grandparent would change how she thought about herself, although being a grandmother would be an extra dimension in her life. In contrast, Stan indicated that he would think about himself differently and hoped that he would be a good example for his grandchild.

While for a small number of the participants there was a more traditional sense of grandparenthood being a major life event, for most of the participants it was more common to feel that grandparenthood was an 'extra dimension', but not necessarily a central dimension to being an older person. Some of the participants saw grandparenthood as a 'privilege' and a 'fulfilling' opportunity, while others were resistant to the normative idea of what a grandparent should be like and how much of their time they should give to their grandchildren, with some like Dianne being quite resistant to the idea of being 'like other grandmothers'. While there was a little more heterogeneity in the views of the participants under the previous two sections, in this final section, there was a lot more similarity between participants in regard to whether or not grandparenthood would change how they saw themselves (with most suggesting it would not). Given that we interviewed some of the grandparents prior to the birth of their (first) grandchild, we cannot know if they did indeed experience a shift in their sense of self, but certainly for the participants we did interview who were already grandparents, there was a sense in which grandparenthood had not changed their sense of self *per se*, even if it was a 'privilege' and brought a sense of joy.

9.6   CONCLUSIONS

This chapter provides an interesting counterpoint to the previous chapters, where we focused on the first-time parents. For the existing or intending grandparents we interviewed, many spoke about having similar experiences as parents to the first-time parents we interviewed for this study. Many of the first-time parents spoke about gender imbalances in carework, the extreme fatigue of being a new parent, and the challenges in accessing support, including for some from their partners. Not surprisingly, for the grandparents we interviewed, who had their children many decades ago, some of the gender norms were much more readily apparent, though some of the women in particular were also very critical of these norms, and hoped that their daughters would experience different journeys as new mothers. When it came to becoming grandparents, then, for many of the participants, grandparenthood offered a path to new ways of relating to their own children, and to their grandchildren, rather than repeating what they saw as mistakes of the past. Grandparenthood thus opened a window to self-reflection, even if most did not see it as engendering a change of sense of self. Perhaps what bridges the gap between these two is that grandparenthood allowed the people we interviewed to reflect on their past and to create change for the future, but that did not necessarily mean that they would view themselves inherently differently. For example, someone might recognise that their parenting was too 'disciplinary', and seek to do things differently with a grandchild, but that did not rewrite their past and change how they parented their own children.

To a certain extent, the people we interviewed suggested that the social flesh of grandparenthood is somewhat more flexible than the social flesh of new parenthood. While most suggested that contemporary parenthood was very different to their own experiences of parenthood, as was evident in the interviews more broadly, this largely related to changes in technology, public conversations about parenthood, and the availability of support. What has not necessarily changed, as the previous chapters would suggest, are the gendered norms that sit around new parenthood and the expectations placed on new parents. In a certain sense, then, the social flesh (Beasley & Bacchi, 2007) of new parenthood remains somewhat similar across generations. By contrast, grandparenthood seems to have undergone a change, at least for the people we interviewed. No longer does grandparenthood automatically classify one as 'old'. No longer is it axiomatic that grandparents must give over their lives to grandchildren. Instead, to a large degree, the people we interviewed reported considerable agency in terms of the support they might provide, their availability to care for grandchildren, how they would provide such care, and whether or not grandparenthood would change their sense of self. Furthermore, grandparenting was viewed as removed from the intensity of parenthood, and some participants, particularly men, were able to connect with grandchildren on a closer level in a different time period to when they parented their child(ren). Ultimately, as we can see from the considerable diversity in the accounts provided, grandparenthood appears to more readily lend itself to a diversity of choices, at least for the people we interviewed.

Nonetheless, there was a sense in which, at least for most of the participants, that grandparenthood functioned as a way to get institutions under the skin, in terms of the affective dimensions of grandparenthood. This was most evident in the idea that for most of the people we interviewed, grandparenthood was seen as a time of joy and fulfilment, and as a desirable part of later life. Here, it is the institutionalisation of generativity that comes under the skin via the pleasurable affective dimensions of new grandparenthood. In other words, while there was considerable diversity in terms of how the participants intended to approach grandparenthood, there was far greater uniformity in terms of the affective aspects, with grandchildren largely viewed as extending reach across generations, and as allowing for the passing on of knowledge and skills. This emphasises the idea that an individual's worth is valued most when it can be shared: when it can be passed on and remembered. Certainly, we are not suggesting that people are not worthy of being remembered, or of having their achievements and knowledges celebrated by successive generations. Rather, what we are emphasising here is that the institutionalised aspects of generativity – where wisdom is seen as cumulative and valuable – serve to enshrine grandparenthood as desirable and as a life achievement. That children sit at the heart of this institutional norm potentially speak less to the actual interests of all children, and more to what Baird (2008) refers to as 'child fundamentalism', namely the idea that much is done by adults in the service of an idealised childhood experience. Again, this is not to devalue the joy that people get from grandparenthood. Rather, it is to emphasise that it is the affective dimensions of grandparenthood that seem to bring such joy, but which are also potentially premised on prevailing institutional norms about generativity, as much as many of the participants actively resisted the idea that grandparenthood would automatically change their sense of self.

10 Reflecting on the Study Findings and Experience

In Chapter 1, we began by sharing the journeys in researching family diversity that brought us to the qualitative longitudinal project *Feeling, Wanting, Having: The Meaning of Children to Heterosexual Couples*. In this chapter, we start by reflecting on how the project itself was a journey. While we were interested in exploring the affective aspects of wanting to have a child and the experiences of becoming a parent, we noticed from the very first interview we conducted that it was very difficult for some participants to talk about such an abstract concept. In part, these experiences of interviewing highlight the very focus of the project – the ways in which middle-class heterosexual couples are centred as the (privileged) norm in relation to having children, making it difficult to discuss their experiences, as we discussed in Chapter 1. As we developed our interview schedules and began speaking more to people, it became evident that no matter how much Clare sought creative ways to ask questions, it was difficult for some of the people we interviewed to think about the affective or unconscious aspects of their journeys to parenthood. Certainly, as we have seen in this book, the affective dimensions did become evident eventually, but this was often as part of the weaving of the conversations between the participants and Clare, rather than necessarily in direct response to an interview question.

These challenges, or at least shifts, in our project over its own lifecourse were perhaps already foreshadowed when it came to finding participants for the study. We had, perhaps naively, thought that given the likely size of the target population, it would be relatively straightforward to find couples willing to participate in the study. And while we certainly did not have to struggle *per se* to find a large enough sample for our qualitative longitudinal focus, it did indeed take longer and require more concerted and creative advertising methods to reach people who might be interested in participating, as we outlined in Chapter 2. Similarly, just as we presumed it would be straightforward to find participants, perhaps reflecting on their own journeys or seeing their journeys as anything remarkable was not a familiar narrative for the many people who saw our materials looking for participants. In other words, perhaps heterosexual parenting is viewed by many as so commonplace or indeed axiomatic that they could not imagine what they might have to contribute to a study on the topic. Another potential reason we have much discussed is that while parenthood was often viewed as 'natural', fears around difficulties conceiving, even if people did not think they would eventuate, may have also made people hesitant to participate in the study. Indeed, previous qualitative longitudinal studies of first-time parenthood have tended to interview people from pregnancy onwards (e.g., Fox, 2009; Lupton & Barclay, 1997; Miller, 2005, 2011).

On our part, the journey through the study came with other twists and turns. We had carefully planned out a qualitative longitudinal study with interviews at four points: (1) when the couples were planning a pregnancy via reproductive heterosex (i.e., without the assistance of reproductive technologies), (2) at the six-month mark of pregnancy, (3) six months after the birth of the child, and (4) eighteen months after the birth of the child. While we were able to complete the study with these interviews, it proved more difficult and time-consuming than we had first anticipated. Going into the initial interviews, we were mindful that journeys to parenthood do not always turn out as planned. We had worked out what we thought were sensitive ways for contacting people who might face challenges in conceiving, and we also reflected on how we would sensitively talk to people who needed to exit the study. This turned out to be the case for one couple, who felt it was better for them and for us if they left the study, although they later rejoined when they were able to conceive. Obviously, this was an upsetting experience for the couple (and one which also had impacts on us as part of the emotion work on conducting such research), as we explored in Chapter 2, but for us, it also pushed us to think more closely about how we engaged with this sensitive topic, and how we gently approached people for follow-up interviews over time. While, as we explored in Chapter 3, some participants experienced miscarriages, we started to think how we might engage with participants if their child was stillborn, or what would happen if couples separated. These were not ethical questions per se (i.e., in terms of institutional ethics), but rather were questions of relationships and care. Over the years of interviewing, Clare established a strong rapport with the couples, and was mindful of how her interactions with the couples potentially carried extra weight and meaning when it came to outcomes for their parenthood journeys. These are the topics that we consider more later in this chapter.

When it came to writing this book, we were presented with another turn in our journey with this study. While it was tempting to write a fairly 'critical' academic book, reflective of our own criticisms about normative assumptions about parenthood and the relative privilege accorded to heterosexual parents in a heteronormative world, we wanted to more deeply and fairly explore the stories of the participants. As Damien read through hundreds of hours of interview transcripts, the complex, meaningful, difficult, and touching aspects of their stories reminded us of how much the participants had shared, and that they too were often as critical of, or affected by, normative assumptions. As such, this book became a somewhat different entity. As evident from the previous chapters, we have certainly been critical of norms about parenting, including how they may have been taken up by some of the participants. But we have sought to situate the experiences of the participants in the context of these norms, while also being sensitive to their experiences. We did not want to simply accept the participants' narratives as taken for granted, but at the same time we wanted to honour their stories. As we explore in the following text, for many of the participants, their involvement in the study became a way to mark experiences that might otherwise remain left unrecorded, or at least would not have been reflected on in such depth. We wanted to contribute to that in a positive way, rather than providing a framing that would be unnecessarily critical of their lives.

As we discuss in Section 10.2, our approach to balancing a critical account of social norms about new parenthood for heterosexual couples with respecting, exploring, and celebrating the experiences of the participants involved comparing expectations about new parenthood (often based on social norms) with the reality of new parenthood. This constant process of juxtaposition, alongside other points of comparison between and within couples, meant that we have been able to tell a story in this book that moves beyond the descriptive, and into a space that pairs rich narratives with critical commentary. In the sections that remain of this chapter, we first provide an overview of the key insights that we gained from this study and our approach to writing this book. We then turn to consider what the participants had to say in their final interviews about what it meant to participate in this study. This again was an idea that we added in as the project progressed: to invite participants to reflect on their experience, given the length of time that they had spent speaking with Clare, and the significant contributions they all made to the study. We conclude the chapter by considering what the findings shared in this book mean for the study of family diversity, and some of the key learnings we feel could inform future research on heterosexual first-time parents.

10.2 NEW INSIGHTS PRODUCED THROUGH THE PROJECT

As we mentioned previously, key to our framing of this book has been an analytic focus on expectations about, as compared to the reality of, new parenthood. Certainly, given that our study adopted a qualitative longitudinal approach, it is not surprising that we had the capacity to look across time points and compare shifts in people's views. Further, our interview schedule included questions that were asked similarly across time points, allowing us to look at differences (and similarities) in responses. Yet, these points of comparison only tell part of the story as to why a comparison between expectations and reality was so salient for this book. More important was the fact that, for the participants, the difference between the two appeared salient. In other words, for several of the participants, they reported quite firm, often idealised, images of what new parenthood would be like during their first interview. Despite gentle probing from Clare, many were wedded to quite traditional or normative understandings of what conception would be like, what pregnancy and birth would be like, and what becoming a parent would be like. The reality of all of these aspects of their journeys to parenthood, by contrast, was often quite starkly different to the expectation. Our focus on expectations as compared to reality in this book, then, is less simply a process of marking change across time, and instead, it is about exploring how the participants were in some ways taken by surprise by the intensity of new parenthood, and by the unexpected emotions that often came with it. In many ways, then, our focus on expectations as compared to reality became a way to draw out the affective dimensions of new parenthood.

Of course, simply stating that there were differences between expectations and reality was never going to be enough to fill a book. Instead, we needed a form of analytic leverage through which we could make the most of these points of comparison. This was where the work of juxtaposition came in, where we looked at diverse accounts of (intending) parenthood in relation to each other, as we outlined in Chapter 1. As Vogel (2021) notes, juxtaposition is a strategy for 'determining how to relate to the dominant theories in our field, and how to avoid strengthening them while still recognising their power' (p. 53). Our take on Vogel's claim maps neatly over from the dominant theories of a field to the dominant accounts of a particular aspect of human life, in this case, heterosexual couples becoming parents. For us, then, juxtaposition has allowed us to determine how we as researchers will relate to the norms that exist about first-time parenthood, and how we can avoid naively endorsing them while still recognising their power in the lives of the participants. By juxtaposing accounts between couples, within couples, and across time, in this book, we have been able to draw out how heterosexual couples come to understand reproduction, how they experience it, and how their experiences are shaped by normative assumptions. For us as researchers, juxtaposition has allowed us to come to know these assumptions more closely, to have a critical standpoint on them, but to do so in ways that recognises their power, while also being respectful of the participants.

In addition to the aspects of juxtaposition mentioned earlier, we also, in many chapters, juxtaposed the experiences and views of women and men. This was not without its problems.

It was a problem because there are more than two genders, and we were often mindful that our writing could make it seem as though we thought otherwise. We have sought to counter this concern by repeatedly emphasising that our focus is on (cisgender) heterosexual couples. To a degree, this is an exclusionary approach (i.e., it only focuses on two genders and people who are cisgender), but as we outlined in Chapter 1, it was done for specific reasons. It was also a problem as so much of the research on 'gender differences' not only assumes that there are only two genders, but that it treats gender as a biological reality. Moving into a space that compares two genders runs the risk of being read as slipping into essentialism. We have sought to counter this by emphasising normative assumptions related to views on gender, and to use our approach to comparing expectations with reality to highlight that these assumptions are the product of social norms. We were also careful not to view gender solely as difference, which would work to erase many similarities between the stories of the participants, both within and between couples. Finally, it can be even more difficult to talk about the affective dimensions of gender without again seeming to resort to essentialism. Our approach to this quandary has been to focus on the doing of gender as a norm: how gender functions through its everyday enactment. In other words, gender is not a free-floating reality that exists, shaping people's experiences in uniform ways. Rather, gender impacts on people's lives in diverse ways, where people may take up and/or challenge expectations and norms in a myriad of ways. The journey to parenthood appeared to force some participants to come face to face with gender norms as they became more salient than previously, such as in expectations around the gendering of carework and housework.

Our way of looking at these forced re-evaluations and decisions was to build on Ahmed's (2010) statement about feelings being a way that institutions get under the skin. This simple statement provided us with significant leverage for thinking about how social norms shape people's experiences, how they come to see them, and how they resist them, reshape them, or continue to work with them. It gave us a way to 'be kind' to the participants, a driving force behind this book. As we said earlier, we wanted to provide a critical account of the stories that the participants shared with us, but we also wanted to respect their journeys. Ahmed's conceptualisation of feelings meant that we could examine how the affective dimensions of new parenthood pushed some participants to further invest in social norms about gender, reproduction, and family, while other people used new parenthood as an opportunity to reflect on their relationships with themselves, with others, and with social norms. In turn, our focus on how institutions get under the skin allowed us to look at institutions themselves, and in particular to look at the social flesh (Beasley & Bacchi, 2007) of parenthood (and grandparenthood). As we have mapped out, the social flesh of parenthood for heterosexual couples in many ways remains unchanging in terms of social norms and expectations, even if some of the services available to new parents have changed, and even if new parents have greater latitude now to resist or rework social norms. In other words, cultural expectations for new parents show great similarities across generations, even if at the same time there is greater scope for new parents to create alternate ways of thinking about themselves and their relationship to social norms. In the concluding section of this chapter, we turn to consider what this continuity and change means for the study of heterosexual first-time parenting into the future.

10.3   PARTICIPANT REFLECTIONS ON THE STUDY

At the conclusion of our final interview with each participant, we asked them to reflect on their experiences of taking part in the study. As they had contributed so much to our study, and had allowed us to share in such a key aspect of their lives, we wanted to ask them how they had experienced taking part in the study and what benefits they may have received from participating, both as individuals and as couples. In the following sections, we explore these two aspects of participation, first looking at the different ways in which the participants spoke about whether or not they shared their experiences of being interviewed with their partner, and then looking at what the participants gained personally from being interviewed. Overall, we would note that all of the participants spoke positively, with none making any negative comments about the interviewing process, although we acknowledge this may have been difficult when speaking with Clare. Some, typically men, mentioned that they had not necessarily expected to enjoy the process so much, noting with some surprise that it had turned out to be a useful process for them. Others, typically women, noted that they had used the interview process as a way to work through their own thoughts. We explore these points of difference in the following section.

10.3.1   *Sharing the Interview Experience with Their Partner*

We first asked the participants if they spoke about the interview process with their partner. We were very clear throughout the study that it was up to participants if they wanted to talk about the interview experience with their partner, but that we were primarily interested in their own views on our interview questions, rather than having a shared consensus on the interview topics. Throughout the study, some participants remarked that they had spoken to their partner about the interviews, while others were very clear that they had sought to keep their responses to themselves, and others again seemed to think little of the study in between interviews so had not thought to speak to their partner about it. When asked about speaking with their partner about the study during their final interview, the participants responded in one of three ways, which we outline in detail now.

10.3.1.1 Nice to Talk about the Interview Process with Partner

A majority of the participants noted that it had been helpful to talk about the interview process with their partner. Gina, for example, shared that 'it's interesting to reflect on everything with somebody. Sometimes Cameron and I will talk about it at the end of the day and be like "what did you say about this?". It's interesting hearing how we both think about it'. Despite Clare reiterating multiple times that couples were welcome to talk about the interviews with each other, Gina nonetheless stated that she felt she knew that such sharing was 'not part of it, I'm not supposed to', which Clare clarified was absolutely fine to do. The point of difference may have been that we tried to be clear in interviews that *Clare* would not share what a partner had said (although responses may be matched in publications), but partners were very welcome to talk about what they had each said to Clare. Interestingly, when we asked Cameron about whether or not he spoke to Gina about the interviews, he initially said that they had not really spoken about the interviews, before then clarifying that 'perhaps there might have been one or two questions'. As such, it would appear that Gina was more interested in talking about the interviews with Cameron and hearing his views, whereas Cameron felt less of a desire to do so.

For Paula, talking about the interviews with her partner Isaac was a good way to get to know him better. As she shared, in the early interviews, there was a sense in which 'we were still getting to know each other's thoughts and expectations at that point'. Talking about the interview topics thus helped the couple to know where each other stood on key parenting decisions. By the time of the last interview, by contrast, Paula shared that 'I think now we'd probably be so much more in tune, I'm pretty confident he would say almost the same things'. Isaac had a similar view about the utility of talking about the interview topics. While he suggested, similar to Cameron, that he and Paula had not really spoken about the interview contents, he nonetheless shared that reflecting on the interviews had allowed the couple to identify any points of difference and to negotiate a middle ground. As Isaac stated, 'we always wanted to have a united approach' to parenting, so talking about their interviews provided them with them a way to ensure they were 'on the same page'.

While Gina spoke about discussing the interviews as a good way to know what her husband thought, and Paula and Isaac spoke about discussing the interviews as a good way to ensure parenting consensus, Alice offered a slightly different take on the utility of talking about the interview experience. For Alice, talking about the interviews was 'a nice way to connect' with her partner Josh. As she shared, 'usually after he's had an interview we'll chat about some of the things and what our responses were'. In a sense this is similar to Gina, in that the couple spoke after they had both been interviewed. The point of difference is that for Alice, it was less about knowing what Josh had said, and more about the conversation offering an opportunity to connect. While Josh noted at first that he had not really spoken to Alice, similar to Cameron he then offered that he did 'remember discussing some of the things and touching on some of the questions' with Alice.

10.3.1.2   *Did Not Feel a Need to Talk with Partner*

While some participants found talking about the interviews useful as a way to connect, to be on the same page, or to learn about their partner's views, a small number of participants felt that there was little need to talk about the interviews with their partner. A good example of this was Jemma and Adam. Jemma had a very interesting take on whether or not she felt the need to talk about the interviews with Adam. While Jemma was clear that she could talk to Adam about the study, it was not necessary as 'I haven't told you [Clare] anything that I wouldn't say to him [Adam]'. This claim by Jemma suggests that everything shared with Clare was something she would share with Adam, if she had not already. Jemma went on to note that she held this view because 'I tend to put enough thought into what I am saying that if I ever have to defend or justify it I can explain why I said it'. This is an interesting account. It would seem less that there was potentially no utility in talking with Adam about the interviews in terms of their relationship and communication, and more that Jemma felt strongly that her views were both clearly thought out and communicated, mitigating any need to share them further. Adam provided a similar response. He noted that 'we haven't needed to talk about too much because we've already talked about it'. Adam did note that he learned something interesting about Jemma in one interview because he was in the house and overheard one of her interviews (she had expressed comfort with him being around and being within hearing distance of the interview). However, he nonetheless maintained that 'we didn't surprise each other at all', thus justifying why there was not much to be gained by talking about the interviews.

10.3.1.3 Taking Part in an Interview Highlights Views about Partner

Finally, some of the participants reflected that *considering* talking about the interviews with their partner brought to attention, whether implicitly or explicitly, some of their broader views about their partner and communication. For two of the women we interviewed, both reported a sense that their partners were not very communicative, so being interviewed was a useful way to get them to talk. Ana noted that her husband Daniel 'is not very forthcoming, he doesn't dwell on things very deeply'. Ana felt this was because Daniel is a 'very private person, not that he's hiding or anything, he's just private'. For Ana, then, the interviews were an opportunity for Daniel to open up, as much as they served as a reminder that Daniel was not very big on sharing. Lara too felt that the interviews were good for her partner Nathan. As she stated, 'women don't mind sitting around talking about our emotions, but for men the interviews might be emotion provoking for some of them'. She went on to note that when she talks to Nathan about his feelings she gets 'one-word answers', so for him being interviewed might be challenging, but might also be a positive experience encouraging him to open up about his feelings.

In a similar yet different vein, for some of the men speaking to someone who was not their partner was an appealing part of the interview process. This is exemplified by John, who noted that speaking with Clare was useful as it provided an opportunity to 'speak openly about a lot of these things without bringing up a whole discussion' because he felt if he raised some of the topics with Lucy she may want to discuss them at length. For John, he felt that he had lost time for himself and for social time with friends and Lucy, an issue that was of concern to him. He was aware of tensions between him and Lucy, so talking about this with Lucy would 'bring up a whole discussion'. By contrast, being able to talk about his feelings with Clare was a way to work through his feelings with someone who was not his partner. Indeed, there was a sense in which Lucy could see this had been useful for the couple. As she noted, she and John each have quite 'unique' views on things related to parenting, and the interview process helped her not to take for granted that they would always share the same views, and that the interview process had encouraged John to 'work through our issues and our differences'.

10.3.2   What Participants Gained from Being Involved in the Study

In addition to asking the participants about whether or not they spoke to their partner about the study and what that meant for them, we also asked the participants what, if anything, they gained from the study. As we noted earlier, all spoke positively about their participation. We now focus on three benefits of engaging in the interviews that participants shared with us.

10.3.2.1   Reflecting on Expectations and Then Reality

Throughout this book, we have consistently focused on the differences (and similarities) between expectations about new parenthood and the reality of new parenthood. When asked to reflect on the experience of being interviewed, many of the participants noted that indeed the greatest benefit was being able to reflect on the reality of new parenthood. Alice, for example, noted that 'it's been really lovely because it forces you to think about things deeper'. As she went on to say, 'I've been able to recognise some of my weaknesses and take a bigger picture view on these things'. Alice's husband Josh too noted that engaging in the interviews had helped him to reflect on the reality of parenthood, not just for himself but for his extended family. He came to see that his own experience of new parenthood was different in some ways to the experience of his parents, and helped him to be more appreciative of the greater support available to new parents now.

Nathan was another participant who noted that the major benefit of being involved in the study was that he could reflect on changes across the transition to parenthood. As he noted, 'being involved starts the thought process, it makes it a little bit real, and then once it happened, reflecting back on how I thought it would be like this but it turned out like this'. For Nathan, this process of reflection was important as it allowed him to see his experience of new parenthood holistically, in a way similar to Alice's focus on the 'bigger picture view'. While some aspects of new parenthood had been challenging for Nathan, the interview process had encouraged him to work through the challenges. His comments support Lara's shared earlier, namely that participating in the interviews had been good for Nathan who generally did not open up about his feelings. As with Nathan, Lara similarly noted that the interview process allowed her to identify what she was not prepared for, and to situate that alongside what she came to experience as 'right' for her. For Lara, this related primarily to 'not feeling very maternal' at the time of the first interview, to 'feeling completely different now'. This had implications for having a second child, as Lara was able to see that while the idea of a second child was daunting, she was open to the idea that her feelings and experience could again change, just as they did with her first child.

10.3.2.2   *Thinking about Things that Might Not Otherwise Be Considered*

Other participants shared similar views about the benefits of the interview process, but focused more on things that might not be otherwise considered. While in the previous section we focused on the differences between expectations about, and the reality of, new parenthood, this section emphasises that for some participants the interview process helped them to identify topics or issues that needed further consideration. Touching on a similar topic to Lara mentioned previously, Cameron noted that when Clare asked about his plans for additional children, being involved in the project had helped them to think about 'our expectation of a future with children and how we would go about it the second time around'. This is not to suggest that Cameron and his wife Gina would not have worked through their thoughts about a second child on their own, but rather that the interview process encouraged them to put conversations about whether or not to have more children at the forefront, rather than just waiting to see what transpired.

Cameron's wife Gina too noted that being involved in the interviews helped her to consider things she might not have otherwise thought about. Gina thought this was especially the case for the first interview, where we asked people to think about what it would mean if conception was harder than expected, or if they might need to utilise assisted reproduction. But Gina also noted that even the later interviews were useful, as they helped her to 'mentally prepare' for the challenges of new parenthood. In a similar way, Isaac noted that engaging in the interviews 'made me realise how much everything affects your parenting'. For Isaac, this related to his own upbringing and how it continued to impact on the decisions he made. Isaac was very mindful that he wanted to make decisions in collaboration with Paula, and to engage in a positive approach to parenting. Reflecting on his upbringing via the interviews allowed him to 'see the cause and effect of other events in our life on how we parent'. This reflection was important for Isaac as it allowed him to engage in the kind of growth he wanted to undertake in order to fulfil his intentions about parenthood.

10.3.2.3 Remembering Things that Might Otherwise Be Forgotten

Beyond reflecting on the differences between expectations and reality, and thinking about things that might not otherwise be considered, some participants also spoke about the interviews as a way to mark or celebrate significant events as part of new parenthood that might otherwise be forgotten. As Catherine noted, 'it's been really great to reflect on our journey, because I remember specifically after the last interview thinking "wow, I hadn't really thought about it until you asked me those things"'. As she went on to share, the interviews covered topics that 'you wouldn't just sit around and ask yourself', meaning that the interviews provided an opportunity for introspection that might otherwise be missed in busy day-to-day life, particularly in the later interviews when they were raising a child. Similar to Catherine's comment that she had not thought about things asked of her, Max noted that the interviews were a good chance to reflect, even though it was 'challenging to think back and remember things that have gone on', alluding to difficulties with conceiving and a traumatic birth experience. While it was at times a challenge for Max to remember some of his experiences as a new parent, it was nonetheless 'good' and 'easy' to talk, even if it was just 'once a year'.

Other participants framed their involvement in the interviews as a way to memorialise events for the future. Lucy shared that it was 'wonderful' to reflect on the emotions of her pregnancy and to be appreciative on the arrival of her child. She went on to state that she very much hoped that her child would be able to read about her experiences one day, and that her involvement in the study allowed for a record of her experiences beyond any records or keepsakes she might have created herself. Nathan too referred to the process of participating in the interviews as a 'good walk down memory lane', one in which he both spontaneously remembered parts of his journey to parenthood and was helpfully prompted to think about things he might have otherwise forgotten. Ultimately, for all of the participants, it was this process of reflecting and remembering that was the most beneficial aspect of taking part in the study. Along with thinking ahead to things they might not have otherwise thought about, the study allowed them to look back in retrospect on their own assumptions and experiences, and to draw on these insights for their future parenting decisions, both in terms of raising their first child and for some in terms of having more children.

We also note here that from the outset of the study we had told the participants that we would individually provide them with the transcripts of their four interviews when all of the couple's interviews had been completed, if they wished to have them as a document of their journey to parenthood. For some participants, such as Lucy, this was a keepsake she really appreciated and which she viewed as a benefit of participating, as mentioned earlier. Others welcomed the chance to have their transcripts, but were perhaps less invested in receiving them. Jemma said 'I think I'll find it really funny', presumably to read her expressed views over the course of the journey to parenthood. Others again thought they would not have time to read them or did not want to read them so did not want to receive them. Daniel's response, for example, emphasised that the challenging journey to parenthood meant he would prefer to leave these conversations in the past: 'Oh, no, I don't want to see how hard that was'.

10.4   CONCLUSIONS

We gained a lot from undertaking this project, and it was a great privilege for us that the participants shared their journeys to parenthood with us and entrusted us with their unfolding stories. As we outlined in Chapter 1, we came into the project inspired by a challenge to move beyond normative presumptions about heterosexual couple parents. When publishing other work in the field of family diversity, Damien and his colleagues had at times been challenged by reviewers about statements we made about heterosexual couple parents. Reviewers asked us how we knew that heterosexual couple parents did things in certain ways, or adhered to certain beliefs. This project was a result of those challenges. It was a way for us to move beyond these presumptions, and to move beyond relying on the large bodies of research that have nominally been about heterosexual parents, but which have not explicitly focused on the social positions of such parents as both normative and privileged, but also diverse. It also allowed us to make a contribution to the body of research that *does* purposively focus on heterosexual parents (as briefly overviewed in the first chapter of this book), by adding a longitudinal and generational focus. It is for all of these reasons that this book makes a substantive contribution to the literature. While our focus was on people living in Australia, our broad focus on social norms likely translates our work in this book across a diversity of related contexts where norms about parenthood, parenting styles, and expectations about new parenthood are broadly similar to those in Australia.

Echoing the work of Morison and Macleod (2015), throughout this book we have emphasised that the enactment of gender through the lens of social norms appears to shape at times the differing experiences of women and men. This is not to suggest an essentialist point of difference, but rather to note that what is expected of women and men differs based on the social flesh of parenthood. That men can be granted leeway to 'learn' what it means to be a father, while women are expected to automatically 'know' what it means to be a mother, is an obvious example of how the social flesh of parenthood shapes experiences. But this also occurs in very small ways. Who is spoken to in the delivery room or antenatal class? Who appears on advertising materials for bottles and formula? Where is information about new parenthood located? Who does the childcare centre call if a child is sick? When we stop and think about these few examples, we can see how it is most often women who are targeted across these examples, placing both privilege and burden on them. While antenatal classes increasingly address the needs of men, we must consider how they are addressed: as co-birthing parents or as supportive partners? While occasionally for marketing purposes greater 'diversity' may be highlighted in baby-related materials, it is still less common to see a man on a pamphlet for a baby carrier. And where does information about new parenthood most commonly appear? Do we see information about new parenthood in places that men might be presumed to frequent?

These points about gender suggest to us the importance of continued research on men's experiences of new parenthood, and the ways in which this can benefit transitions to parenthood for heterosexual couples. As we have suggested in this book, while it was at times challenging to engage men, especially when it came to talking about emotions and in the early interviews when having a child was an abstract concept, it is only through such engagement that we can learn more about how to support men to be knowledgeable about new parenthood. Otherwise, we run the risk of reinforcing normative assumptions. If we were to naively suggest that the answer is to put information about new parenthood in gyms, or in a mechanic workshop, this would simply reinforce the idea that men only enter specific traditionally masculine spaces, and that they would welcome information about parenthood there. Such a strategy certainly would not have reached several of the men in our study. Similarly, putting images of men in advertisements about baby-related items may not actually reach men. Like the work of Miller and Nash (2017), needed is research that looks at what men actually value, what men are engaged by, and how this information can be used to better provide information to men about new parenthood, all the while being mindful of the diversity between men and what they might find useful. Similarly, the study reported in this book gives a clear indication of the types of information that is less than helpful to women. This includes both unsolicited advice giving and a lack of information (premised on the assumption that women automatically 'know' how to care for children). It includes questions that treat it as axiomatic that all women can and want to breastfeed, and that all women can conceive relatively easily when they want to. While it might seem that there is a plethora of information available to women (as we seemed to suggest earlier), in this book, we have suggested that what is actually needed is information that speaks to the experiences of women, rather than to normative presumptions about mothers.

As we have highlighted at multiple junctions in this book, this project repeatedly raised questions about the ethics of care. What did it mean in particular for Clare to engage in sustained relationships with the participants? How did she show care for their diverse experiences, both their joys and their challenges? And what does this mean for those conducting research in this field? We would suggest that any qualitative longitudinal project must from the onset consider the affective dimensions of the project. Certainly, we were very attuned to affect when it came to participants, as we noted at the start of this chapter. But it was only with time that we came to better conceptualise the emotion work of running the study, particularly for Clare, alongside the positive emotional experiences and connections with participants. Of course, in all research, there is an emotional component for the researcher, and we are very aware of this. Coming back to the participants' narratives to write this book was another moment when we had to grapple with our ethical responsibility to the participants, and to find a way to share their stories in ways that were respectful. We also note again the importance of people who are intending parents and then first-time parents having an outlet to talk about their feelings and experiences. For some participants, the interviews were a chance to reflect on things they had rarely or never discussed with anyone apart from their partner or sometimes with anyone at all, which they found beneficial. In the context of our interviews, participants often found it useful to talk and reflect on aspects without the need for counselling-type responses. At the same time, we suggest that opportunities for further counselling and support should be made available to people in their first-time parenting journeys.

To bring us back to the first chapter of this book, we want to consider the question of what this book means for the study of family diversity. Elsewhere Damien has argued for the importance of including heterosexual families within the remit of family diversity (Riggs & Due, 2018). There we argued that treating 'family diversity' as everything *other than* heterosexual families simply repeats the treatment of heterosexual families as the norm. Yet at the same time, and as we have demonstrated in this book, simply collapsing hetero-sexual families into family diversity is also not the answer, as it then ignores the considerable privilege accorded to heterosexual families in heteronormative societies. Instead, what we have done in this book is to situate heterosexual parenthood as itself 'diverse', while at the same time highlighting how the social flesh of parenthood promotes heterosexual parenting as the norm (a norm that impacts all parents, including heterosexual parents). To include heterosexual families within 'family diversity' is thus to recognise that such families are diverse, as much as it is to recognise that they occupy a place within an imagined norm that has very real impacts, one which places privilege on heterosexual couples, but also enforces norms upon them.

Lastly, what this book teaches us is that the social flesh of par-enthood often seems to try to enforce a singular narrative of new par-enthood, premised on the experiences of heterosexual people. Yet, this narrative is rarely the reality for most parents, and even when it is, the affective dimensions of new parenthood are highly individualised while nonetheless speaking to broader social norms about reproduction. Looking at a group of heterosexual couples across time has allowed us to map out both the broad contours of these norms and examine in detail how individual heterosexual first-time parents take up or resist these norms. This book is thus a story of difference as much as it is a story of sameness. It is a story of how differing experiences are made to matter according to their alignment with social norms, and it is a story of how all people are affected by social norms, even if the effects are differentiated. To speak of 'heterosexual first-time parents', then, is important as it helps us to acknowledge and interrogate a privileged norm, while at the same time it is reductionist in that it overlooks the diversity between heterosexual first-time parents. The generic category 'heterosexual first-time parents' belies the immense diversity of experi-ences that we have explored in this book. It is this diversity, combined with critical attention to norms and privilege, that we hope continues to grow as the hallmark of research on heterosexual parenting.

References

Ahlborg, T., & Strandmark, M. (2001). The baby was the focus of attention: First-time parents' experiences of their intimate relationship. *Scandinavian Journal of Caring Sciences, 15*(4), 318–325.

Ahmed, S. (2010). *The promise of happiness*. Durham: Duke University Press.

Arnold-Baker, C. (2019). The process of becoming: Maternal identity in the transition to motherhood. *Existential Analysis: Journal of the Society for Existential Analysis, 30*(2), 260–274.

Australian Bureau of Statistics. (2020). Population and COVID-19. December. Canberra: ABS. www.abs.gov.au/articles/population-and-covid-19

Australian Bureau of Statistics. (2017). *2071.0 – Census of Population and Housing: Reflecting Australia – Stories from the Census,* 2016. Canberra: ABS.

Bäckström, C., & Wahn, E. H. (2011). Support during labour: First-time fathers' descriptions of requested and received support during the birth of their child. *Midwifery, 27*(1), 67–73.

Baird, B. (2008). Child politics, feminist analyses. *Australian Feminist Studies, 23*(57), 291–305.

Balint, P., Eriksson, L., & Torresi, T. (2017). State power and breastfeeding promotion: A critique. *Contemporary Political Theory, 17*(3), 306–330.

Bartholomaeus, C., & Riggs, D. W. (2020). Intending fathers: Heterosexual men planning for a first child. *Journal of Family Studies, 26*(1), 77–91.

Bartholomaeus, C., & Riggs, D. W. (2019). Embryo donation and receipt in Australia: Viewing on the meanings of embryos and kinship relations. *New Genetics and Society, 38*(1), 1–17.

Bartholomaeus, C., & Riggs, D. W. (2017a). Daughters and their mothers: The reproduction of pronatalist discourses across generations. *Women's Studies International Forum, 62*(4), 1–7.

Bartholomaeus, C., & Riggs, D. W. (2017b). Terms of endearment: Meanings of family in a diverse sample of Australian parents. In R. Harding, R. Fletcher, & C. Beasley (Eds.), *ReValuing care in theory, law and policy: Cycles and connections* (pp. 182–197). London: Routledge.

Bartholomaeus, C., & Tarrant, A. (2016). Masculinities at the margins of 'Middle-Adulthood': What a consideration of young age and old age offers masculinities theorizing. *Men and Masculinities, 19*(4), 351–369.

Bayes, S., Fenwick, J., & Hauck, Y. (2012). 'Off everyone's radar': Australian women's experiences of medically necessary elective caesarean section. *Midwifery, 28*(6), e900–e909.

Beasley, C., & Bacchi, C. (2007). Envisaging a new politics for an ethical future: Beyond trust, care and generosity – towards an ethic of social flesh. *Feminist Theory, 8*(3), 279–298.

Bell, S. A., Lori, J., Redman, R., & Seng, J. (2016). Understanding the effects of mental health on reproductive health service use: A mixed methods approach. *Health Care for Women International, 37*, 75–96. doi: 10.1080/07399332.2015.1061525

Bhamani, S. (2017). Educating before birth via talking to the baby in the womb: Prenatal innovations. *Journal of Education and Educational Development, 4*(2), 368.

Bhrolcháin, M. N., & Beaujouan, É. (2019). Do people have reproductive goals? Constructive preferences and the discovery of desired family size. In R. Schoen (Ed.), *Analytical family demography* (pp. 27–56). Netherlands: Springer.

Birch, M., & Miller, T. (2000). Inviting intimacy: The interview as therapeutic opportunity. *International Journal of Social Research Methodology, 3*(3), 189–202. doi: 10.1080/13645570050083689

Brady, M., Stevens, E., Coles, L., Zadoroznyj, M., & Martin, B. (2017). 'You can spend time … but not necessarily be bonding with them': Australian fathers' constructions and enactments of infant bonding. *Journal of Social Policy, 46*(1), 69–90.

Braun, V., & Clarke, V. (2006). Using thematic analysis in psychology. *Qualitative Research in Psychology, 3*(2), 77–101.

Bresnahan, M., Zhu, Y., Zhuang, J., & Yan, X. (2020). 'He wants a refund because I'm breastfeeding my baby': A thematic analysis of maternal stigma for breastfeeding in public. *Stigma and Health, 5*(4), 394.

Brubaker, S. J., & Dillaway, H. E. (2009). Medicalization, natural childbirth and birthing experiences. *Sociology Compass, 3*(1), 31–48.

Brouwer, M. A., Drummond, C., & Willis, E. (2012). Using Goffman's theories of social interaction to reflect first-time mothers' experiences with the social norms of infant feeding. *Qualitative Health Research, 22*(10), 1345–1354.

Brook, P. (2009). In critical defence of 'emotional labour': Refuting Bolton's critique of Hochschild's concept. *Work, Employment and Society, 23*(3), 531–548.

Butler, J. (2002). *Gender trouble*. New York: Routledge.

Caldas-Coulthard, C. R., & Moon, R. (2016). Grandmother, gran, gangsta granny: Semiotic representations of grandmotherhood. *Gender & Language, 10*(3), 309–339.

Callister, L. C., Holt, S. T., & Kuhre, M. W. (2010). Giving birth: The voices of Australian women. *The Journal of Perinatal & Neonatal Nursing, 24*(2), 128–136.

Carolan, M. (2005). 'Doing it properly': The experience of first mothering over 35 years. *Health Care for Women International, 26*(9), 764–787.

Centrelink. (2019a). Newborn upfront payment and newborn supplement. Retrieved June 30, 2020, from www.servicesaustralia.gov.au/individuals/services/centrelink/newborn-upfront-payment-and-newborn-supplement

Centrelink. (2019b). Parental leave pay. Retrieved June 30, 2020, from www.servicesaustralia.gov.au/individuals/services/centrelink/parental-leave-pay/how-much-you-can-get

Charpentier, M., Quéniart, A., & Marchand, I. (2013). Meaning and practice of grandmotherhood: A theoretical study based on older women in Quebec. *Canadian Journal on Aging, 32*(1), 45–55.

Choi, P., Henshaw, C., Baker, S., & Tree, J. (2005). Supermum, superwife, super-everything: Performing femininity in the transition to motherhood. *Journal of Reproductive and Infant Psychology, 23*(2), 167–180.

Chonody, J. M., & Gabb, J. (2019). Understanding the role of relationship maintenance in enduring couple partnerships in later adulthood. *Marriage & Family Review, 55*(3), 216–238.

Clarke, V. (2002). Sameness and difference in research on lesbian parenting. *Journal of Community & Applied Social Psychology, 12*(3), 210–222.

Crossley, M. L. (2009). Breastfeeding as a moral imperative: An autoethnographic study. *Feminism & Psychology, 19*(1), 71–87.

Cunen, N. B., Jomeen, J., Poat, A., & Xuereb, R. B. (2021). 'A small person that we made'-Parental conceptualisation of the unborn child: A constructivist grounded theory. *Midwifery*, 103198. https://doi.org/10.1016/j.midw.2021.103198

Dahlen, H. G., Barclay, L. M., & Homer, C. S. (2010). The novice birthing: Theorising first-time mothers' experiences of birth at home and in hospital in Australia. *Midwifery, 26*(1), 53–63.

Daniels, P., & Weingarten, K. (1982). *Sooner or later: The timing of parenthood in adult lives.* New York: W. W. Norton & Company.

DeVault, M. L. (1999). Comfort and struggle: Emotion work in family life. *The ANNALS of the American Academy of Political and Social Science, 561*(1), 52–63. Doi: 10.1177/000271629956100104

Dolan, A., & Coe, C. (2011). Men, masculine identities and childbirth. *Sociology of Health & Illness, 33*(7), 1019–1034.

Donath, O. (2015). Regretting motherhood: A sociopolitical analysis. *Signs: Journal of Women in Culture and Society, 40*(2), 343–367.

Dudová, R., Hašková, H., & Klímová Chaloupková, J. (2020). Disentangling the link between having one child and partnership trajectories: A mixed-methods life-course research. *Journal of Family Studies*, 1–22.

Due, C., & Riggs, D. W. (2009). Moving beyond English as a requirement to 'fit in': Considering refugee and migrant education in South Australia. *Refuge*, 26(1), 55–64.

Duggan, L. (2012). *The twilight of equality?: Neoliberalism, cultural politics, and the attack on democracy*. New York: Beacon Press.

Dun, T. (2010). Turning points in parent-grandparent relationships during the start of a new generation. *Journal of Family Communication*, 10(3), 194–210.

Dun, T., & Sears, C. (2017). Relational trajectories from parent and child to grandparent and new parent. *Journal of Family Communication*, 17(2), 185–201.

Edhborg, M., Friberg, M., Lundh, W., & Widström, A. M. (2005). 'Struggling with life': Narratives from women with signs of postpartum depression. *Scandinavian Journal of Public Health*, 33(4), 261–267.

Eliasson, M., Kainz, G., & Von Post, I. (2008). Uncaring midwives. *Nursing Ethics*, 15(4), 500–511.

Elmir, R., Schmied, V., Wilkes, L., & Jackson, D. (2010). Women's perceptions and experiences of a traumatic birth: A meta-ethnography. *Journal of Advanced Nursing*, 66(10), 2142–2153.

Eisikovits, Z., & Koren, C. (2010). Approaches to and outcomes of dyadic interview analysis. *Qualitative Health Research*, 20(12), 1642–1655. doi: 10.1177/1049732310376520

Evans, A., Barbato, C., Bettini, E., Gray, E., & Kippen, R. (2009). Taking stock: Parents' reasons for and against having a third child. *Community, Work & Family*, 12(4), 437–454.

Faircloth, C. (2015). Negotiating intimacy, equality and sexuality in the transition to parenthood. *Sociological Research Online*, 20(4), 144–155.

Fenwick, J., Burns, E., Sheehan, A., & Schmied, V. (2013). We only talk about breast feeding: A discourse analysis of infant feeding messages in antenatal group-based education. *Midwifery*, 29(5), 425–433.

Finkler, K. (2000). *Experiencing the new genetics: Family and kinship on the medical frontier*. Philadelphia: University of Pennsylvania Press.

Finn, M., & Henwood, K. (2009). Exploring masculinities within men's identificatory imaginings of first-time fatherhood. *British Journal of Social Psychology*, 48(3), 547–562.

Fischer, O. J. (2020). Non-binary reproduction: Stories of conception, pregnancy, and birth. *International Journal of Transgender Health*, 22(1–2), 77–88.

Forbat, L., & Henderson, J. (2003). 'Stuck in the middle with you': The ethics and process of qualitative research with two people in an intimate relationship. *Qualitative Health Research, 13*(10), 1453–1462. doi: 10.1177/1049732303255836

Fox, B. (2009). *When couples become parents: The creation of gender in the transition to parenthood.* Toronto: University of Toronto Press.

Gamgam Leanderz, Å., Hallgren, J., Henricson, M., Larsson, M., & Bäckström, C. (2021). Parental-couple separation during the transition to parenthood. *Nursing Open, 8*(5), 2622–2636.

Garncarek, E. (2020). 'Living with illegal feelings'—Analysis of the internet discourse on negative emotions towards children and motherhood. *Qualitative Sociology Review, 16*(1), 78–93.

Gartrell, N., & Bos, H. (2010). US National Longitudinal Lesbian Family Study: Psychological adjustment of 17-year-old adolescents. *Pediatrics, 126*(1), 28–36.

Gerber-Epstein, P., Leichtentritt, R. D., & Benyamini, Y. (2008). The experience of miscarriage in first pregnancy: The women's voices. *Death Studies, 33*(1), 1–29.

Gold, K. J., Sen, A., & Hayward, R. A. (2010). Marriage and cohabitation outcomes after pregnancy loss. *Pediatrics, 125*(5), e1202–e1207. doi: 10.1542/peds.2009-3081

Goldberg, W. A. (2014). *Father time: The social clock and the timing of fatherhood.* Basingstoke: Palgrave.

Haggis, J. (1990/2013). The feminist research process – defining a topic. In L. Stanley (Ed.), *Feminist praxis: Research, theory and epistemology in feminist sociology* (pp. 67–79). London and New York: Routledge.

Hanser, A., & Li, J. (2017). The hard work of feeding the baby: Breastfeeding and intensive mothering in contemporary urban China. *The Journal of Chinese Sociology, 4*(1), 1–20.

Harrison, S. (2021). The tyranny of life milestones. *BBC Worklife,* March 23. www.bbc.com/worklife/article/20210315-the-tyranny-of-life-milestones

Heaphy, B., & Einarsdottir, A. (2012). Scripting civil partnerships: Interviewing couples together and apart. *Qualitative Research, 13*(1), 53–70. doi: 10.1177/1468794112454997

Henwood, K., Neale, B., & Holland, J. (2012). Advancing methods and resources for qualitative longtitudinal research: The Timescapes initiative. *Qualitative Research, 12*(1).

Herrera, F. (2020). 'A horror movie with a happy ending': Childbirth from the father's perspective. *NORMA, 15*(3–4), 251–266.

Hertz, R. (1995). Separate but simultaneous interviewing of husbands and wives: Making sense of their stories. *Qualitative Inquiry, 1*(4), 429–451. doi: 10.1177/107780049500100404

Hochschild, A. R. (1979). Emotion work, feeling rules, and social structure. *American Journal of Sociology, 85*(3), 551–575.

Hochschild, A. R. (1983/2003). *The managed heart: Commercialization of human feeling.* Twentieth anniversary edition. Berkeley: University of California Press.

Holland, J., Thomson, R., & Henderson, S. (2006). Qualitative longitudinal research: A discussion paper. Families & Social Capital ESRC Research Group, London South Bank University. London.

Hollway, W. (1989). *Subjectivity and method in psychology: Gender, meaning and science.* London: SAGE Publications.

Holton, S., Fisher, J., & Rowe, H. (2011). To have or not to have? Australian women's childbearing desires, expectations and outcomes. *Journal of Population Research, 28*(4), 353.

Horsfall, B., & Dempsey, D. (2015). Grandparents doing gender: Experiences of grandmothers and grandfathers caring for grandchildren in Australia. *Journal of Sociology, 51*(4), 1070–1084.

Hubbard, G., Backett-Milburn, K., & Kemmer, D. (2001). Working with emotion: Issues for the researcher in fieldwork and teamwork. *International Journal of Social Research Methodology, 4*(2), 119–137. Doi: 10.1080/13645570116992

Hunter, S., Riggs, D. W., & Augoustinos, M. (2017). Hegemonic vs. a caring masculinity: Implications for understanding primary caregiving fathers. *Social and Personality Psychology Compass, 11*(1), 1–9.

Iwata, H. (2009). The experiences of Japanese men during the transition to fatherhood. Unpublished PhD thesis, Duquesne University.

Johnson, S. A. (2014). 'Maternal devices', social media and the self-management of pregnancy, mothering and child health. *Societies, 4*(2), 330–350.

Johnson, M. P. (2002). An exploration of men's experience and role at childbirth. *The Journal of Men's Studies, 10*(2), 165–182.

Karlström, A., Nystedt, A., & Hildingsson, I. (2015). The meaning of a very positive birth experience: focus groups discussions with women. *BMC pregnancy and childbirth, 15*(1), 1–8.

Kerrick, M. R., & Henry, R. L. (2017). 'Totally in love': Evidence of a master narrative for how new mothers should feel about their babies. *Sex Roles, 76*(1–2), 1–16.

Kevin, C. (2005). Maternity and freedom: Australian feminist encounters with the reproductive body. *Australian Feminist Studies, 20*(46), 3–15.

Klapdor M. (2013). Abolishing the baby bonus. Retrieved June 30, 2020, from www
.aph.gov.au/About_Parliament/Parliamentary_Departments/Parliamentary_
Library/pubs/rp/BudgetReview201314/BabyBonus

Kruger, L., Beer, C. L.-D., & Du Plessis, A.-B. (2016). Resilience in gay and lesbian
parent families: Perspectives from the chrono-system. *Journal of Comparative
Family Studies, 47*(3), 343–356.

Kwok, K., & Kwok, D. K. (2020). More than comfort and discomfort: Emotion work
of parenting children with autism in Hong Kong. *Children and Youth Services
Review, 118*, 105456. https://doi.org/10.1016/j.childyouth.2020.105456

Larkin, P., Begley, C. M., & Devane, D. (2012). 'Not enough people to look after
you': An exploration of women's experiences of childbirth in the Republic of
Ireland. *Midwifery, 28*(1), 98–105. doi: 10.1016/j.midw.2010.11.007

Laurent, J., Human, O., Guzmán, C. D., Roding, E., Scholtes, U., Laet, M. d., &
Mol, A. (2021). Excreting variously: On contrasting as an analytic technique.
In A. Ballestero & B. R. Winthereik (Eds.), *Experimenting with ethnography: A
companion to analysis* (pp. 186–197). Durham: Duke University Press.

Letherby, G. (2002). Claims and disclaimers: Knowledge, reflexivity and represen-
tation in feminist research. *Sociological Research Online, 6*(4). Retrieved from
www.socresonline.org.uk/

Lovett, L. (2010). Pronatalism. In A. O'Reilly (Ed.), *Encyclopedia of motherhood*
(pp. 1028–1029). Thousand Oaks: SAGE Publications.

Lowe, P. (2016). *Reproductive health and maternal sacrifice: Women, choice and
responsibility*. Basingstoke: Palgrave Macmillan.

Luppi, F. (2016). When is the second one coming? The effect of couple's subjective
well-being following the onset of parenthood. *European Journal of Population,
32*(3), 421–444.

Lupton, D. (2020). Caring dataveillance: Women's use of apps to monitor pregnancy and children. In L. Green, D. Holloway, K. Stevenson, L. Haddon, & T.
Leaver (Eds.), *Routledge companion to digital media and children* (pp. 393–
402). London: Routledge.

Lupton, D. (2000). 'A love/hate relationship': The ideals and experiences of first-
time mothers. *Journal of Sociology, 36*(1), 50–63.

Lupton, D., & Barclay, L. (1997). *Constructing fatherhood: Discourses and experiences*. London, Thousand Oaks, and New Delhi: SAGE Publications.

MacAdam, R., Huuva, E., & Berterö, C. (2011). Fathers' experiences after having
a child: Sexuality becomes tailored according to circumstances. *Midwifery,
27*(5), e149–e155.

Mann, R., Tarrant, A., & Leeson, G. W. (2016). Grandfatherhood: Shifting masculinities in later life. *Sociology, 50*(3), 594–610.

Mannix, J., & Jackson, D. (2003). Mothering and women's health: I love being a mother but … there is always something new to worry about. *Australian Journal of Advanced Nursing, 20*(3), 30–37.

Margolis, R., & Myrskylä, M. (2015). Parental well-being surrounding first birth as a determinant of further parity progression. *Demography, 52*(4), 1147–1166.

Marhankova, J. H. (2019). 'I want (to be) an active grandmother': Activity as a new normative framework of subjective meanings and expectations associated with the grandmother role. *Ageing & Society, 39*(8), 1667–1690.

Matley, D. (2020). 'I miss my old life': Regretting motherhood on Mumsnet. *Discourse, Context & Media, 37*(1), 1–8.

Mauthner, N. S. (1999). 'Feeling low and feeling really bad about feeling low': Women's experiences of motherhood and postpartum depression. *Canadian Psychology, 40*(2), 143.

Mellor, R. M., Slaymaker, E., & Cleland, J. (2013). Recognizing and overcoming challenges of couple interview research. *Qualitative Health Research, 23*(10), 1399–1407. doi: 10.1177/1049732313506963

Meyers, D. T. (2001). The rush to motherhood: Pronatalist discourse and women's autonomy. *Signs, 26*(3), 735–773. doi: 10.1093/0195140419.003.0002

Miller, T. (2015). Going back: 'Stalking', talking and researcher responsibilities in qualitative longitudinal research. *International Journal of Social Research Methodology, 18*, 293–305. doi: 10.1080/13645579.2015.1017902

Miller, T. (2012a). Balancing caring and paid work in the UK: narrating 'choices' as first-time parents. *International Review of Sociology, 22*(1), 39–52.

Miller, T. (2012b). Reconfiguring research relationships: Regulation, new technologies and doing ethical research. In T. Miller, M. Birch, M. Mauthner & J. Jessop (Eds.), *Ethics in qualitative research* (2nd ed., pp. 29–42). London: SAGE Publications.

Miller, T. (2011). *Making sense of fatherhood: Gender, caring and work.* Cambridge: Cambridge University Press.

Miller, T. (2005). *Making sense of motherhood: A narrative approach.* Cambridge: Cambridge University Press.

Miller, T., & Bell, L. (2012). Consenting to what? Issues of access, gate-keeping and 'informed' consent. In T. Miller, M. Birch, M. Mauthner & J. Jessop (Eds.), *Ethics in qualitative research* (2nd ed., pp. 61–75). London: SAGE Publications.

Miller, T., & Nash, M. (2017). 'I just think something like the "Bubs and Pubs" class is what men should be having': Paternal subjectivities and preparing for first-time fatherhood in Australia and the United Kingdom. *Journal of Sociology, 53*(3), 541–556.

Miller, W. B., Severy, L. J., & Pasta, D. J. (2004). A framework for modelling fertility motivation in couples. *Population Studies, 58*(2), 193–205. doi: 10.1080/0032472042000213712

Mobbs, E. J., Mobbs, G. A., & Mobbs, A. E. (2016). Imprinting, latchment and displacement: A mini review of early instinctual behaviour in newborn infants influencing breastfeeding success. *Acta Paediatrica, 105*(1), 24–30.

Moore, L. J. (2008). *Sperm counts: Overcome by man's most precious fluid.* New York: New York University Press.

Moore, J., & Abetz, J. S. (2019). What do parents regret about having children? Communicating regrets online. *Journal of Family issues, 40*(3), 390–412.

Morell, C. (2000). Saying no: Women's experiences with reproductive refusal. *Feminism & Psychology, 10*(3), 313–322. doi: 10.1177/0959353500010003002

Morison, T. (2013). Heterosexual men and parenthood decision making in South Africa: Attending to the invisible norm. *Journal of Family Issues, 34*(8), 1125–1144.

Morison, T., & Macleod, C. (2015). *Men's pathways to parenthood: Silence and heterosexual gendered norms.* Cape Town: HSRC Press.

Morison, T., Macleod, C., Lynch, I., Mijas, M., & Shivakumar, S. T. (2016). Stigma resistance in online childfree communities: The limitations of choice rhetoric. *Psychology of Women Quarterly, 40*(2), 184–198.

Munz, E. A. (2017). Grandparents' perspectives on parent-adult child relationships during the transition to grandparenthood. *The Open Family Studies Journal, 9*(1), 37–48.

Nash, M. (2007). From 'bump' to 'baby': Gazing at the foetus in 4D. *Philament, 10*(1), 1–25.

Newman, L. (2008). How parenthood experiences influence desire for more children in Australia: A qualitative study. *Journal of Population Research, 25*(1), 1–27.

Nilsson, C. (2014). The delivery room: Is it a safe place? A hermeneutic analysis of women's negative birth experiences. *Sexual & Reproductive Healthcare, 5*(4), 199–204.

Nordqvist, P., & Smart, C. (2014). *Relative strangers: Family life, genes and donor conception.* Basingstoke: Palgrave Macmillan.

Oakley, A. (2016). Interviewing women again: Power, time and the gift. *Sociology, 50*(1), 195–213. doi: 10.1177/0038038515580253

Oakley, A. (1986). *From here to maternity: Becoming a mother.* Hammondsworth, Middlesex: Penguin.

Oakley, A. (1974). *The sociology of housework.* Bristol: Policy Press.

Olsson, A., Lundqvist, M., Faxelid, E., & Nissen, E. (2005). Women's thoughts about sexual life after childbirth: Focus group discussions with women after childbirth. *Scandinavian Journal of Caring Sciences, 19*(4), 381–387.

Olsson, A., Robertson, E., Björklund, A., & Nissen, E. (2010). Fatherhood in focus, sexual activity can wait: New fathers' experience about sexual life after childbirth. *Scandinavian Journal of Caring Sciences, 24*(4), 716–725.

Orb, A., & Davey, M. (2005). Grandparents parenting their grandchildren. *Australasian Journal on Ageing, 24*(3), 162–168.

Palmer, J. (2009). Seeing and knowing: Ultrasound images in the contemporary abortion debate. *Feminist Theory, 10*(2), 173–189.

Peng, Y. (2020). Should we have a second child? Reproductive decisions and family negotiation under China's two-child policy. *Journal of Contemporary China, 29*(125), 792–807.

Peters, K., Jackson, D., & Rudge, T. (2008). Research on couples: Are feminist approaches useful? *Journal of Advanced Nursing, 62*(3), 373–380. doi: 10.1111/j.1365-2648.2007.04558.x

Qu, L. (2021). *Impacts of COVID-19 on pregnancy and fertility intentions*. Families in Australia Survey: Towards COVID Normal: Report no. 4. Australian Institute of Family Studies. https://aifs.gov.au/sites/default/files/publication-documents/2106_4_fias_pregnancy_and_fertility_intentions.pdf

Read, D. M., Crockett, J., & Mason, R. (2012). 'It was a horrible shock': The experience of motherhood and women's family size preferences. *Women's Studies International Forum, 35*(1), 12–21.

Reid, J., Schmied, V., & Beale, B. (2010). 'I only give advice if I am asked': Examining the grandmother's potential to influence infant feeding decisions and parenting practices of new mothers. *Women and Birth, 23*(2), 74–80.

Reiger, K., & Lane, K. (2013). 'How can we go on caring when nobody here cares about us?' Australian public maternity units as contested care sites. *Women and Birth, 26*(2), 133–137. doi: 10.1016/j.wombi.2012.11.003

Riggs, D. W. (2020). *Diverse pathways to parenthood: From narratives to practice*. Cambridge: Academic Press.

Riggs, D. W. (2010). 'I'm not gay, but my four mums are': Psychological knowledge and lesbian-headed families. *Radical Psychology, 9*(1).

Riggs, D. W., Augoustinos, M., & Delfabbro, P. (2007). 'Basically it's a recognition issue': Validating a foster parent identity. *Family Matters, 76*, 64–69.

Riggs, D. W., & Bartholomaeus, C. (2020). 'That's my job': Accounting for division of labour amongst heterosexual first time parents. *Community, Work and Family, 23*(1), 107–122.

Riggs, D. W., & Bartholomaeus, C. (2018). 'It's just what you do': Australian middle class heterosexual couples negotiating compulsory parenthood. *Feminism & Psychology, 28*(3), 373–389.

Riggs, D. W., & Bartholomaeus, C. (2016a). *Australian family diversity: An historical overview 1960–2015.* Adelaide: Flinders University.

Riggs, D. W., & Bartholomaeus, C. (2016b). The desire for a child amongst a sample of heterosexual Australian couples. *Journal of Infant and Reproductive Psychology, 34*(5), 442–450.

Riggs, D. W., & Peel, E. (2016). *Critical kinship studies: An introduction to the field.* Basingstoke: Palgrave Macmillan.

Riggs, D. W., Bartholomaeus, C., & Due, C. (2016). Public and private families: A comparative thematic analysis of the intersections of social norms and scrutiny. *Health Sociology Review, 25*(1), 1–17.

Riggs, D. W., Delfabbro, P. H., & Augoustinos, M. (2009). Negotiating foster families: Identification and desire. *British Journal of Social Work, 39*(1), 789–806.

Riggs, D. W., & Due, C. (2018). Support for family diversity: A three-country study. *Journal of Infant and Reproductive Psychology, 36*(3), 192–206.

Riggs, D. W., & Due, C. (2015). White Australian adoptive mothers' understandings of birth cultures and families. *Adoption Quarterly, 18*(2), 273–290.

Riggs, D. W., & Due, C. (2013). Representations of reproductive citizenship and vulnerability in media reports of offshore surrogacy. *Citizenship Studies, 17*(2), 956–969.

Riggs, D. W., & Peel, E. (2016). *Critical kinship studies: An introduction to the field.* Basingstoke: Palgrave.

Riggs, D. W., Worth, A., & Bartholomaeus, C. (2018). The transition to parenthood for Australian heterosexual couples: Expectations, experiences and the partner relationship. *BMC Pregnancy and Childbirth, 18*(1), 342.

Roberto, K. A., Allen, K. R., & Blieszner, R. (2001). Grandfathers' perceptions and expectations of relationships with their adult grandchildren. *Journal of Family Issues, 22*(4), 407–426.

Røseth, I., Bongaardt, R., Lyberg, A., Sommerseth, E., & Dahl, B. (2018). New mothers' struggles to love their child: An interpretative synthesis of qualitative studies. *International Journal of Qualitative Studies on Health and Wellbeing, 13*(1), 1–10.

Saldaña, J. (2003). *Longitudinal qualitative research: Analyzing change through time.* Walnut Creek: AltaMira Press.

Schmied, V., & Lupton, D. (2001). The externality of the inside: Body images of pregnancy. *Nursing Inquiry, 8*(1), 32–40.

Seery, B. L., & Crowley, M. S. (2000). Women's emotion work in the family: Relationship management and the process of building father-child relationships. *Journal of Family Issues, 21*(1), 100–127.

Sevón, E. (2012). 'My life has changed, but his life hasn't': Making sense of the gendering of parenthood during the transition to motherhood. *Feminism & Psychology, 22*(1), 60–80.

Shakespeare, J., Blake, F., & Garcia, J. (2004). Breast-feeding difficulties experienced by women taking part in a qualitative interview study of postnatal depression. *Midwifery, 20*(3), 251–260.

Sheehan, A., & Schmied, V. (2011). The imperative to breastfeed: An Australian perspective. In P. Liamputtong (Ed.), *Infant feeding practices: A cross-cultural perspective* (pp. 55–76). Netherlands: Springer.

Símonardóttir, S., & Gíslason, I. V. (2018). When breast is not best: Opposing dominant discourses on breastfeeding. *The Sociological Review, 66*(3), 665–681.

Símonardóttir, S., & Rúdólfsdóttir, A. G. (2021). The 'good' epidural: Women's use of epidurals in relation to dominant discourses on 'natural' birth. *Feminism & Psychology, 31*(2), 212–230.

Sorensen, P., & Cooper, N. J. (2010). Reshaping the family man: A grounded theory study of the meaning of grandfatherhood. *The Journal of Men's Studies, 18*(2), 117–136.

Spencer, M. L. (2016). Lived experiences of becoming and being a young maternal grandmother: An interpretative phenomenological analysis. Unpublished PhD thesis, University of Northampton.

Spinelli, M., Frigerio, A., Montali, L., Fasolo, M., Spada, M. S., & Mangili, G. (2016). 'I still have difficulties feeling like a mother': The transition to motherhood of preterm infants' mothers. *Psychology & Health, 31*(2), 184–204.

Stearns, C. A. (2009). The work of breastfeeding. *Women's Studies Quarterly, 37*(3/4), 63–80.

StGeorge, J. M., & Fletcher, R. J. (2014). Men's experiences of grandfatherhood: A welcome surprise. *The International Journal of Aging and Human Development, 78*(4), 351–378.

Sweeny, K., Andrews, S. E., Nelson, S. K., & Robbins, M. L. (2015). Waiting for a baby: Navigating uncertainty in recollections of trying to conceive. *Social Science & Medicine, 141*(2), 123–132. doi: 10.1016/j.socscimed.2015.07.031

Thomson, R., Kehily, M. J., Hadfield, L., & Sharpe, S. (2011). *Making modern mothers*. Bristol: Policy Press.

Thomson, R., & McLeod, J. (2015). New frontiers in qualitative longitudinal research: An agenda for research. *International Journal of Social Research Methodology, 18*(3), 243–250. doi: 10.1080/13645579.2015.1017900

Turner, B. S. (2001). The erosion of citizenship. *The British Journal of Sociology, 52*(2), 189–209.

Ulrich, M., & Weatherall, A. (2000). Motherhood and infertility: Viewing motherhood through the lens of infertility. *Feminism & Psychology, 10*(3), 323–336.

Ussher, J. M. (2006). *Managing the monstrous feminine: Regulating the reproductive body.* New York: Routledge.

Vogel, E. (2021). Juxtaposition: Differences that matter. In A. Ballestero & B. R. Winthereik (Eds.), *Experimenting with ethnography: A companion to analysis* (pp. 53–65). Durham: Duke University Press.

Walsh, T. B., Davis, R. N., Palladino, C. L., Romero, V. C., & Vijay Singh, M. D. (2014). Moving up the 'magic moment': Fathers' experience of prenatal ultrasound. *Fathering, 12*(1), 18.

Weaver, J. J., & Ussher, J. M. (1997). How motherhood changes life: A discourse analytic study with mothers of young children. *Journal of Reproductive and Infant Psychology, 15*(1), 51–68.

Weston, R., Qu, L., Parker, R., & Alexander, M. (2004). 'It's not for lack of wanting kids ...': A report on the Fertility Decision Making Project. Report No. 11. Melbourne: Australian Institute of Family Studies.

Whitehead, K. (2016). Motherhood as a gendered entitlement: Intentionality, 'othering', and homosociality in the online infertility community. *Canadian Review of Sociology, 53*(1), 94–122.

Willing, I. (2004). The adopted Vietnamese community: From fairytales to the diaspora. *Michigan Quarterly Review, 43*(4), 648–664.

Younane, S. (2008). 'Working families' and the 'opportunity society': Political rhetoric in the 2007 Australian federal election campaign. *Communication, Politics & Culture, 41*(2), 62–83.

Index